Bud

by
Julia Kluge-Fabényi
and
Hella Markus

Prestel
Munich – New York

This guide contains 146 full-color and 37 black-and-white illustrations, 1 double-page color map, 6 plans, and a map of the metro system.

Front cover: The Széchenyi Chain Bridge, the Danube, and Parliament House
Photo: Image Bank

Inside front cover: Fishermen's Bastion, reflected in the facade of the Budapest Hilton
Photographer: János Eifert, Budapest

Back cover: The Millennium Monument on Hősök tere
Photographer: Magyar Képek, Budapest

Originally published as *Prestel Führer Budapest,* © 1992 Prestel
Other Prestel Guides in this series: **Berlin, Munich, Prague,** and **Vienna**

Edited by Ian Robson, Merklín u. Přeštic, with Barbara Jürgensen
Translated from the German by John Gabriel, with Nancy Norwood

Prestel-Verlag, 16 West 22nd Street, New York, NY 10010, USA
Tel. (212) 627 81 99; Fax (212) 627 98 66
and Mandlstrasse 26, 80802 Munich, Germany
Tel. (89) 381 70 90; Fax (89) 38 17 09 35

Distributed in continental Europe by Prestel-Verlag
Verlegerdienst München GmbH & Co. KG, Gutenbergstrasse 1, 82205 Gilching, Germany
Tel. (81 05) 38 81 17; Fax (81 05) 38 81 00

Distributed in the USA and Canada on behalf of Prestel by te Neues Publishing Company, 16 West 22nd Street, New York, NY 10010, USA
Tel. (212) 627 90 90; Fax (212) 627 95 11

Distributed in Japan on behalf of Prestel by YOHAN Western Publications Distribution Agency, 14-9 Okubo 3-chome, Shinjuku-ku, Tokyo 169, Japan
Tel. (3) 32 08 01 81; Fax (3) 32 09 02 88

Distributed in the United Kingdom, Ireland, and all remaining countries on behalf of Prestel by Thames & Hudson Limited, 30-34 Bloomsbury Street, London WC1B 3 QP, England
Tel. (71) 636 54 88; Fax (71) 636 16 95

Photograph credits: p. 191

Design: Norbert Dinkel, Munich
Maps: Franz Huber, Munich
Color separations: PHG Lithos GmbH, Martinsried
Typesetting: Typodata, Munich
Printing, and binding: Passavia Druckerei GmbH, Passau

Printed in Germany

ISBN 3-7913-1329-0 (English edition)
ISBN 3-7913-1203-0 (German edition)

Contents

Maps

Introduction

An Outline Chronology

Facts and Figures

Castle Hill: Royal Palace and Borough

Greater Buda

Danube Bridges and Margaret Island

Downtown Pest

Greater Pest

City Park (Városliget) and Outskirts of Pest

Óbuda

Practical Tips *149*

Index *188*

A medieval find: two lions with a single head, at the corner of Úri utca and Anna utca

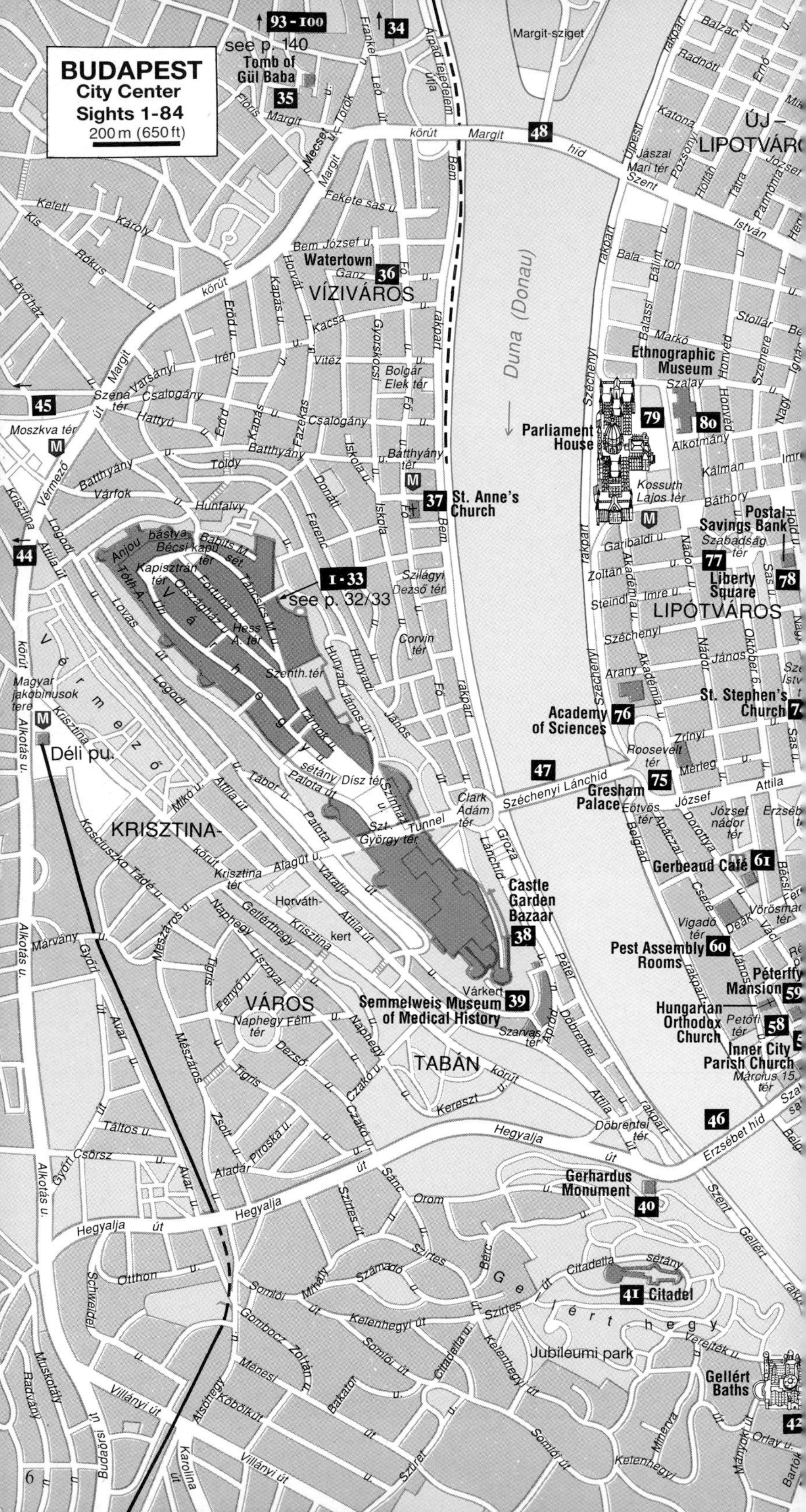
BUDAPEST
City Center
Sights 1-84
200 m (650 ft)
93 - 100
see p. 140
34
Tomb of Gül Baba
35
Margit-sziget
48
Margit híd
ÚJ-LIPÓTVÁROS
Watertown
36
VÍZIVÁROS
Duna (Donau)
Ethnographic Museum
79
80
Parliament House
Kossuth Lajos tér
St. Anne's Church
37
45
Moszkva tér
44
I - 33
see p. 32/33
Postal Savings Bank
77
Liberty Square
78
LIPÓTVÁROS
Academy of Sciences
76
St. Stephen's Church
47
Széchenyi Lánchíd
Clark Ádám tér
Gresham Palace
75
Roosevelt tér
Déli pu.
KRISZTINA-VÁROS
Vérmező
Várhegy
Gerbeaud Café
61
Castle Garden Bazaar
38
Pest Assembly Rooms
60
Péterfy Mansion
59
Semmelweis Museum of Medical History
39
Hungarian Orthodox Church
58
Inner City Parish Church
TABÁN
46
Erzsébet híd
Gerhardus Monument
40
Hegyalja út
Gellért-hegy
41 Citadel
Jubileumi park
Gellért Baths
42

see 85 - 92 p. 132
Városliget
Heroes' Square
Hősök tere
83
Városligeti-tó
Little Subway
84
82
Ferenc Hopp Eastern Asia Museum
ERZSÉBETVÁROS
81
West Station
Nyugati tér
Kodály körönd
82
TERÉZVÁROS
Lövölde tér
Oktogon
73
Hall of Fashion
70
69
Music Academy
Liszt Ferenc tér
Opera
Ernst Museum
71
72
János Arany Theater
Almássy tér
Bethlen Gábor tér
Keleti pu.
Baross tér
Klauzál tér
Orthodox Synagogue
65
ERZSÉBETVÁROS
New York Café
68
Madách Imre tér
Deák F. tér
62
Protestant Church
Great Synagogue
64
Blaha Lujza tér
Köztársaság tér
ELVÁROS
63
Central Town Hall
66
Rákóczi Road
Franciscan Church
JÓZSEFVÁROS
55
University Library
53
Gutenberg tér
56
Clothilde Mansions, Paris Court
51
Hungarian National Museum
Mátyás tér
Egyetem tér
52
University Church
54
Serbian Church
Mikszáth Kálmán tér
32-esek tere
Kálvin tér
Horváth Mihály tér
Central Market
50
Losonci tér
Csarnok tér
49
University of Economic Sciences
Fővám tér
Museum of Applied Art
67
Duna (Donau)
Technical University
43
Petőfi híd
Bakáts tér
FERENCVÁROS
Ferenc tér

Budapest — Queen of the Danube

A good many Hungarians, with their endearing propensity to exaggeration, claim that there is only one city in their country — that city, obviously, being the capital: Budapest. Cultural, academic, and political life is concentrated here to such an extent that all other population centers are merely part of the "provinces."

The course of Budapest's rapid-paced development into a European metropolis began about 120 years ago, with the union of the disparate municipalities of Buda (with Óbuda) and Pest. The luminous ribbon of the Danube — not truly blue, though on some days silvery — is the interface between the two halves of the city, uniting more than dividing. Eight bridges span the river; the buildings that line the embankments — lavish facades in the revival styles of the late nineteenth century and massive "carbuncles" of more recent date — are reflected in its waters. Budapest's magical charm has again and again earned it such sentimental titles as "Queen of the Danube." Grandeur and triviality, semblance and reality — all exist side by side in this incomparable city. Budapest

Top left: *Music students in historical costume entertaining tourists with old Hungarian folk music.*

Top right: *The equestrian monument of Stephen I by Alajos Stróbl on Fishermen's Bastion*

Turul, the emblem of the princely dynasty of Árpád, has graced

the gate to the court above the Habsburg Steps since 1903

and "her" river encapsulate the fleeting moment, show us the pulse of time monumentalized into history.

A lot of water has flowed under Budapest's bridges since the Magyars took possession of their new homeland in the Carpathian Basin eleven hundred years ago, causing most of Europe to quake with fear at the speed, dexterity, and tactical finesse of their horsemen. By the beginning of the eleventh century, however, the founder of the Hungarian state, King István I, was urging his son Imre "to be well-disposed toward, to protect, and to esteem" the foreign "newcomers" to his court, "so that they would prefer to stay and reside with him, rather than elsewhere." These foreigners with their various languages, customs, and talents, would bring "great benefit and ornament" to the realm. Today's visitor to the country can be equally as-

Top left: *The national culture is cultivated by young people too*

Top right: *The glass dome of the Museum of Applied Art [No. 67]*

Above: *This relief on Lord Street is a reminder of the former Turkish presence in Buda*

Left: *Fortuna Street, view of the building of the Hungarian State Archive*

sured of such a positive, friendly welcome. But it is certainly no disadvantage for the visitor to know of another traditional skill attributed to the Hungarian: he will courteously allow you to step first into the revolving door—only to emerge before you on the other side. Might this also be a throwback to the times of the nomadic horsemen?

The Magyars—described in historical sources from the tenth century as "handsome, spirited, quick to anger but just as quickly placated"—are proud of their city.

Top left: *Budapest is sometimes called the "Paris of the East" for its nightclubs such as the Cabaret Orfeum*

Top right: *A portrait of Franz Liszt in the National Gallery*

Above: *A female first violinist*

Right: *The* Large Hungarian Wedding, *performed at the Budapest Spring Festival*

Like all the tourists—but their rapture perhaps tinged with melancholy—they are entranced by the shimmering panorama of Budapest by night that unfolds below the Citadel and other viewpoints. But the next moment, with some caustic re-

mark or witticism, they will draw attention to the more inglorious aspects of their metropolis: the traffic congestion, the air pollution, the run-down buildings, the cunning auto thieves with their fondness for silver-metallic models, the anachronistic banking and chaotic telephone systems, the latest corruption scandal, the humiliating performance of the national football team. But woe to the foreigner who even vaguely agrees with them: in Budapest, the right to grumble is the prerogative of the locals!

This guide, however, does not dwell overmuch on the glamour, the goulash, the gypsy violinists, and the other clichés associated with Hungary, but attempts to present a wide-ranging and cohesive portrait of the metropolis on the Danube. Our "100 Places of Interest" are arranged in the form of a tour, which takes the visitor first of all to the plateau of Buda's Castle

Women from Transylvania selling embroidered goods in the center of the city

Left: *Typical inner court of a building from the 1870s*

Hill. Here we find the former palace of the kings and the sleepy lanes of the castle quarter, with a wealth of historic buildings [Nos. 1-33]—most however only presenting vestiges of their original substance. Here we can well appreciate the special position of Budapest: centuries of sieges and devastation, the precariousness of the borderland situation, tragic historical entanglements, and not least, linguistic isolation led over a long period of time to the underestimating or even ignoring of the Hungarian contribution to the cultural history of Europe.

The next section of our guide directs the visitor toward that part of Buda outside the castle fortifications [Nos. 34-45], and especially offers the opportunity to discover the city's baths, characterized by their effervescent and medicinal thermal springs. Then, after a commentary on the aesthetic and technical qualities of the Danube bridges and a visit to Margaret Island with its splendid park [Nos. 46-48], we cross over to the inner city of Pest [Nos. 49-65], where a tour of the most important examples of ecclesiastical architecture provides an insight into the religious diversity and tolerance of the city. The important principal secular buildings to be seen here illustrate the "National Style" of the turn-of-the-century Hungarian Secessionist movement. No tour of Pest would be

Above: *Braids of garlic and peppers are popular at Budapest's markets*

Right: *The famous New York Café in all its glory [No. 68]*

Below: *The Széchenyi Baths: From the days when swimming was a civilized affair [No. 87]*

complete without a visit to one of its famous coffeehouses such as the New York Café [No. 68]. The city's concert hall and its repositories for cultural treasures also lie outside the Inner Ring [Nos. 66-84]. Worthwhile as well is an excursion to the charming City Park with its impressive monuments [Nos. 85-92]. The oldest district of the city, Óbuda ("Old Buda"), will stir the imagination of the traveler with its relics of a Roman settlement.

The "Practical Tips" section provides the essential information the visitor needs to plan his stay; it includes a mini-phrasebook, which should additionally ease encounters with the exceptionally outgoing and friendly people of Budapest. We hope that a glance through this guide will convince you that one of the most useful words to know is *gyönyörű*—"fantastic!"

An Outline Chronology

c. 12,000 B. C. Stone Age settlements along the banks of the Danube and on the slopes of the Buda Hills, in which there are a large number of caves and hot springs.

c. 1250 B. C. Lusatian tribes invade from the north and establish themselves in the caves of the Buda Hills.

4th-3rd century B. C. Settlement of the area by Celtic Eravísci.

c. 10 A. D. The Romans conquer the region and set up a military base on the site of present-day Óbuda.

106 The Roman garrison Aquincum (Celtic *Ak-ink*, "with abundant water") becomes capital of the province of Pannonia Inferior.

194 Aquincum, with a population of between 30,000 and 60,000, is elevated to the status of a colony.

409 With the decline of the Roman empire, Aquincum falls into the hands of the Huns (to 453). Legend has it that Attila had his younger brother, Bleda/Buda, murdered when he named the town after himself. After Attila's death the area is occupied by Ostrogoths and Langobards.

Copy of a Roman altar with a depiction of Mars, on Kórház utca, Óbuda. The original, from the latter half of the 2nd century, is in the Aquincum museum

569 Beginning of two hundred years' Avar rule. Subsequent settlement of Bulgarian Slavs and other peoples on and around Gellért Hill and on the opposite bank of the river.

769 The region becomes a frontier territory of the Frankish empire.

896 Magyar tribes originating from the region between the Volga and the Urals cross the Carpathians into the Danube basin and begin settlement under princes Kurszán and Árpád (Árpád dynasty, 896-1301).

955 Otto I defeats the Magyars at the battle of Lechfeld. Prince Géza (972-97) converts to Christianity.

1000 On Christmas Day, Stephen (István) I (heathen name Vajk, son of Géza, reigned 997-1038) receives from the pope the holy crown (St. Stephen's Crown), with which he is crowned first king of Hungary. He encourages the spread of Catholicism in the country and is later canonized.

1046 The missionaries, especially Benedictine monks, brought to Hungary by Stephen include Bishop Gerhardus (Gellért). Heathen nomads resisting christianization cast the bishop into the Danube from the cliff that now bears his name, Gellért-hegy.

1061 First documentary mention of the city of Pest, on the left (east) bank of the Danube.

12th century Merchants from central and western Europe establish themselves in Buda and Pest.

c. 1204 Master P (known as Anonymus), the scribe of Béla III, writes the first surviving chronicle of the Hungarian people, in Low Latin.

1222 The nobility succeed in gaining more comprehensive rights, which are recorded by King Andrew (András) II in the Golden Bull.

c. 1225 Earliest document in the Hungarian language, the "Funeral Oration."

1241/42 Mongol invasion and destruction of the city.

1242-44 King Béla IV attempts to revive the devastated land and its agriculture by means of a liberal settlement policy. The German population of Pest are accorded full privileges and relocated on Castle Hill in Buda. Fortification of the city begins.

1243 Dominican friars settle in Buda.

1247-65 Construction of Buda's first royal castle.

1255 Buda receives market and customs privileges.

1255-69 Building on Castle Hill of St. Mary's Church (later Matthias Church) as German parish church and of St. Mary Magdalen's Church as parish church for the Hungarian congregation.

c. 1300 The "Old Hungarian Lament of the Virgin" reflects the piety of the mendicant religious orders. An outstanding representative is St. Margaret (Margit), daughter of Béla IV, who spent her life as a Dominican nun on the Danube island that now bears her name.

1301 Internal dissension follows upon the death of the last king of the Árpád dynasty.

1308-87 Angevin rule brings a renewed strengthening of central power vis-à-vis the nobility.

1308-42 Charles Robert (Róbert Károly, Charles I) king of Hungary. The forint as unit of Hungarian currency still survives today as a reminder of the Florentine-style gold coins Charles began to mint in 1325. Trade with the West flourishes.

1342-82 Louis (Lajos) I, the Great; in 1347 he moves his residence from Visegrád to Buda.

1387-1437 Sigismund (Zsigmond) of Luxemburg king of Hungary (from 1410 German king, and from 1433 Holy Roman Emperor). He launches an ambitious building program for Buda Castle. His international prestige is confirmed at the Council of Constance, where in 1417 papal prerogatives over the Hungarian church are largely rescinded at his instigation.

1438 Equal rights for Hungarian and German citizens are decreed by the Buda diet.

1446 János Hunyadi appointed regent.

1456 Hunyadi's armies vanquish the Turks under Mehmet II at Nándorfehérvár (now Belgrade). His victory is still commemorated today by the ringing of church bells at noon.

1458-90 Matthias (Mátyás) Corvinus, 15-year-old son of János Hunyadi, becomes king of Hungary. Patriot, gifted diplomat, and connoisseur of the arts, Matthias transforms Buda into a center of Renaissance culture. The royal castle is rebuilt and extended, and the Bibliotheca Corviniana becomes one of Europe's leading libraries.

Gyula Benczúr, The Baptism of Vajk, *1875*

Portrait of Matthias Corvinus. Miniature from the Codex Marlianus Mediolanensis, 15th century (Volterra, Biblioteca Guarnacci)

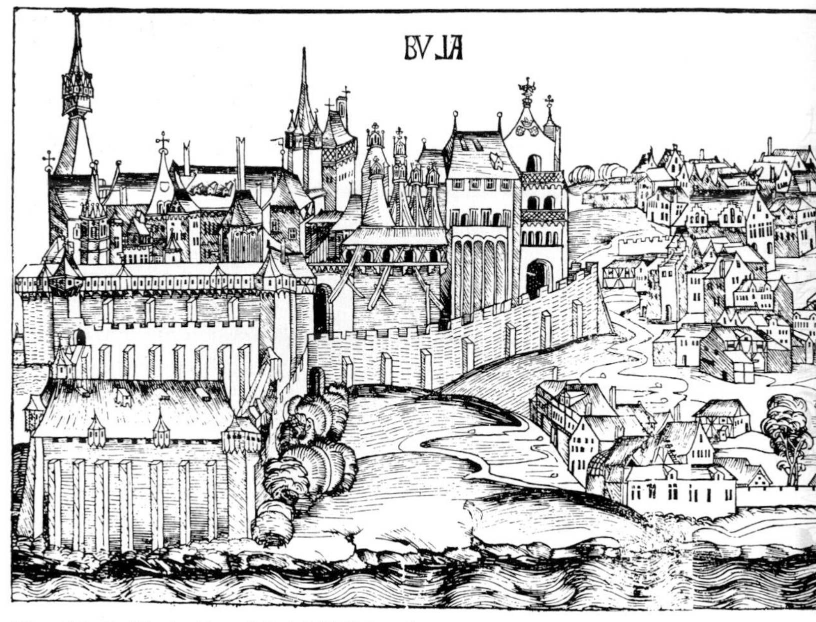

View of Buda. Woodcut from Schedel's Weltchronik, *1493*

1468 King Matthias grants Pest the privileges of a royal free city.

1471 New gold coins are minted under Matthias, who keeps a standing mercenary army and has an estimated annual income from taxes of one million florins, more than the kings of England and France.

Earliest surviving example of the Hungarian coat of arms. Found during excavations in the castle district

1473 Publication of the *Chronica Hungarorum,* the first book printed in Hungary, by András Hess of Buda.

1477 By royal charter, the Dominican college becomes the first university in Buda.

1478 The opulent royal castle is further enlarged. A law is passed threatening landlords who neglect to keep up their property with dispossession.

c. 1480 The first poems of Janus Pannonius are published.

1490-1526 Successional disputes weaken the governmental and defense system established by Matthias Corvinus. Aristocratic despotism leads to a peasant revolt under György Dózsa (1514), which is suppressed with great bloodshed by János Zápolya (Szápolyai).

1526 The Hungarian armies are defeated by the Ottoman Turks at Mohács. Buda is plundered and set to the torch. Its conquerors turn over the ravaged city to János Zápolya.

1541-1686 After Zápolya's death Buda is occupied by the Turks under Sultan Süleyman II, the Magnificent. The face of the city changes as baths, fortifications, a *medrese* (Islamic university of law and theology), and a number of barracks are built. All of its churches are converted into mosques.

1686 Charles of Lorraine and troops of the Holy League expel the Turks. The castle is heavily damaged in the fighting.

1687 At the Diet of Pozsony (Pressburg, now Bratislava) the estates assign the Hungarian crown to the house of Habsburg. The Jesuits establish themselves in Buda and open a seminary.

1694 Pest receives permission to hold four trade fairs a year, and in 1696 a national fair in addition.

1703 Both Buda and Pest obtain the royal prerogative of free cities, yet only Roman Catholics enjoy the status of free burghers.

1710/11 Blockade of the city during a revolt led by Ferenc II Rákóczi. Plague epidemic.

1712 Disastrous flood.

1724 The combined population of Buda and Pest numbers 12,200.

1730 The first German-language newspaper is published in Buda, the *Ofnerischer Mercurius.*

1731 An urban planning code is enacted.

1738-42 Great plague epidemic.

1740-80 During the reign of Maria Theresa there is a modest economic upswing, encouraged by the immigration of artisans and merchants especially from German-speaking regions. Large Jewish community in Óbuda.

1749 Cornerstone of the new royal palace laid.

1752 Regular postal coach service instituted between Buda and Vienna.

1766 A pontoon bridge links Buda and Pest.

1777 The university moves from Nagyszombat (now Trnava, Slovakia) to Buda.

View of Buda during Ottoman rule. Engraving from the workshop of Georg Houfnagel, 1617

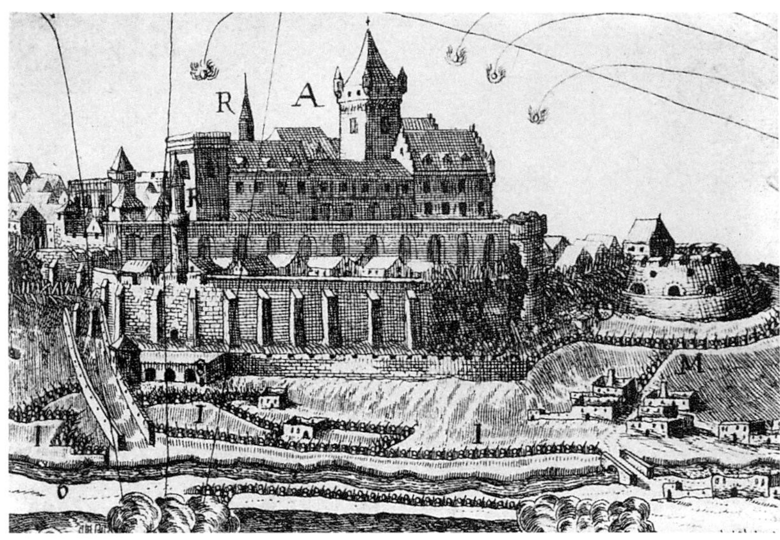

M. Wening, Recapture of Buda Castle, *1686. Etching after L. N. de Hallart*

The city obtains street lighting in the form of oil-burning candelabra.

1784 The university is relocated in Pest. Major administrative bodies are transferred from Pozsony to Buda.

1787 Castle Theater inaugurated in Buda.

1788 First newspaper in the Hungarian language published in Pest, the *Magyar Merkurius.*

Ferenc II Rákóczi, prince of Transylvania (1676-1735)

1790 The national diet convenes in Buda.

1795 Execution of Hungarian Jacobin leaders on the Vérmező ("Blood Meadow") on May 20.

1796 The 20-year-old Prince Joseph is appointed palatine of Hungary. He enjoys great popularity among the Hungarian populace.

1800 The population of Buda reaches approximately 24,000, and that of Pest 30,000. Haydn conducts the *Creation* in the royal palace; Beethoven gives a concert in the Castle Theater.

1802 Establishment of the Széchényi Library.

1805 Royal Chancellery relocated from Vienna to Budapest.

1807 The Vienna government entrusts János Hild with the architectural planning of the city; a "Beautification Commission" is formed.

1809 The royal court flees from Vienna to Buda before Napoleon's armies.

1820 Initiation of a national reform movement dedicated to a moderate liberalism and led by Count István Széchenyi.

1838 Great flood (the water level is recorded on plaques on St. Roch's Hospital and the Százéves restaurant).

1846 First railway built to connect Pest with Vác.

Count István Széchenyi (1791-1860)

The poet Sándor Petőfi (1823-49)

1848 Sándor Petőfi, poet and advocate of liberty, declaims his "Song of the Nation" at the entrance to the National Museum. Lajos Kossuth demands a Hungarian government independent of Austria. A cabinet is formed unter the leadership of Count Lajos Batthyány.

1849 General Windischgraetz's troops capture Castle Hill on January 5. Great devastation results from the fighting. April 14: Hungarian declaration of independence. The Austrians, with Russian aid, suppress the revolt.

The Széchenyi Chain Bridge (Széchenyi lánchíd) is opened to traffic.

1851-57 Ignaz Philipp Semmelweis heads the obstetric clinic at St. Roch's Hospital. In 1847 he had discovered the cause of puerperal fever.

1861 The diet is reconvened in Pest. Ferenc Deák attempts to reach a peaceful solution of the Austro-Hungarian conflict.

1861-69 Franz Liszt serves as chairman of the music academy founded at his instigation.

1867 The Austro-Hungarian Compromise results in a Hungarian constitution and the reorganization of the empire in the form of a dual monarchy.

The Great Flood of 1838

Ignaz Semmelweis, who discovered the cause of puerperal fever

1871 International competition for the redesign of Buda-Pest, with particular attention to the sewer system, streets, and power supply.

1873 The three townships of Pest, Buda, and Óbuda, whose population totals about 300,000, are amalgamated.

1876 Margaret Bridge constructed.

1877 West Station built.

1878 Electric street lighting introduced.

1881 The first telephone exchange goes into operation.

1887 First electric streetcar line built from West Station to Király utca.

Franz Liszt, most famous Hungarian composer of the Romantic era, and father-in-law of Richard Wagner

1893 Telephone news service inaugurated.

1896 The Hungarian millennium is celebrated with a great exhibition. Opening of first subway on the European continent. Franz Joseph Bridge (now Liberty Bridge) built.

1897 Kaiser Wilhelm II visits Budapest.

1900 Population of Budapest 733,843.

1905 St. Stephen's Church consecrated.

1909 First airport opens in Rákos (now Kőbánya).

c. 1910 Economic upswing; industries and services expand.

1918 November 16: Proclamation of an independent Hungarian republic.

1919 Workers' council government survives for only a few months. Romanian troops occupy Budapest in August.

1920-40 Miklós Horthy head of state; he proclaims the country a monarchy with vacant throne.

1920 The Treaty of Trianon deprives Hungary of two-thirds of her territory, which falls to Czechoslovakia, Romania, and Yugoslavia.

1941 Hungary enters the war on the side of the Axis.

1944 March 19: German troops occupy the country; deportation of the Jewish population begins. October 15: Following Horthy's abortive attempt to extricate Hungary from the war, the pro-Nazi Arrow-Cross party takes control.

1945 Budapest is occupied by Soviet troops; much of the city is in ruins.

1945-49 Coalition governments are dominated by the Communists; expropriation of estates and nationalization of banks and industry. Cardinal Mindszenty sentenced to life imprisonment.

1946 Liberty Bridge (Szabadság híd) is the first Danube bridge to be rebuilt.

1949 Rigged elections create overwhelming majority for Hungarian Workers' Party (hard-liner Mátyás Rákosi general secretary, to 1956). August 20: Hungary becomes a "People's Republic." Purges of "subversive" elements, e.g. former foreign secretary László Rajk (executed October 15).

1950 Ferihegy Airport opened.

A moment of triumph in the abortive Hungarian Uprising of 1956

1953 After Stalin's death a "new course" is promulgated. Imre Nagy replaces Rákosi as prime minister; he closes the internment camps and plans further reforms.

1955 Nagy deposed by pro-Moscow faction.

1956 Earthquakes in January and June. October 23: A student demonstration escalates into a full-scale revolt; Nagy is returned to power. November 4: Soviet tanks enter Budapest; the popular uprising is brutally suppressed.

The rehabilitation and reburial of ex-premier Imre Nagy, executed in 1958, was an important step on the way to the new Hungary

1956-88 Under János Kádár Hungary is again a loyal member of the Soviet bloc, but from the sixties onward tentatively begins to liberalize conditions at home and seek more contacts with the West.

1958 Nagy and associates condemned for high treason and executed.

1968 The "New Economic Mechanism" represents a departure from rigidly orthodox Communist principles. Rebuilding of Buda Castle completed.

1972/73 Hundredth anniversary of the unified city of Budapest. East-west subway line completed. The city's population reaches the two-million mark.

1975 Slum clearance program inaugurated; the old cores of Buda and Pest are restored.

1978 The USA returns St. Stephen's Crown and other national treasures to Hungary.

1987 A meeting of liberal intellectuals in Lakitelek results in the formation of the Hungarian Democratic Forum (HDF).

1989 Opening of the border to Austria. Hungary becomes a democratic republic. Imre Nagy is rehabilitated.

1990 The first free elections after the demise of the one-party state return the HDF to power.

1991 June 30: The last Soviet troops leave Hungary.

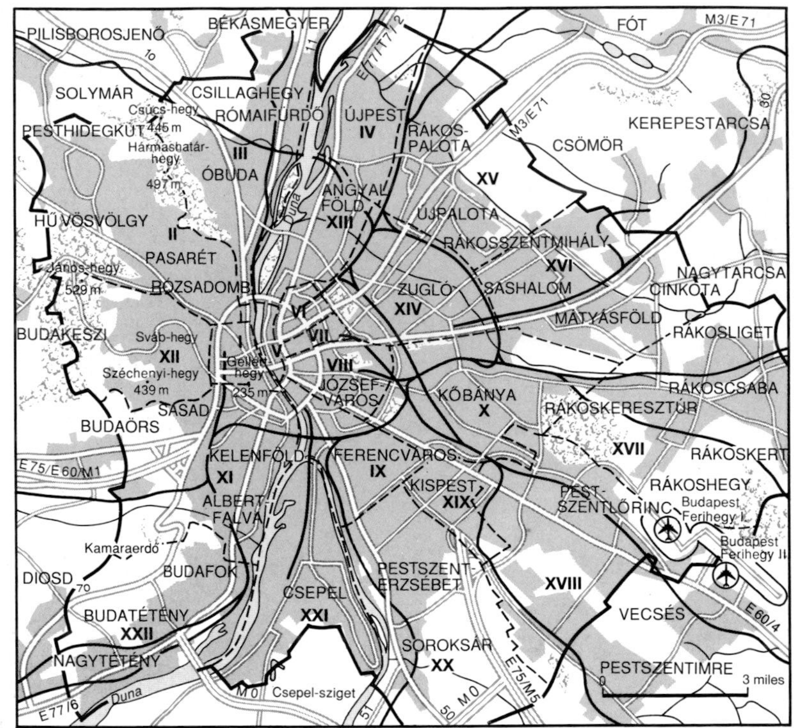

Facts and Figures

Status: Budapest is the capital of the Hungarian Republic, and also the country's largest industrial center.

Location: Longitude 19°08′ E, latitude 47°29′ N. Height above sea level: from 97 m/318 ft. (Csepel Island) to 529 m/1,734 ft. (János Hill).

Municipal area: 525 km²/202 sq. mi., of which Pest comprises 351 km²/135 sq. mi. and Buda 174 km²/67 sq. mi. Residential area 182 km²/69 sq. mi.; industrial area 45 km²/17 sq. mi; water 30 km²/12 sq. mi.; green areas 67 km²/26 sq. mi.

The **Danube** flows through Budapest for 28 km/17 mi. of its course, with an average width of 400 m/1,312 ft. and depth of 5.8 m/19 ft.

Local time: Greenwich Mean Time plus one hour (Central European Time). In summer, Budapest goes on daylight saving time, setting clocks ahead one hour.

Climate: Continental climate, with an average annual temperature of 10.9°C/52°F (January –1.2°C/30°F, July 22°C/71°F).

Population: 2,015,955 (as of January 1, 1992). About a fifth of the country's inhabitants live in Budapest, whose ethnic groups include Gypsies, Germans, Slovaks, Southern Slavs, and Romanians.

Religion: Approximately 50% Roman Catholic, 30% Protestant, 10% Orthodox, Jewish, and other faiths; the remaining 10% unaffiliated.

Transportation: 3,700 km/2,300 mi. of roads, and a good public transportation system, including 159 km/99 mi. of tramways, 68 km/42 mi. of trolleybus lines, 743 km/462 mi. of bus lines, 31 km/19 mi. of subways, and 110 km/68 mi. of suburban railways. Two airports, located in Ferihegy.

Cultural institutions: 95 public libraries, 22 theaters, 127 movie theaters, 87 museums.

Coat of arms: On New Year's Day 1991 Budapest received a new coat of arms [illustration p. 3] based largely on its traditional emblem. The shield is in the colors red, gold, and blue, and the transverse silver band symbolizing the Danube now appears without the five-pointed red star of socialism. Auxiliary emblems are, at the top, St. Stephen's Crown and, flanking and bearing the shield, lambent figures of animals: a lion and a griffon.

Postal code: H-1xxx. The second and third digits denote the district.

Fishermen's Bastion ▷

100 Places of Interest

Castle Hill: Royal Palace and Borough

A flat rocky eminence rising some 180 feet above the Danube, Castle Hill is about a mile long but relatively narrow; the plateau is guarded by perimeter walls. The northern part is occupied by a self-contained township of historic burgher houses, while the extensive royal palace crowns the southern extremity. Of the many accesses to Castle Hill, which is largely closed to automobile traffic, we recommend the pedestrian route that begins on Szarvas tér near Erzsébet híd (Elizabeth Bridge). Skirting the round bastion, steps lead up to the Ferdinand Gate, which is guarded to the west by the Buzogány (Mace) Tower; the ascent ends at the entrance to the Budapest Historical Museum.

History: The origins of Buda Castle extend back to the period after 1241/42, when Mongol tribes had invaded Hungary and left devastation and poverty in their wake. King Béla IV made valiant attempts to lead the country out of its lethargy and economic ruin, and to revive a cultural life that had been well-nigh extinguished. To defend the Danube harbor against further attack, he had a fortress with keep surrounded by high walls built on the southeast tip of the Buda plateau, which since the eleventh century had been occupied by an unfortified farming community, Minor Pesth. The six-foot-thick walls of stone that began to go up in 1243 soon secured the entire plateau and the town of Buda, also founded by Béla IV. Under the Ange-

vin dynasty the thirteenth-century castle walls had to make way for new fortifications. Construction of the medieval palace was largely due to the status-consciousness of King Louis (Lajos) the Great; unlike his father, Charles Robert of Anjou, he resided not in Visegrád but, from 1347, in the castle at Buda. The ruins of a Gothic dwelling tower (obliquely set before the south front of the Budapest Historical Museum) named after his younger brother, Stephen (d. 1354), and the lower part of a two-story chapel on the Danube side, which was finished in 1366, attest to the king's building activity. During the fifty-year reign of Sigismund of Luxemburg (1387-1437) the Angevin castle was considerably expanded and converted into one of the most formidable and magnificent royal palaces in Europe. A complex fortification system with reinforced walls and sophisticated defenses not only sealed off the battlemented castle and its three courtyards from the Danube side and along the western edge, but also isolated it from the town. Where the "New Palace"

"Breather" Gate, one of the earliest still extant features of Buda Castle

Castle Hill and the royal palace from the Pest side of the river. The Matthias Church and Fishermen's Bastion are visible at the far right

Ferdinand Gate, the southern entrance to the castle. To its left, the Mace Tower

abutted on the marketplace, Sigismund ordered a moat to be dug, sixty feet wide and twenty deep. In the north courtyard, a tower was planned as a bulwark in front of the west wing, and masons were apparently hired from Prague cathedral lodge, headed by Peter Parler; never finished, it was known as the "Rump Tower." King Sigismund received a number of illustrious foreign guests in his Buda Palace — in 1395 crusaders against the Turks, including Jean sans Peur, who later became Duke of Burgundy. It was the site of key diplomatic negotiations, such as the peace talks of 1412 between Poland and the Order of Teutonic Knights, and developed into a center of international cultural exchange in the fields of music, architecture, and sculpture. In the Chronicle of the Hungarians (1488), János Thuróczy describes their "foreign king" fifty years after his death as an imposing man with a handsome face, kindly eyes, and wavy, bluish hair, who let his beard grow long out of affection for the Hungarians.

Ever aware of the Ottoman threat, Sigismund had his smiths forge a heavy iron chain, which, stretched across the Danube from bank to bank, barred the river passage. Another example of the engineering feats he encouraged was the town's first water supply system. Work began in 1416, when Hartmann Steinpeck of Nuremberg developed a special pump, followed a short time later by a horse-driven hydraulic elevator that supplied the palace with Danube water. For heating, the Angevin building had had conduits in the floor, while under Sigismund the palace was equipped with large dutch ovens.

During the reign of King Matthias Corvinus (1458-90), Buda Castle rose to new glory. Among those who sang its praises was court historian Antonio Bonfini, who in his *Rerum Ungaricarum Decades* (1491-96) wrote: "King Matthias ordered the repair of Buda Castle, in which, apart from Sigismund's magnificent buildings, there was nothing very remarkable. He had the rear of the palace renovated with great splendor and, on the Danube side, had a chapel fitted out with a water organ and ornamented with a double font of marble and silver.... Upstairs he installed his library, which was exceedingly rich in Greek and Latin books. He had palaces built that are more than a match for the splendid palaces of Rome, furnished grand dining rooms and superb bedchambers, likewise fitted with all variety of gilded ceilings, and ornamented with diverse coats of arms, fine doors embellished at the top with inlay work, and magnificent fireplaces.... Below are the ground-floor rooms and treasuries and, to the east, various pantries and bedchambers.... Then come the council chamber and assembly hall. As one proceeds, various high, vaulted living rooms, many winter and summer rooms follow, as do sunny terraces, gilded niches, and also deep, secret chambers, silver couches, silver thrones." The court of Buda during Matthias's reign was not only the seat of a politically well-founded royal power but provided new stimuli to European trade, economy, art, culture, and even fashion.

Records indicate that King Matthias used the two-aisle Great Hall in Sigismund's New Palace — at 240×60 feet the largest interior in all of Hungary — on a variety of official and festive occasions, including his own wedding celebrations. By installing stairways and portals of red marble, and bronze candelabra and door leaves, he updated the Gothic interiors in the Renaissance style. Sigismund's Rump Tower, on the other hand, served Matthias as a prison. To the south of the New Palace

Aerial view of Castle Hill, with the Víziváros quarter behind. Also visible are the Danube island Margit-sziget and three bridges: Széchenyi lánchíd in the foreground, Margit híd, and Árpád híd

Matthias had new wings built around an arcaded courtyard. To the east projected the chapel with Holy Sepulcher mentioned by Bonfini (excavated between 1947 and 1955). Adjacent to the chapel, on the second floor of the east wing, there was an observatory and a royal library, the Bibliotheca Corviniana, whose priceless stocks of richly illustrated manuscripts grew—particularly after Matthias married the Neapolitan princess Beatrix of Aragon in 1476—to over two thousand volumes and attracted scholars from far and wide, including the Florentine humanist Taddeo Ugoleto. The palace also harbored workshops devoted to copying and illumination, majolica ceramics, goldsmith work, glassblowing, inlay work, and furniture making, done in a shop whose carved and gilded coffered ceilings were extolled by all who saw them. From the royal gardens on the southwest slope of the hill a covered passageway led down to the royal baths. According to Bonfini, the gardens included not only a vineyard, fruit trees, and plots of vegetables imported from Italy, but the Villa Marmorena, a gem of Renaissance architecture whose roof of silver-plated copper gleamed in the sun.

The beauty of Buda Castle during Matthias's reign is no longer immediately evident, as none of its structures have survived intact. Still, its predominant Florentine and Tuscan style has been recorded in descriptions, building plans, drawings, and prints, and is reflected especially in the architectural fragments that remain. These finds include pieces of pilaster and column capitals in the manner of Filippo Brunelleschi, Michelozzo di Bartolomeo, and Leon Battista Alberti, door frames embellished with garlands of fruit, balustrade posts, and friezes in styles echoing those of Bernardo and Antonio Rossellino, Desiderio da Settignano, and Benedetto da Majano. Giovanni Dalmata (Ioannes Duknovic de Tragurio) was the most renowned of the Dalmatian stonemasons who worked for the Hungarian king in Buda. A key phase of building activity under Matthias is associated with the name of Chimenti Camicia, an architect from Florence. Made chief supervisor of works about 1479 Camicia was active in Buda until 1491 and played a considerable part in the rapid influx of Renaissance art from Florence during this period. King Matthias Corvinus in turn sent Hungarian masters to Florence to study the new arts, sciences, and humanistic teachings at their source. A patron and purchaser of art, he also corresponded with Lorenzo Medici. It

Turkish gravestones on the southern slope of Castle Hill

was another Italian who praised the Hungarian capital of the day in the words: "The three most beautiful cities in all of Europe are Venice by the sea, Buda on the hill, and Florence in the plain."

Although the Turks called the palace "Kazil Elma" (palace of the "Golden Apple") on account of its gilded roof tiles, they let it completely deteriorate in the period of Ottoman rule from 1541 to 1686. During a spring thunderstorm in 1578, the gunpowder stored in the New Palace exploded, destroying the most significant building of Sigismund's era. By the time Budapest was recaptured, all that remained of the palace was an imposing ruin.

When King Charles III of Habsburg (1711-40) decided to build a new, Baroque palace, the crumbling walls of a structure that had once been famous throughout Europe were torn down, and the site required for its successor razed as far as the Great Court to the north. Of the buildings erected to plans by Fortunato de Prati under the supervision of Johann Hölbling from 1714 to 1723, none have survived but the south wing (Historical Museum). The only way now to walk in the steps of the ancient kings of Hungary and gain a sense of the eventful history of this site is to descend into the subterranean levels.

The life and times of Empress Maria Theresa (1740-80), daughter of Charles III, are also associated with the architectural development of the castle. She had the last remnants of the old royal palace razed, and added to her father's, to the north, a two-story extension with central projection. The plans were drawn up by Jean-Nicolas Jadot, architect to the Viennese court, and Nikolaus Pacassi. Franz Anton Hillebrandt and Ignác Oracsek designed a salient wing on the Danube side. Completed by 1770, the building accommodated a convent from 1762 to 1772, and from 1779 to 1784 it housed the university after its move to Budapest from Nagyszombat.

After 1790 the court in Vienna designated the palace residence of the palatine, or viceroy. The great fire of 1810 and the attack by the Honvéd army during the Hungarian rising in May 1849 both severely damaged the new palace. When Emperor Franz Joseph was crowned king of Hungary in 1867, after the Compromise between Vienna and the Hungarian nation, the desire arose to rebuild and enlarge the castle on a grand scale. The project was entrusted to the architects Miklós Ybl (active 1869-91) and Alajos Hauszmann (1893-1905). In 1875, on the western flank of the hill above Krisztinaváros, Ybl began a new wing in the Neo-Renaissance style. Through Hauszmann's contribution the main facade on the Danube was given a unified, Neo-Baroque treatment and extended to a length of 1,000 feet. A domed and colonnaded central block linked the Charles III and Maria Theresa structures with the extension, and an integrated roof design crowned the whole.

Shortly before the end of the Second

World War the palace was gutted by fire. In parallel with reconstruction work, excavation began — and continues to this day — of parts of the medieval complex, bringing to light a variety of architectural fragments and thousands of examples of decorative art. Restoration in the 1950s was based on an eclectic approach; the domed main facade on the Danube side is magnificently effective. Since the late 1960s a number of cultural institutions have taken up quarters in the castle complex: wing A — Museum of Contemporary History with Ludwig Collection; wings B, C, and D — Hungarian National Gallery; wing E — Budapest Historical Museum; and wing F — Széchényi National Library.

Sculpture fragment from the era of King Sigismund

I Budapest Historical Museum

Budapesti Történeti Múzeum

Wing E of Buda Castle

Illustrates the history of Budapest and particularly of Castle Hill, and houses notable Gothic sculptures discovered during excavations.

On the upper floors of the museum, original documents, finds from archaeological excavations, and samples of visual art illustrate the history and territorial development of the settlements on the banks of the Danube that now constitute the metropolis of Budapest, created by the amalgamation in 1873 of the towns of Pest, Buda, and Óbuda. The museum gives an interesting overview of the inhabitation of the area before the Magyars and its subsequent development after Hungarian colonization. Periodic exhibitions are devoted to key epochs of Hungarian history.

When we explore the basement of the museum, which is built on the foundations of the original royal palace, it is like traversing the ages of Hungary's history as reflected in the construction phases of the castle. The rebuilt lower section of an orig-

15th-century floor tiles found during the excavation of Buda Castle

Castle Hill
(the numbers correspond to the articles in the text)

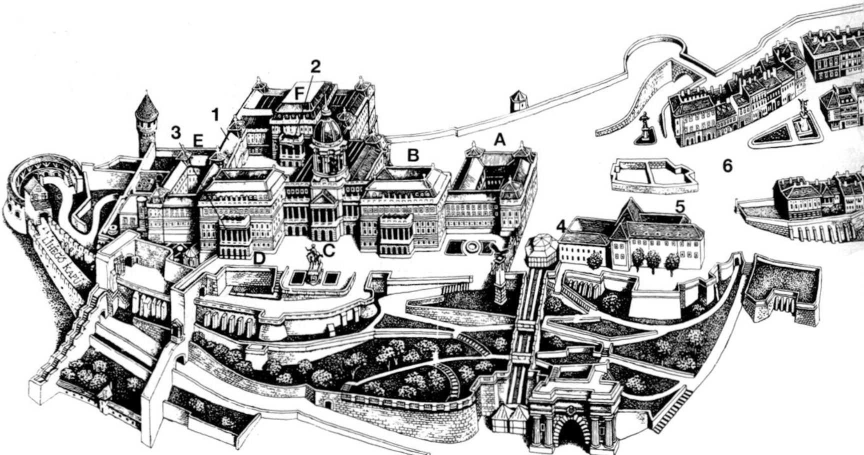

1 Budapest Historical Museum
2 Széchényi National Library
3 Hungarian National Gallery
4 Sándor Palace
5 Castle Theater
6 Parade Square (Dísz tér)
7 Treasurer Street (Tárnok utca)
8 Matthias Church
9 Fishermen's Bastion
10 Hilton Hotel
11 András Hess Square
12 The Red Hedgehog
13 Mihály Táncsics Street
14 Old Barracks
15 The Jewish Quarter
16 Mihály Babits Promenade
17 Vienna Gate Square (Bécsi kapu tér)
18 Fortuna Street

inally two-story Gothic chapel of 1366 stems from the palace of Louis the Great; reconsecrated on August 18, 1990, as St. Stephen's Chapel (Szent István kápolna), it is now used for ecumenical services. The two-aisle Gothic Great Hall, once the queen's chambers, is a fascinating architectural experience.

The coats of arms, stove tiles, and carved fragments of red limestone displayed in their original or reconstructed settings reflect the superb craftsmanship and specifically national character that Hungarian art had attained by the time the palace of King Matthias was built. As recent research indicates, the formal canon of Italian quattrocento architecture did not pass to Central Europe by way of France or the Alpine region, as was long thought, but initially via Hungary.

Among the most significant items on display in the museum are the forty or so Gothic sculptures exhibited in a suitably awe-inspiring ambience in one of the ground floor rooms, the remnants of a series of figures commissioned by Emperor Sigismund in Buda. The sculptures came to light in 1974, in the course of excavations in the northern castle forecourt. It was a sensational find, because it revealed the Hungarian royal court in the period around 1400 to have been a center of European rank as regards Gothic sculpture in the International Style. Made of limestone from the environs of Buda and 35 to 50 inches in height, the figures represent saints, bishops, and knights and ladies of the court, whose garments reflect European fashions of the 1360s to 1370s. They were probably done by French stonema-

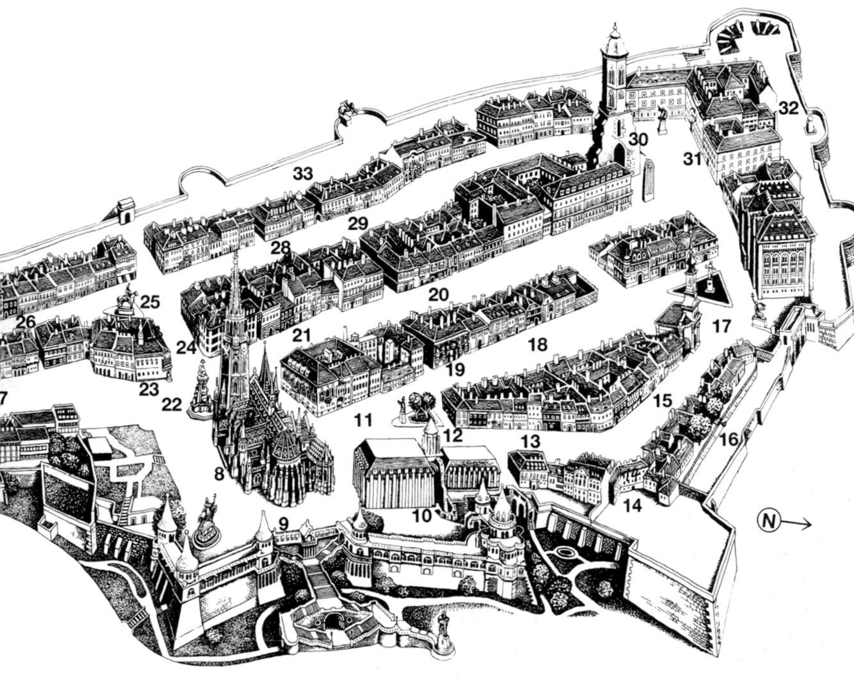

19 Museum of Commerce and Catering
20 Parliament Street (Országház utca)
21 Országház utca 2
22 Trinity Square (Szentháromság tér)
23 Old Town Hall
24 Ruszwurm Pastry Shop
25 Hadik Monument
26 Lord Street (Úri utca)
27 Buda Castle Labyrinth and Panopticum
28 Hölbling House
29 Lord Street (Úri utca) north
30 St. Mary Magdalen's Church
31 Capistrano Square (Kapisztrán tér)
32 Anjou Bastion
33 Árpád Tóth Promenade

sons who had an extremely detailed knowledge of the figure program on the Tour Maubergeon of the duc de Berry's castle in Poitiers (1385). While a few of the pieces in this unique collection show traces of original painting and gilding, other fragments were apparently left unfinished, or perhaps were smashed or disfigured in an act of iconoclasm. They were buried or used as filling material for new buildings during the period of discord that preceded Matthias's accession to the throne in 1458. One controversial early dating associates the rediscovered sculptures with the inital phase of King Sigismund's reign, prior to 1397. Married into the kingdom, this ruler from the house of Luxemburg was embroiled from the start in political conflict with the leading magnates of the Hungarian court. When Sigismund's crusade suffered defeat at the hands of the Turks in the battle of Nikopolis in 1396, a clique of nobles in Buda fomented a revolt to rid the country of the unpopular king. The wrath directed against Sigismund, whose extensive building activity fueled accusations of prodigality, may not have stopped short of the sculptures created and displayed in his palace.

The fortifications of Buda Castle, most of which date from Sigismund's era, can be viewed to best advantage from the terrace of the Historical Museum. Visible to the right of the ruin of the St. Stephen Tower (c. 1330) are sections of the inner wall and, abutting on the Mace Tower, remnants of the outer wall. On the Danube side the outer wall is intersected by two lateral walls ("curtains"), which ended at the riverbank in two massive bastions. The south curtain once housed a horse-driven waterworks, designed by Hartmann Steinpeck, a hydraulic engineer from Nuremberg, and built in 1416. The huge circular bastion (130 feet in diameter, with fifteen-foot-thick walls) with its gate tower—nicknamed by the Turks "Breather Gate" on account of the steep ascent—guards the carriageway that leads to the south gate of the castle. Running around the top of the bulwark is a (reconstructed) parapet, or "murder walk" as it used to be known for the opportunities it afforded the defending garrison; this type of high bastion (*cavaliero*), with embrasures between projecting spurs of masonry and a wood-roofed ledge along the inner side, was the brainchild of the military engineer Domenico da Bologna (before 1541).

In the interior courtyard of the Historical Museum, differently colored paving stones mark the outlines of the destroyed medieval buildings. The garden below the south facade of the museum is graced by the Beatrix Fountain, a stone cistern installed here after 1476, the year of King Matthias Corvinus's marriage. It bears a double coat of arms surmounted by a crown, carved delicately and in great detail. The right-hand shield bears the family arms of the queen's house, Aragon; Matthias's arms feature the national emblem with the Hungarian stripes, the Hungarian two-armed cross, lions' heads signifying Dalmatia, the Bohemian lion, and finally, in a superimposed, heart-shaped field, the raven from the arms of the Hunyadi family.

The entrance to the Historical Museum from Lion Court may be seen as a metaphor of the turbulent history of the Hungarian royal palace: the allegory *War and Peace* flanking the portal is a 1900 work by Károly Senyei, the sculptor who in 1912 also created the fountain sculpture *Children Fishing* (located in front of the east facade of wing A).

2 Széchényi National Library

Országos Széchényi Könyvtár

On Lion Court in wing F of Buda Castle

Repository of one of the world's finest Renaissance libraries and of a modern scientific collection; venue of important exhibitions.

Entering Lion Court by way of the north gate, for a second we might well feel we have strayed into the lions' den. The highly naturalistic sculptures, created by János Fadrusz (1901/02), have given the spacious courtyard its apt name. On the western side, Lion Court is bordered by the National Library, a building from the 1890s designed by Miklós Ybl and Alajos Hauszmann. The library was founded in 1802 by Count Ferenc Széchényi. Its most prized possession is a collection of manuscripts from the era of Matthias Corvinus.

The royal library, Bibliotheca Corviniana, has been a byword among scholars here and abroad since the latter half of the fifteenth century. Its name derives from the raven (*corvus*) with a ring in its beak that graced the arms of King Matthias, a Renaissance monarch and erudite humanist. Taddeo Ugoleto, his court librarian from Florence, had every codex in the collection adorned with this emblem. A gem of artisanry in gold-plated silver with baked enamel inlays, it shines on bindings of gilded, tooled, or embroidered leather, on purple velvet, on red or green silk. The manuscripts, written in Greek or Latin with abundant illuminations and marvellous calligraphy, are devoted to topics in the fields of philosophy, poetry, rhetoric, medicine, astronomy, geography, architecture, and military history.

A few of the valuable and coveted books were given away by King Matthias's successors. Sultan Süleyman II, after his victory at Mohács in 1526, had a portion of the library taken to Turkey; the remaining

---

Eyewitness report of 1485: *"Let it be known that Matthias, King of the Hungarians, in the Year 1485 of Our Lord, at eight o'clock in the morning on the eve of Corpus Christi Day, entered the City of Vienna in order to capture it. Firstly, he sent 32 wagons with provisions ahead, and then, 2000 selected horseman. These were followed, thirdly, by 24 camels bearing the king's treasury. Fourthly came 400 foot-soldiers, fifthly 24 bishops with 1000 horsemen, all selected men. Sixthly King Matthias entered the city accompanied by 1000 horsemen. They followed him well armed and on steeds decked in caparisons that reached to the ground. Seventhly the king was followed by 200 very select troops on foot. Eighthly came 1000 oxen for the provisioning of said city.... Vienna, seat of Austria, fell into Hungarian hands. So had God pleased it to be."*

On the north wall of wing C of the royal palace, the Matthias Fountain depicts the king on a hunting expedition (Alajos Stróbl, 1904)

manuscripts were carefully looked after by the pashas of Buda, as seventeenth-century sources record. In 1877, Sultan Abdul Hamid made a diplomatic gesture by returning a number of Corviniana treasures to Austria-Hungary. The Renaissance king's superb library contained over two thousand items. Today, the National Library is in possession of 32 of the 216 surviving originals; the others are dispersed among 47 libraries in 16 countries.

3 Hungarian National Gallery

Magyar Nemzeti Galéria

Wings B, C, and D of Buda Castle

Hungarian visual arts from the Romanesque era to the present day.

An autonomous institution devoted to the collection, preservation, study, and presentation of the country's art, the Hungarian National Gallery was established in 1957 and initially housed in a building on Kossuth Lajos tér. Its nucleus was formed by various private and public collections, including a municipal collection that had existed since 1880. In the meantime, the gallery's stocks have grown to almost seventy thousand works in the fields of painting, sculpture, drawing, printmaking, and medallions. It moved to its present location in the palace in 1975.

Displayed on the first floor of wings C and D are medieval Hungarian sculpture and painting. Among the most outstanding pieces are two wood sculptures in the International Style of the early fifteenth century, a St. Dorothy from Barka and a Madonna from Toporc. Great artistic and documentary value attaches to the medieval stonemason's work, fragments of applied sculpture, and architectural ornamentation originating from major Hungarian churches, cathedrals, and monasteries, such as the late Romanesque pieces from Ják Abbey (first half of the thirteenth century). The collection is supplemented by carvings from the Renaissance centers of Buda, Visegrád, Vác, Nyék, and Diósgyőr.

On the second floor of wing D, in the former ceremonial hall of Empress Maria Theresa (known since 1856 as the "Great Throne Room"), Late Gothic altarpieces are on display. A major work is to be found in the vestibule of the hall, a Visitation by Master M.S., dating from 1506; the panel was originally part of an altarpiece in Selmecbánya.

Hungarian Baroque art is on view in the adjacent rooms of the former Emperor's Suite, including the opulent bedchamber. Portraits of rulers, funerary sculptures, domestic altars, and devotional pictures bear witness to avid patronage of the arts on the part of the Hungarian nobility.

Leaving the Baroque gallery, we find nineteenth-century painting and sculpture on the second floor of wings B and C. Romantic painting is well represented, with landscapes by Károly Makó and Károly Kisfaludy, as is the Biedermeier period, with Miklós Barabás's discreetly respectful portraits and exuberant genre paintings (*Arrival of the Bride*, 1856). A salient trait of Hungarian painting, a profound love of country not infrequently tinged with transfiguring melancholy, is especially evident in the large-format history paintings of the latter half of the century (Viktor Madarász's *Mourning of László Hunyadi*, 1859; Bertalan Székely's *Women of Eger*, 1867). The potential of impressionistic, plein-air painting was explored by Pál Szinyei Merse, an artist associated with the Leibl circle in Munich (*Picnic in May*, 1873). As regards Hungarian Realism, the outstanding rank of Mihály Munkácsy is underscored by a presentation of his work in a special room. *The Condemned Cell* won the artist a gold medal at the 1870 Paris Salon.

The development of Hungarian art in the twentieth century is traced in displays on the third and fourth floors. The top floor is also devoted to changing exhibitions from the rich holdings of the department of prints and drawings (comprising about forty thousand works on paper).

The Ludwig Collection (sponsored by a German patron) features contemporary Hungarian and international art; since 1991 it has been installed on the second floor of wing A (Museum of Contemporary History).

The schedule of the Hungarian National Gallery also includes large special exhibitions, one of the main focuses of which is art around 1900. Art Nouveau in Hungary was a euphoric movement that lasted from about 1896 to 1914 and encompassed highly diverse but characteristic styles. In a historicism suffused with patriotic fervor, artists living a millennium after the Hungarian colonization exalted the nomadic life into the realm of myth. Yet this strongly cultic approach was parallelled by an art devoted to the beauties of everyday life and of great painterly sophistication. The major figure in this context is unquestionably Tivadar Csontváry Kosztka. Three of his idiosyncratic, visionary paintings (including *The Ruins of the Greek Theater in Taormina*, 1904/05) are displayed in the stairwell between the third and fourth floors, where the marvelous brilliance of their colors fascinates visitors. In the paintings of József Ripple Rónai, a Post-Impressionist pointillism of French inspiration is combined with graceful stylization and mysterious symbolism (*Woman with a Birdcage*, 1892).

The Habsburg Palatine Crypt (entrance from wing C of the National Gallery): During the reign of Maria Theresa, a chapel dedicated to St. Sigismund with crypt was erected in the interior courtyard of the north block of the new palace, to a design by court architect Nicolas Jadot. In the course of conversion and expansion under Nikolaus Pacassi and F. A. Hillebrandt, the chapel was incorporated in the western part of what is now wing C. The crypt served until 1777 as a burial place for the nuns of the Mary Ward order. From 1820 it was used as a family vault by the palatines who represented the house of Habsburg in Hungary; alterations were subsequently made by Franz Hüppmann, Miklós Ybl, and Alajos Hauszmann, who took the Medici Chapel in Florence as their inspiration. The three vaulted rooms with a total area of 80 × 25 ft. are faced with marble; the ceiling represents the star-studded heavens, and the spandrels are painted with figures of angels. The sculptures are by Alajos Stróbl, Károly Senyei, and György Zala (statue and relief on the tomb of Palatine Joseph, d. 1847). A large part of

Master M. S., The Visitation, *early 16th century. Hungarian National Gallery*

the exquisite and finely crafted furnishings were lost to theft in 1972; the mortal remains of the palatines were vandalized. The crypt was restored at the expense of great time and effort in the late 1980s.

In the northwest forecourt that lies between wings A and C, the **Matthias Fountain** built onto the north facade of the former St. Sigismund's Chapel invokes the bygone glory of the royal palace. Often compared with the Fontana di Trevi in Rome, this 1904 work by Alajos Stróbl is a paean of praise to the popular Renaissance monarch, whose life is shrouded in legend. In majestic pose, accompanied by his chief hunter and the Italian court poet Galeotto Marzio (on the left), Matthias is depicted as an unknown hunter who gains

Pál Szinyei Merse, Picnic in May, *1873*

the love of a Hungarian country girl, the lovely Ilonka (on the right). This idealization had a long tradition, extending back to Antonio Bonfini's eyewitness descriptions: "The late Matthias was physically somewhat taller than average; his body was well-shaped and possessed great endurance and strength in bearing cold, heat, and hunger. He suffered nothing easier than exertions in war, and nothing harder than inactivity at home. His glance was open and frank, like that of a lion. Yes, even to the cut of his eyes and his youthfulness he very much resembled the man whom he had ever taken as an ideal for his life — Alexander the Great."

In the course of postwar reconstruction a number of sculptures were removed from the sites originally determined by palace architect Alajos Hauszmann. These include *The Horseherd*, a chased-copper sculpture of about 1898 by György Vas-

Tivadar Csontváry Kosztka, Ruins of the Greek Theater in Taormina, *1904/05. Hungarian National Gallery*

tagh the Younger, which was shown with success at the Paris World Fair of 1899/1900, and which, since 1983, has graced the northwest forecourt in front of wing B. The two bronze figures *Csongor and Tünde*, pieces by Miklós Ligeti based on the romantic fairy tale of the same name by Mihály Vörösmarty, now located near the Danube-side gallery entrance in wing C, were unfortunately torn out of a very effective architectural context on the side landings of the Habsburg steps (where they had stood since 1903). On the other hand, *Prince Eugene of Savoy* still surveys the city from his charger outside the main entrance of the National Gallery, as he has since the turn of the century. The equestrian statue commemorates the general who liberated Hungary from the Turks in the late seventeenth century. Originally ordered by the town of Senta (now in Serbia), scene of Eugene's greatest victory, it was purchased for Buda Castle by Emperor Franz Joseph from its creator, József Róna. The exit to Szent György tér is marked by a majestic mythical bird atop a column rising above the Habsburg Steps, a hunting falcon with outstretched wings modelled in 1903 by Gyula Donáth. Known as the Turul, it is the emblem of the princely dynasty of Árpád: according to legend, the primeval mother of the Hungarian people bore a child by the Turul, Álmos, the progenitor of the clan, whose son Árpád led the Hungarian settlement of the country.

4 Sándor Palace

Sándor palota

Szent György tér 1-2

Residence of the prime ministers of Hungary from 1867 to 1944.

Beneath Szent György tér runs the thirty-foot-wide tunnel that was bored through Castle Hill in 1853-57, to plans by the British engineer Adam Clark; at its eastern edge is the station of the funicular railway, which — inaugurated in 1870 and destroyed in the Second World War — has since 1986 again been carrying passengers up from the Danube embankment. In medieval times the venue of jousts and fairs, thousands of years earlier the site of the square was the bed of a lake fed by hot springs. In 1806, Count Vincent Sándor commissioned Michael Pollack with the construction of a Neoclassical mansion. The building was originally connected with the theater across the narrow lane by a covered bridge. Its architect, trained in Vienna and Milan, had settled in Pest in 1799, and contributed materially to shaping the city's aspect with buildings in the Neoclassical style.

Spectacular balls and festivities took place in the Sándors' mansion. The most illustrious guests of the noble family were Friedrich Wilhelm III of Prussia, the Russian czar Alexander I, and Emperor Franz of Austria, who met under their roof in autumn 1814. The first owner's son, Count Móric Sándor, gained a reputation as a paragon of Hungarian living at its wildest. His breakneck feats on horseback, galloping up palace stairs or across ice floes on the Danube, both fascinated and dismayed

Sándor Palace, main elevation

the audience he loved. Ending his life as a cripple after the inevitable accident, the count lives on in the town annals as the "Hell Rider" of Buda.

In 1867 Sándor Palace was converted by Miklós Ybl and served as seat of government for several decades. Badly damaged in the Second World War, it has been under restoration since the late 1980s. A decision as to its future occupancy is still pending.

5 Castle Theater

Várszínház

Szinház utca 1-3

Budapest's first permanent theater, located in a former Carmelite church.

The building history of what is now the Castle Theater extends back to the inception of Buda itself. Its site was occupied as early as the thirteenth century by a Franciscan friary, in whose living quarters the pashas resided during Ottoman rule. The church, dedicated to St. John the Evangelist, was used as a mosque, and suffered such damage in the siege of Buda that it collapsed in 1686, the year of the city's recapture. From 1725 to 1736 a new Carmelite church in the late Baroque style was erected over its foundations. After abolishing the religious order, Emperor Joseph II decreed in 1786 that the monastery be converted into a casino and the church into a theater. This task was entrusted to the versatile artist Farkas Kempelen, who designed a Rococo facade and installed sophisticated wooden structures inside with the aid of which, for instance, the former burial vault was used to accommodate the movable stage in its lowered position and the galleries were transformed into boxes for aristocratic families. During his lifetime Kempelen's name was known far beyond the borders of Hungary, for the mysterious speaking machine and chess-playing automaton he invented were favorite party attractions at many European courts.

Budapest's first permanent theater, the Castle initially only presented plays in the German language. The first performance in Hungarian—on October 15, 1790—was a significant event in the social life of the capital, which by then had a large Hungarian majority. Another red-letter day in the theater calendar was May 7, 1800, when Ludwig van Beethoven gave a concert.

Zsigmond Kisfaludi Strobl, The Old Hussar, *created 1926, erected on Dísz tér 1932*

The renovation completed in 1978 restored the state of the building after the Neoclassical extensions in the nineteenth century. The number of seats was reduced to a quarter of the original capacity (264, as compared to 1,200 at the theater's inception). The theater is today used for plays and concerts. In recent years the courtyard of the former Carmelite monastery (Színház utca 5-11) has been used for open-air performances on summer evenings, especially rock musicals with a spiritual message. The erstwhile refectory contains frescoes from the first half of the eighteenth century, recently restored.

6 Parade Square

Dísz tér

A "parade" of burgher houses and mansions.

Dísz tér might be described as the hub of Castle Hill. Accessible through two gates — Víziváros Gate to the east and Fehérvár Gate to the west — this is the juncture where burgher quarter and palace precinct meet. The plaza, originally in front of St. George's Church, is haunted by the ghosts of many a poor wretch executed here as people watched from the houses around. The church, located on the northern side, burned down in the late summer of 1686. In 1893 a monument was unveiled on the site, the **Honvéd Monument**, whose inscription reads "May 21, 1849 / For a free homeland." The bronze figures by György Zala and the high limestone pedestal by Albert Schickedanz commemorate those who died in the struggle for Hungarian independence.

The aspect of the square today is dominated by palatial residences of the Baroque and Neoclassical periods. The two-story Baroque mansion at **No. 3** belonged to the Batthyány family until 1945. It was built for Count Lajos Batthyány as governor in 1743; the architect was Joseph Giessl, Vienna, and the supervisor of works Martin Sigl, Buda. The lot had been in possession of the high aristocracy since medieval times, and was formerly occupied by a late-seventeenth-century residence designed by the Italian architect Venerio Ceresola. He also built, in collaboration with Christopher Griuzenberg, the neighboring building, Kremsmünster House, at **No. 4-5**. The lot was presented by the city to the Upper Austrian abbey of Kremsmünster in 1686, as a sign of gratitude for the services they had rendered during the recapture of Buda. Remnants of medieval house walls were integrated in the new mansion, whose gateway thus contains the earliest seat niches in the borough, which date from the latter half of the thirteenth century.

Across the square (**No. 11**) Venerio Ceresola built his own residence toward the end of the seventeenth century, likewise using the walls of preceding medieval houses. In the course of later renovation the building received a Neoclassical facade.

Also located on the western side, at **No. 15**, next to Buda's oldest pastry shop, Korona, is the Schultz Mansion. Remains of medieval masonry may still be seen on the ground floor, which is now occupied by a post office. In the early sixteenth century the building came into the possession of the archbishop, and after a fire in 1723 it was purchased by János Schultz, to whom it owes the Baroque wing facing on the square. The idiosyncratic present facade with passageway and the romantic interior court surrounded by arcades date from the succeeding owner, Baron de la Motte, an army officer and engineer who bought the Baroque palais in 1760.

Merchant's house at Tárnok utca 14

Seat niches are found in many entryways on Tárnok utca

7 Treasurer Street

Tárnok utca

A medieval market street.

Tárnok utca connects Dísz tér with Szentháromság tér. The widest street in the borough, it runs roughly parallel to the town walls along the edge of the Castle Hill plateau, which in turn follow the sinuous natural contours of the cliffs. The history of Tárnok utca goes back to the thirteenth century, when in the wake of the Mongol invasion Buda was founded by King Béla IV. The market that grew up near the now fortified and defended Danube harbor burgeoned into a center of international trade; its merchants formed guilds, enjoyed special rights, and were protected by royal privileges. In the Middle Ages, Tárnok utca was a hub of trade and commerce. When the German merchants held their Wednesday market, the stalls crowded the street from one side to the other, and extended all the way down to St. George's Church on Dísz tér, where a further market was under way. Some historians explain the width of Buda's streets by pointing out that many townspeople of the time were farmers as well: narrow lanes would have been clogged by herds of cattle and wagons bearing crops from the outlying fields, orchards, and vineyards. The bustling activity of the multinational and mutilingual society that congregated here in medieval times found a parallel in the bright color schemes of the merchants' houses, guildhalls, market buildings, and mansions, whose living quarters upstairs were not continuously occupied but whose shops at street level generally kept their doors open year round.

The merchants' houses at **Nos. 14 and 16** are typical examples of this early phase of the town's history. Originally they were only one story high, and had roofs sloping to the street. Toward the end of the fifteenth century the shops with their fourteenth-century display windows received a projecting upper floor supported by stone corbels and articulated by a row of segmental arches. The brightly colored painted decoration of both interiors and exteriors, with ornamental patterns or imitated ashlarwork in geometric designs in black, green, white, or yellow, was characteristic of Gothic domestic architecture in Buda. An idea of this former splendor may be

The Matthias Church and, behind, the Hilton Hotel, which incorporates the ruins of a medieval Dominican monastery ▷

gathered from No. 14, whose murals dating from around 1500 have been restored on the basis of original paint traces. The two commercial establishments, now occupied by restaurants with an olde-worlde atmosphere, have since been given a common entryway with a trap door leading down to the medieval cellars, which are used to store wine. Fragments of medieval murals dating from Emperor Sigismund's reign have survived on the buildings at **Nos. 3 and 5**. Visible on **Nos. 6, 7, 10, and 13** are Romanesque elements that have been conserved and integrated in the new structures.

The originally Gothic trading house at **No. 18** has a shop on the ground floor decorated in an exuberant Baroque style. Location of the Golden Eagle pharmacy for over 160 years, it has survived almost unaltered and is now open to visitors as a pharmacy museum.

8 Matthias Church

Mátyás templom

Coronation church of Hungarian kings, restored in nineteenth-century Neo-Gothic by Frigyes Schulek; one of Budapest's main landmarks.

At about the same time as the palace of Béla IV was under construction at the south end of Castle Hill, the fortified town to the north began to grow rapidly, necessitating the building of a church for its primarily German immigrant population. According to extant records, a parish church dedicated to St. Mary went up on this site between 1255 and 1269.

Stylistically, the original building apparently combined elements of northern French Gothic with the late Romanesque style of Burgundy, which had been brought here by Cistercian monks. In the course of its conversion into a High Gothic aisled church sometime after 1370, a portal was built at the western end of the south side with a pediment relief depicting the Death of the Virgin. During a service in 1384 the southwest tower collapsed. The stonemasons of the Parler lodge in Prague whom King Sigismund had summoned to work on his palace also sculpted the architectural figures in St. Mary's and raised the aisles to the height of the nave. The roof of the now fully fledged hall church was clad with colored Viennese glazed tiles about 1443.

The Matthias Church

1 West portal
2 Nave
3 Transept
4 Choir
5 Choir chapels
6 Sacristy
7 Tomb of Béla III
8 St. Emeric Chapel
9 North vestibule
10 North portal
11 Loreto Chapel
12 South vestibule
13 St. Mary Door
14 Southeast portal
15 Chapter sacristy
16 St. Stephen Chapel
17 Stairs to oratorium of the Maltese Knights

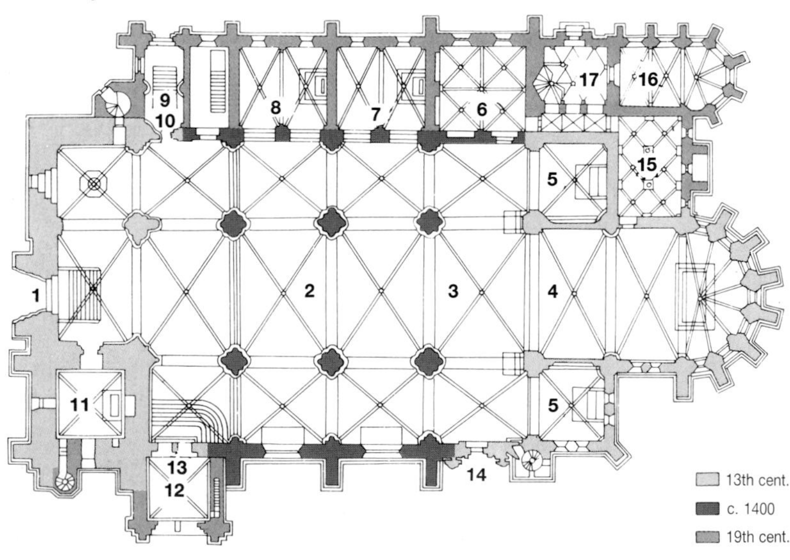

Detail of an altarpiece by Mihály Zichy, 1894. St. Emeric Chapel in the Matthias Church

With numerous additions made under Matthias Corvinus—a royal oratory above the north choir aisle and a five-story tower finished in 1470 to replace the ruined southwest tower—the church has since been known by its present name. After being sacked and burned by the Turks in 1526, and converted into a mosque with whitewashed walls in 1541, it briefly came into Franciscan hands when Buda was recaptured, and then passed to the Jesuits. It was they, between 1688 and 1714, who built a college to the north and a seminary to the south, and who gave the church its Baroque interior.

Its present form reflects the well-meant but sometimes misguided efforts of the nineteenth-century historical revival. In the course of extensive restoration to commemorate the thousand-year anniversary of Hungarian colonization, Frigyes Schulek attempted between 1874 and 1896 to restore the Matthias Church to its medieval state. This entailed not only the removal of Baroque substance but also the replacement of original architectural elements by replicas. After suffering heavy war damage in 1944/45, the church remained closed for a long period. Reconstruction required sixteen years, from 1954 to 1970.

Today, the church again reflects the significance it had as one of the coronation churches of the kings of Hungary. Charles Robert of Anjou was crowned here in 1309, Sigismund of Luxemburg in 1387. It was during the latter's reign that the custom arose of draping the church with enemy banners captured in war. In 1444 these began to be supplemented with generals' escutcheons hung near the high altar. The church has witnessed moving ceremonies, as when King Matthias Corvinus wed Katherine Podiebrad in 1463 and, after her untimely death, took Beatrix of Aragon as his wife in 1476.

The city's conquerors also made use of the Matthias Church, for example in 1541,

when the Ottoman Turks gathered here under Sultan Süleyman for a prayer of thanksgiving for their successful entry into Buda. Of great political significance was the coronation of Franz Joseph and Queen Elisabeth in 1867, for which Liszt composed his *Coronation* mass. The coronation of the last king of Hungary, Charles IV of Habsburg, was celebrated here in 1916.

The twin-towered **west front** of the church, with its tripartite articulation, forms its dominant aspect. The pointed arch of the west portal, ornamented with a vine-leaf design along its outer rim, has a modern tympanum relief depicting the Virgin flanked by kneeling angels. Based on medieval models, it was created by Lajos Lantai in 1890. The early Gothic stained-glass rosette was restored by Schulek. The center of the west facade is topped by a cornice and pediment, lined with crockets and bearing a finial at its apex. It is articulated vertically by seven pointed-arch apertures and horizontally by a dwarf gallery with trefoil arches. The walls of the north (left) Béla Tower date from the thirteenth century; the arcades above the cornice and the helm with its colorful tile patterns reveal the imaginative touch of Frigyes Schulek. The south Matthias Tower is also an example of Schulek's late-nineteenth-century Gothic Revival style. While the two lower stories echo those of the north tower, the finely articulated octagonal upper ranges seem to render the 250-foot-high tower with its filigree spire almost weightless. King Matthias's arms, bearing the date of completion of the tower, 1470, are now on display inside the church, at the west end of the south aisle (the emblem on the tower is a replica).

The **south facade** is also effectively terminated by the Matthias Tower. A further accent is provided by the St. Mary Door, which is protected by a vestibule designed by Schulek. This cross-vaulted porch is entered by way of a pointed-arch portal, whose delightful sculptural ornament — a round window with triskele tracery, two hovering angels — is the work of Ferenc Mikula. The restoration of the St. Mary Door, with its tympanum relief depicting the Death of the Virgin, can be easily distinguished from the original medieval elements by their brownish hue. The south facade has a second portal, further to the right, ornamented with zigzag and diamond designs and lent depth by six flanking inset columns with flower-bud capitals. In this case, too, an impression of the original southeastern portal, dating from about 1250, is conveyed by a Schulek reconstruction.

◁ *The interior of the Matthias Church glows in deep golden hues*

The **interior** presents the aspect of a hall church, modified by a row of chapels off the north aisle. That closest to the choir, the Trinity Chapel, contains the tomb of Béla III and his wife, Anne de Châtillon; the mortal remains of the Hungarian king (1172-96), discovered in the basilica at Székesfehérvár in 1848, were buried in the Budapest chapel with great ceremony on October 21, 1898. The Loreto Chapel, named after the popular place of pilgrimage in Italy, contains a Baroque madonna in ebony and a seventeenth-century Virgin with Child in red marble.

The frescoes on the church walls, by Bertalan Székely and Károly Lotz, were completed in 1896. These two artists were also responsible for the design of the stained glass in the choir, which was executed by Ede Kratzmann. Schulek, in his capacity of "reinventor" of the Matthias Church, replaced the Baroque pews with historicizing furnishings, and was also responsible for the Neo-Gothic high altar.

A flight of steps just inside the southeast portal leads to the crypt, which houses a collection of sculptures. Emerging from the crypt to the north of the choir, we ascend the stairs to the gallery where the church treasures are displayed, including replicas of the Hungarian royal crown and orb.

9 Fishermen's Bastion

Halászbástya

A major Budapest landmark, this popular terrace with its six round towers offers a breathtaking view of the city.

An example of historical revival architecture at its virtuoso best, Fishermen's Bastion conveys the romantic atmosphere of knights' castles and monastery cloisters as they must have been during the Middle Ages. Built between 1899 and 1905, the structure proves Frigyes Schulek (1841-1919) to have been not only a restorer of historical monuments but a gifted architect in his own right. Schulek was a native of Budapest who trained in Vienna, where his fascination with medieval architecture began. When a committee to preserve Hungarian monuments was formed in 1872, with Imre Henszlmann, the pioneer Hungarian art historian, as its chairman, Schulek was appointed chief national conservator. In this capacity he restored a number of the country's churches, investing most effort in the Matthias Church, work on which was completed in 1896. Restored to its former glory, the church called out for surroundings to compare. A practical and architecturally convincing solution also had to be found for shortening the ascent to Buda's main church from the winding approach road (Hunyadi János út). A third aspect of the plan that Schulek submitted to the municipal council in 1894 related to the restoration of a crumbling section of the ancient walls on the Danube side of Castle Hill. In the Middle Ages, this strategically important point had been defended by the fishermen's guild, whose marketplace was located behind St. Mary's; they lived in the southern part of "Watertown" (Víziváros) on the embankment. On the site of the original Fishermen's Bastion Schulek erected a massive substructure in a revival style harmonizing with that of the Matthias Church, enlivening the 130 yards of walling with a skillfully articulated cascade of steps, whose central section is formed by a 25-foot-wide bridge oriented toward the church; divergent limbs constitute the upper and lower reaches, and the climb is interrupted by several landings where one can rest and enjoy the view. The central parapet gives rise to L-shaped arms that bound terraces to the north and south. Schulek transformed the former defenses into a peaceful, aesthetic *objet d'art*; the inexhaustible formal richness of the mullions in the arched window openings provides an interesting lesson in architectural history.

In the course of excavations a large number of skillfully carved stones were discovered — relics from a medieval monastery. Some of these are now on display in the cloister of the Hilton Hotel, while others, such as a lion relief, were incorporated into the walls of Schulek's bastion. His architectural concept also included the installation of sculptures. On the northern limb of the lower steps, for instance, there is a copy of the Prague St. George group by the brothers Martin and George of Cluj (the original dates from 1373), and down by the road stands István Tóth's monument (1899-1903) to János Hunyadi, who defeated the Turks at Belgrade in 1456. For the equestrian statue of St. Stephen, first king of the Hungarian nation, Schulek had originally planned a domed hall, but the sculpture by Alajos Stróbl (1898-1903) now stands in the open air on the south terrace. Schulek designed for it an oval stone balustrade and a rectangular pedestal with four lions and reliefs on the sides depicting scenes from the life of St. Stephen: coronation, proclamation of laws, homage of Vienna, and building of the church (the figure holding the model of the church is a self-portrait of the architect). Above this

Fishermen's Bastion

rises a second pedestal, with gilded medallions between paired columns bearing reliefs of the symbols of the evangelists, an Agnus Dei, and the Hungarian two-armed cross. Finally, a stepped plinth bears Stróbl's bronze statue of King Stephen on horseback.

10 Hilton Hotel

Hess András tér 1-2

Successful synthesis of historic monument and modern architecture.

When the Budapest Hilton opened on New Year's Eve, 1976, not only did a first-class international hotel go into operation, but an unusual project in the field of conservation also came to fruition. The modern structure of steel, concrete, and glass by Béla Pinter was convincingly integrated in an urban setting heavy with the tradition of centuries. While the copper-toned panes of the exterior reflect the architectural monuments around the hotel to great effect, the interior harbors elements of medieval buildings that have been excavated and conserved.

Prior to the erection of St. Mary's (Matthias) Church, a Dominican church already stood on this site. Dedicated to St. Nicholas and built between 1243 and 1254, in the course of the urban development initiated by King Béla IV, this early church had a square ground plan and, initially, no tower. The Dominican order held a general chapter in Buda as early as 1254. By the time of the second general chapter in Buda (1382), the lower stories of the west tower were already standing, and a long monks' choir had been added. In a further building phase in the last quarter of the fifteenth century, the upper stories of the tower went up and the vaulting and the cloister were completed.

Monkish meditation, combined with a sense of aesthetics and the spirit of the medieval masons' lodges, characterized

Fishermen's Bastion, the Matthias Church, and the Hilton Hotel form an imposing architectural ensemble

the tradition of the Dominican order. These traits bore fruit on Castle Hill in the early fourteenth century in the form of a college dedicated to the furtherance of the arts and humanities. Thanks to the efforts of Matthias Corvinus, the school became an educational institution of international renown. To commemorate its royal patron, a replica of the relief portrait of the king (by Briccius Gauske, 1486) on the tower of Bautzen Palace in Lusatia, eastern Germany, was installed in 1930 on the west wall of the restored tower of the former church; it shows the diplomatically skilled soldier-king, who as the opponent of Frederick III even cast an eye on the imperial crown, enthroned and crowned by angels, with a lion as footrest, and in possession of the royal titles of Bohemia, Moravia, Styria, Carinthia, Lower Austria (including Vienna), Silesia, and (from 1478) Lusatia.

The last written mention of the Dominican monastery dates from 1539. Over the following century and a half, instead of harboring friars with a penchant for the arts, its walls housed war-horses, weapon caches, and grain for bread. Between 1688 and 1702 the Jesuits had a college erected to plans by Konrad Kerschenstein on the debris-strewn site between the Matthias and the Dominican churches. Its Italianate late Baroque facade has been preserved in the south wing of the hotel building, begun in 1974, while the section north of the tracery-ornamented Late Gothic tower follows its historic predecessors of the thirteenth to fifteenth centuries in terms of ground plan and roofline, and provides access to the excavated portions of the earlier structure (turn right after the inner glass door). In one corner of the medieval cellar system a bar has been installed.

The cloister now serves the recreation of the guests, who may admire a Matthias Fountain, specimens of faience tiles, and architectural relics. The stark ruins of the monk's choir now frame the Dominican Court (accessible from the north terrace of Fishermen's Bastion), which provides a delightful ambience for the concerts and operas performed here in the summer months. Here we find the figure group

King Matthias Corvinus, 15th-century relief (copy) on the tower of the former Dominican church

entitled *The Monks Julianus and Gerardus* (1937), an early work by Károly Antal recalling the origins of the Hungarian people. It was Dominican monks who in 1235 first set out for the Volga territory on a search for the homeland of the Magyars and their surviving kinsfolk. The journey was long and arduous, and Gerardus did not return. Julianus, on his second attempt, discovered the land of his forefathers in 1237, devastated and deserted as a result of the Mongol storm.

11 András Hess Square

Hess András tér

Budapest was an early center of printing.

In the middle of the square, a **statue** of Pope Innocent XI created by József Damkó in 1935 recalls a painful caesura in Hungarian history, from which point onwards it has been divided into periods "before the Turks" and "after the Turks." St. Innocent (he was canonized in 1956) initiated the Holy League, whose armies recaptured Buda for Christian Europe on September 2, 1688, after a siege of 75 days.

House **No. 4**, opposite the Hilton, belongs to the period "before the Turks." It and the square are named after a man who was active here over five hundred years ago: András Hess, whose name is associated with an invention made shortly before the accession of Matthias Corvinus, that of printing from movable type. Despite his definite preference for beautifully ornamented manuscripts, the king also ordered printed volumes for his library, for instance from Anton Koberger of Nuremberg, from Moritz Brandis and Konrad Kachelofen of Leipzig (Royal Book of Laws, 1486), from Erhard Ratdold of Augsburg (Thuróczy Chronicle, 1488), from Johannes Filipecz of Brno, or from printers in Strasbourg and Nuremberg, where in 1477 and 1485 Matthias had pamphlets printed attacking Frederick III. Right here, however, at No. 4, the first book printed in Hungary and dedicated to the king, the *Chronica Hungarorum*, came off the press in 1473. The printer, András Hess, had trained in Italy and was called to Buda from Latium in 1472 by Vice-Chancellor László Karai. By 1480, when the letter of indulgence of Canon Johannes Han of Pressburg (Bratislava) was printed in this shop, it had already changed hands. The substance of the house derives from three smaller predecessors from the fourteenth century; surviving medieval elements include two quadruple seat niches in the south entryway, dating from around 1340, and barrel vaults in the cellars (used by the Fortuna restaurant). The building was restored after the Second World War. The fact that the university press was once located in the rear building (Országhaz ucta 3), and that one can enjoy a cup of coffee while browsing through the books and records at Litea in the courtyard (where a charming carillon rings out every half hour), evokes Buda's lasting significance as a European center of publishing and the book trade.

12 The Red Hedgehog

Vörös sün ház

Hess András tér 3

One of the oldest houses in the quarter, with an original restaurant.

Sited at the top of the square, the Red Hedgehog received its name in 1696, ten years after the expulsion of the Turks. For a century it remained the only inn in the castle district, and was also used for theater performances and balls. In 1810 the building received its present Neoclassical facade, and for a brief period it harbored the reliquary of St. Paul the Hermit of Budaszentlőrinc, patron saint of the Hungarian order of the Paulines. The house emblem over the entrance also dates from the early nineteenth century, but the structural history of the house extends much further back in time, to the fourteenth century. In the course of recent restoration work the walls of four medieval houses were discovered, as were rooms with groined vaults, leading off the entryway and Gothic doors and windows on the upper floor. A wrought-iron hedgehog over the side entrance, a few yards down Táncsics Mihály utca, invites visitors to enjoy modern Hungarian hospitality in a delightful historical ambience.

Emblem of the Red Hedgehog

13 Mihály Táncsics Street

Táncsics Mihály utca

Charming old-town lane with houses from the Baroque and Neoclassical periods.

In 1948 the street leading from Hess András tér to Vienna Gate was renamed after a writer who played a committed role in the 1848/49 struggle for Hungarian emancipation. For centuries it had been known as Jew Lane, being closely associated with the history of the Jewish community in Buda.

House **No. 1** is a late Baroque mansion erected in 1774 for the municipal judge of Buda on the foundations of two medieval dwellings. From 1922 the building housed the British embassy. Gutted by fire in 1944/45, it is now headquarters of the National Commission for the Preservation of Monuments. A relief on the side wall commemorates the art historian Imre Henszlmann, who was active around 1900 in the maintenance and restoration of the castle district. Along Ibolya utca (past the Hilton parking lot) one can reach the wooden staircase that leads through a park down to the embankment in Víziváros.

The passage at **No. 5**, an early Neoclassical building, gives access to a courtyard where the studio and residence of the sculptor Amerigo Tot (d. 1983) are located. Tot was influenced by the Dessau Bauhaus and spent the main years of his career in Rome, where he created reliefs for the central station; he enjoyed late recognition in his own country. His Budapest residence is now occupied by a private gallery devoted to contemporary Hungarian art.

Nr. 7 is the home of the Institute of Musicology of the Hungarian Academy of Sciences, the Bartók Archive, and the Museum of Music History, which has a fine collection of instruments. The Baroque mansion was built over the foundations of two medieval houses between 1750 and 1769. Designed by Buda's leading architect of the day, Matthäus Nepauer, it has superb facades on the courtyard, Danube, and street sides. Ludwig van Beethoven stayed here when he came to Buda for a concert in 1800. The concert hall on the

Táncsics Mihály utca looking south. In the background, the towers of the former Dominican church and the Matthias Church

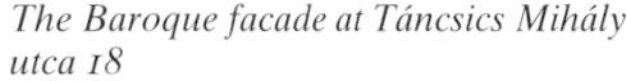

The Baroque facade at Táncsics Mihály utca 18

second floor provides a noble and exclusive setting for musical events.

The lively color scheme of **No. 16** (built about 1700 over a medieval structure and converted about 1770) is effectively contrasted by ornaments and moldings in yellow stucco. An eyecatching feature of the exterior is a Baroque mural with a scene from the Life of the Virgin (Christ and Mary as sovereigns of heaven, surrounded by saints). The barrel-vaulted entryway contains earlier architectural and sculptural fragments let into the masonry.

The entryways of **Nos. 6 and 24** are noteworthy for the seat niches from the period of Emperor Sigismund preserved there.

14 Old Barracks

Táncsics Mihály utca 9

Revolutionaries and patriots were jailed here in the nineteenth century.

Now in American private ownership, the plot extends to the edge of the hill and includes the Erdély Bastion, a fortification comparable to the ancient Fishermen's Bastion, with a network of subterranean tunnels. The street-side wing was built in 1810 as part of the Joseph Barracks, and was used during the 1848/49 war of liberation as a prison; its inmates included leading Hungarian politicians, advocates of national independence such as Lajos Kossuth and Count Lajos Batthyány, and the writers Mihály Táncsics and Mór Jókai.

The site was first built on during the original settlement of Castle Hill. Here stood the Magna Curia, or Great Court, which was probably the queen's residence. Recent excavations have corroborated the existence of a building erected sometime after 1243, which included a chapel dedicated to St. Martin and — according to records of 1255 — the royal mint. Some historians maintain that in the wake of the Mongol invasion King Béla IV built his first fortress on this site, that Buda thus developed from the north to the south end of the hill, and that the earliest palace buildings had their inception in the fourteenth century, under the Anjous. This hypothesis, however, remains speculative.

15 The Jewish Quarter

Táncsics Mihály utca 23 and 26

Two commemorative sites reflecting a history that oscillated between tolerance and persecution.

In an emancipation decree of 1251, King Béla IV granted the Jewish populace of Buda a number of privileges, including freedom of religion, self-determination in the appointment of rabbis and judges, and permission to conduct trade. The Jews for their part were good taxpayers, who contributed materially to the national revenues. They lived at the southwest end of town, in the vicinity of the Fehérvár Gate and today's Szent György utca, where they built their first synagogue in 1307 (no longer extant). In 1360, Louis I of Anjou expelled them from Buda. Permitted to return in 1364, the exiles were assigned the northeastern area of the castle district, along the present-day Táncsics Mihály utca. The Jewish ghetto extended to the city wall at Vienna Gate, and was separated from the rest of the town by a strong wooden fence. Wary of further persecution, the inhabitants of the ghetto built an

Táncsics Mihály utca 26. Drawings with Hebrew script from the 17th century have survived on the synagogue walls

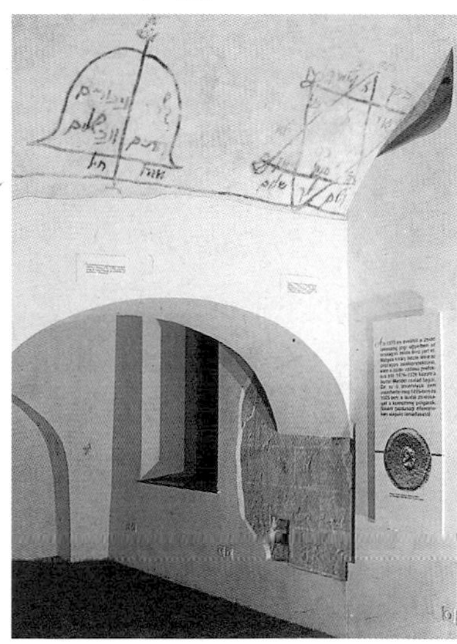

extensive network of escape routes connecting the basements and first and second floors of their houses. During periods of economic and financial prosperity—as under King Matthias—the Jewish community of Buda lived a peaceful and respected life. Even the Turks, who called the street Jehudi-mahalle, showed themselves tolerant in religious and mercantile matters. From the reconquest in 1686 until Joseph II's Edict of Tolerance (1781), however, the lot of the Jews was not always so happy.

Through the entryway of the former Zichy Mansion at **No. 23** we come to a chestnut-shaded garden with a Hercules statue next to the Baroque gateway. This was the site of the Great Synagogue built by the Jewish community in 1461. The remains of the Late Gothic structure—a two-aisle vaulted hall based on the Regensburg synagogue, measuring 85×35 feet in area and about thirty feet in height—were excavated in 1964. Fragments of columns from the synagogue are displayed in the courtyard of **No. 26** (opposite). On the first floor of this Baroque building portions of another synagogue are preserved. The house was owned by the Mendels, leading figures in the Jewish community, from the end of the fourteenth century, and was later known as Kleinmendel House, after one of their descendants. Over the years it was used as a prayer house, pawnshop, and prison. The hall on the ground floor is divided by Gothic piers into three vaulted bays. From the Turkish character of the drawings discovered on the walls and the Hebrew inscriptions dating from the seventeenth century, historians presume that the Kleinmendel House was used as a temple during the Turkish occupation by a group of Syrian Sephardic Jews. About a third of the 75 Jewish families listed as inhabitants of Buda in a Turkish register of 1547 were refugees taken in by the Turks, whose ritual differed from that of the established Ashkenazi community; this explains the existence of two synagogues in the Jewish quarter of Buda. The Budapest Historical Museum uses the premises for an exhibition on the life and history of the Buda Jewish community. The vaults south of the entryway contain gravestones from Jewish cemeteries of the medieval era and the Turkish occupation.

16 Mihály Babits Promenade

Babits Mihály sétány

Historic lane on the northern edge of Castle Hill.

Between Táncsics Mihály utca 17 and 21 an alley called Babits köz leads to a look-out-point that offers a marvelous view of Budapest. Babits Mihály sétány ends to the south in a cul-de-sac, where an iron gate prevents entry into the Erdély Bastion and the former Great Court, now private property. Proceeding to the north we emerge at Vienna Gate. This section of the fortifications was always among the most hotly contested on the entire hill. The houses, now occupied largely by diplomats, were for the most part built over the walls or foundations of destroyed medieval buildings.

Below the ramparts the greenery of Europe Park offers a respite from historic stones. In 1973, to celebrate the hundredth anniversary of the unification of Buda, Pest, and Óbuda, the mayors of European capitals planted trees typical of their countries as symbols of peaceful growth and prosperity. The park also contains a number of commissioned sculptures, including a portrait of Zoltán Kodály by Imre Varga (1982). Influenced by Pop Art, the bronze sculpture is a favorite photo motif, and the stone bench beside it invites visitors to stop and consider the achievement of the great teacher, collector, and arranger of Hungarian folk music (1882-1967). "A profound musical culture," wrote Kodály in 1941, "could emerge only in places where singing formed the basis. The human voice, an instrument accessible to everyone, free of charge, and yet the most beautiful of all, can alone provide the nourishing soil for a general and comprehensive musical culture." Kodály's teaching methods have since found acceptance at music schools around the world.

17 Vienna Gate Square

Bécsi kapu tér

Foyer of the castle district.

The best view of this Baroque square—actually a triangle—is from the platform of the Vienna Gate, where the turn-of-the-century buildings that disturb its homogeneous effect are less in evidence. On the

Bécsi kapu tér with the Protestant church

right is the massive Neo-Romanesque building of the Hungarian State Archive, which in 1915-18 supplanted a number of smaller, earlier structures. To the left rises a Neoclassical Protestant church (built in 1896). Vienna Gate, designed by Jenő Lechner, was built as north entrance to the castle district in 1936, the 250th anniversary of the liberation of Buda from Turkish rule. This event is also commemorated by a monument by Béla Ohmann dating from the same year and located between the gate and the State Archive. In the thirteenth century, when Buda was being fortified, the site was occupied by the "Saturday Gate," so called after the weekly market held here on that day. Later known as "Jew Gate" on account of the nearby ghetto, the original main northern entrance to the district was not designated "Vienna Gate" until the eighteenth century; it was demolished in 1896.

The loveliest feature of Bécsi kapu tér is the row of late Baroque buildings on the west side, modest but finely proportioned and making subtle use of the play of light and shadow.

Lobner House (**No. 5**): A master blacksmith by the name of János Pál Lobner had this residence with Rococo garlands on the facade and a wide gateway built over medieval ruins in 1780. Inside is an interesting Rococo stairwell and a homely courtyard with an open gallery on the second floor.

No. 6: Patron saint of this house, once owned by Kristof Szeth, commandant of Buda Castle, is St. John of Nepomuk, who was canonized in 1729. His statue has stood since the last quarter of the eighteenth century in a niche between two windows on the second floor. The only surviving feature of the previous fifteenth-century building on the site is the Gothic vaulting in the entryway.

No. 7: Parts of the cellars stem from a fifteenth-century building, and walls dating from 1741 were likewise integrated in this magnificent two-story mansion of 1807. The Neoclassical medallions with portraits of Virgil, Cicero, Socrates, Quintilian, and Seneca, along with the allegorical motifs of the reliefs over the upper-floor windows, evidently reflect the humanist leanings of its then owner, the Piarist priest József Grigely. Between the two world wars it

Courtyard of the Lobner House, Bécsi kapu tér 5

was the residence of Baron Lajos Hatvany, a well-to-do sugar manufacturer and patron of literature and art. The wrought-iron grille in the entryway may well have caught the eye of Thomas Mann during one of his visits here, in January 1935 and in June and November 1936.

A celebrated reformer of the Hungarian language, Ferenc Kazinczy (1759-1831), is commemorated in the Neoclassical **fountain** on Vienna Gate Square. Created in 1931 by János Pásztor, its design harmonizes well with the house just described.

No. 8: The special charm of this Neoclassical residence, built by Mihály Weixelgärtner in 1824 for the tailor Florian Appel, resides in its illusionistic facade painting on the mezzanine and oriel. During restoration work in 1959, Late Gothic architectural elements were discovered on the ground floor, in the entryway, and in the window frames, as were remnants of imitation painted ashlar dating from the sixteenth century.

18 Fortuna Street

Fortuna utca

One of the four parallel north-south streets in the walled borough.

Around the year 1400 this street was the home of French artisans brought here by King Sigismund to work on the royal palace and St. Mary's Church. Today its aspect is Baroque, with Neoclassical touches. The homogeneous effect of the whole derives largely from the warm hues of the buildings, most of them with roofs sloping to the street, which in the eighteenth century were occupied mainly by middle- to high-ranking officials. The facades are articulated by projecting bays and pilaster-strips, and several buildings boast finely crafted ornaments, such as stucco rosettes, leafy garlands, coats of arms, and massive carved portals. Visible on some of the Baroque buildings are formal details of their medieval predecessors: Nos. 5 (seat niches), 7, 9, 11, 13, and 25, and Nos. 8 (entryway), 10, 12, 14, and 18. Characteristic examples of the Baroque conversion of late-fourteenth-century houses of the Sigismund era are Nos. 12 and 14, whose gables face on the street. At No. 14 (whose facade and oriel date from 1840) the present eighteenth-century portal marks the site of a narrow medieval lane, which was converted into an entryway with vaulted ceiling in the early fifteenth century. It is worth taking a glance behind other doors on Fortuna utca. Those of **No. 6** (built about 1820), with its charming relief of a cupid on the facade, conceal an especially delightful Buda courtyard with Neoclassical fountain.

19 Hungarian Museum of Commerce and Catering

Magyar Kereskedelmi és Vendéglátóipari Múzeum

Fortuna utca 4

A homage to the perennial shopper and sweet tooth in all of us.

Over the foundations of three medieval buildings—evinced by Gothic seat niches in the entryway—an imposing structure went up on this corner site in 1700. In 1784 it was acquired by the Buda municipal administration for use as an inn and christened "Fortuna." The first-floor rooms

The entrances on Fortuna utca abound in beautiful wood carvings, keystones, and doorjambs

were converted in 1966 into museum premises. The attractions of the Museum of Catering (left of entrance) include the original furnishings of a Buda pastry shop dating from 1870. The founder of the most famous coffee shop in Pest, Emil Gerbeaud, is commemorated in a bust by Alajos Stróbl. A display of tools of the confectioner's trade conveys a vivid impression of how gingerbread, parfaits, and chocolates were traditionally made. There is also a fascinating collection of Easter bunny molds, some of them over a foot and a half tall. One master of the art was János Rorarius, whose candy model of Fishermen's Bastion took a silver wreath of honor at a 1937 exhibition. In the **Museum of Commerce** (to the right), shoppers' temptations from the Austro-Hungarian era are represented by advertising posters and a turn-of-the-century chocolate caramel dispenser. An advertising pillar with interior lighting records 1920s innovations in the field. Also on display is a model of the city's first flashing illuminated sign, an ad for Dreher Bock Beer (Dreher Bak Sör) installed in 1926 on the corner of Rákóczi út and József körút. Hungarian consumers must have been charmed by the 1926 gramophone ad in which a little mechanical dog caught their attention by beating its paws on the display window. Photographs record the development of the great department stores of Pest: a fashion shop (Magyar Divatcsarnok) on Andrássy út; the Corvin Áruház, which opened in 1926 and boasted 33 display windows on three frontages; and the hosiery department of Gólya's, where in 1928 the elegant ladies of Budapest were waited on by deferential male assistants. What a contrast to the village general store from before the Great War, with its coffee roaster, mustard dispenser, yeast slicer, hard soap, and shoe polish sold by the ounce.

20 Parliament Street

Országház utca

Traces of medieval Buda.

The street was named after a late Baroque building at the northern end, **No. 28**. Part of a convent of Poor Clares until the order was dissolved, it was rebuilt between 1783 and 1807 and used by the Hungarian parliament. The Academy of Sciences now holds international colloquia in its auditorium, whose style is a good example of an Empire interior.

As this northern part of Buda's former main street was inhabited in the fifteenth and sixteenth centuries primarily by merchants, architects, and artists from Florence, it was also known as Olasz utca (Italian Street). The Italian colony included four Florentine booksellers, who also sold Venetian prints and manuscripts. Other products made on Olasz utca were equally popular at the court of King Matthias and his wife, Beatrix: gold and silver jewelry, woven silk fabrics, gold brocade, and tapestries. The Florentine merchant Bernardo Vespucci, entrusted in 1488 with the accounting of the stonemasons' workshop by the palace architect, Chimenti Camicia, lived here as well.

Other house owners on Italian Street included representatives of the Medici bank, through whom in 1465 Hungary received funding from the pope and the Signoria of Venice for the war against the Turks.

During Ottoman rule, a portion of the street was named "Haman Yolu" (Bath Street) after the municipal baths located here, and another section "Baker Street" for its bakehouse (the symbol of the bakers' guild is still visible on the portal keystone of No. 17).

The best impression of the "Italian phase" is conveyed by Nos. 18, 20, and 22. **No. 18** still has a fifteenth-century facade, with a solid-looking projecting bay and three late Gothic windows, two of which have been reconstructed. The business premises on the ground floor were reached by way of a stone portal and a second door with Late Gothic frame leading off the vaulted entryway.

The Gothic walls of the adjacent house, **No. 20**, built in the late fourteenth century, with its corbel table of pointed arches supporting the upper story, likewise survived the checkered history of the castle district relatively unscathed. Adjacent to the barrel-vaulted entryway with its four seat niches with trefoil arches, a room with a Gothic cross-vault is still extant. The Ba-

Országház utca 18-22, houses combining elements from the Gothic to the Baroque

roque ornament of the facade was added in 1771.

Surviving fifteenth-century features of **No. 22** are the consoles supporting the bay, and the masonry framing of the portal. The archivolt of the bay is ornamented in sgraffito—the sole surviving remnant of this technique in Buda, which was extremely widespread on Buda houses during the Renaissance. The original medieval building had more than two consoles, because the entire upper story once projected over the street to the depth of the bay. The year in which the present facade

Courtyard of Országház utca 2

Facade detail of Országház utca 20

with its Baroque stucco ornament was erected is recorded on the bay as 1751.

Across the street, at **No. 5**, two medieval structures were integrated by the addition of a Rococo/Neoclassical facade about 1770. The exterior features garlands in various materials — in stucco at the upper end of the pilasters, in sandstone around the portal, and in carved wood on the door leaves. The entryway leads to another courtyard exhibiting the typical Buda flair, with a gallery extending around the second floor.

A unique feature of Hungarian architecture and a jewel of the medieval builder's art are the double seat niches with unusually rich Late Gothic tracery that have survived in the entryway of **No. 9**, only a few steps further north. A plaque on the facade records the fact that the two-story mansion with a large second-floor dining room was presented by King Sigismund to a despot with whom he was allied between 1389 and 1427, the Serbian prince Stephan Lazarevic.

At the south end of Országház utca another mansion from Sigismund's era forms the core of No. 3. The facade of **No. 10** (with an over hundred-year tradition as a restaurant, continued today by the Fekete Holló, or Black Raven) is a good example of the insouciant and unpedantic Rococo architecture typical of Buda.

21 Országház utca 2

A palais from the era of King Sigismund.

Alabárdos (Halberdier) is the name of the restaurant now occupying this two-story building with fine early Neoclassical facade, which was renovated in 1960. Its nucleus is thought to date from the early period of Castle Hill settlement (latter half of the thirteenth century). During King Sigismund's reign an imposing mansion in the international Gothic style rose on the site; but as so often, only fragments of what must have been a sterling achievement of early-fifteenth-century Buda architecture survived the Turkish siege and occupation. These include tracery-ornamented pointed-arch niches flanking the barrel-vaulted entryway, the ground floor of the courtyard wing with spacious arcades resting on octagonal pillars, and ornamental murals on the second floor. Beneath the courtyard paving lie subterranean chambers with barrel vaulting, passageways carved into the bedrock, and a cavern cellar with a well. The conversion of the original cellar system and restora-

Horse-drawn cabs can be hired at Trinity Column for tours of the castle district ▷

tion of the upper story took place after 1700. Another hundred years passed before the colonnade was added to the upper floor on the courtyard side and the entrance passageway was redesigned.

22 Trinity Square

Szentháromság tér

Tourist attractions like Fishermen's Bastion and the Matthias Church ensure that this plaza, in the heart of the castle district, is well frequented all year round.

Trinity Square is flanked on the east by the Matthias Church and on the north by the massive Neo-Gothic hulk of the former ministry of finance (now occupied by the new Hungarian Central Archive and other institutions). On the northwest corner stands a modern building designed by György Jánossy and László Laczkovich, erected in 1981; the form of the roof, the small windows, the vertical emphases, and the stepped profile were all intended to reflect medieval plot divisions and the Italianate architecture that formerly stood here. On the opposite corner of Szentháromság utca stands the Old Town Hall of Buda. To the southeast lies a small park; until the Second World War, this was the site of a grand mansion owned by Count József Brunszvik, last of the Hungarian treasurers (*magister tavernicorum*). Beethoven was a frequent guest here, and dedicated his *Appassionata* sonata to the son and brother of his "immortal beloved."

For almost three centuries the center of the square has been marked by the **Trinity Column**, which was restored in 1967. Forty-five feet in height, it dates from 1710-13, when it was donated by grateful survivors of the plague epidemic of 1709 and created by Philipp Ungleich, a sculptor from Würzburg. (The spot was previously occupied by a votive monument of 1706, recalling the earlier plague that swept Buda in 1691.) Above swarms of cherubim, the hexagonal obelisk is crowned with the Trinity group — Christ with the cross, God the Father, and the dove in a gloriole symbolizing the Holy Spirit. At the corners of the plinth stand statues of Sts. Emeric, Christopher, Augustine, Joseph, Sebastian, and John of Nepomuk; on the consoles above are Sts. Rosalie, John the Baptist, and Francis Xavier, the most popular Jesuit saint.

The Hungarian coats of arms and the reliefs on the sides of the plinth were created by Antal Hörger in 1713. The latter depict King David begging forgiveness of his sins and an end to the pestilence, the horrors of the plague, and the erection of the column.

23 Old Town Hall of Buda

Régi budai városháza

Szentháromság utca 2

A Baroque structure with decorative oriel.

The Old Town Hall played a key role in the history of Buda after its liberation from the Turks, when the city was gradually bureaucratized along Austrian lines. The two-story Baroque building is flanked by three streets and encloses two interior courts.

In constructing the building between 1702 and 1710, Venerio Ceresola, imperial court architect, made use of the scant remains of five Gothic buildings, including the medieval town hall, that once stood here (e.g. the foundations and vaulted entryway with seat niches). The sculptural work on the corner oriel (which burned out in 1723 and was restored the following year) and the upstairs windows, which are topped alternately by segments and triangles, reveal the touch of Franz Josef Barbier. The bell of the little clocktower sounds on the quarter hour to commemorate the friend of the poor, St. John the Almoner, patron saint of a Baroque chapel decorated with stucco reliefs on the second floor.

The town hall was enlarged from 1770 to 1774 by the city architect of Buda, Matthäus Nepauer. The previously single-story west wing on Úri utca was raised to the height of the east wing, and the stairwell received its double flight of stairs with balustrade. The building continued to serve as town hall from the first council meeting in 1710 until 1873, when Buda, Óbuda, and Pest were united. At present it houses the Collegium Budapest, an international institute of advanced studies.

Since 1928 the niche on the corner of Szentháromság tér has been graced by Carlo Adami's statue of Pallas Athene. Garbed in long robe, sandals, and helmet, the seated figure holds a shield bearing the Buda arms, indicating that the city has been placed under the aegis of the Greek goddess of war. Adami, a native of Como,

Old Town Hall of Buda

Italy, finished his sculpture in 1785. It was commissioned by the Buda city council for installation on a pink marble fountain on the southwest side of the square, which had supplied pure spring water from the Buda Hills to the town since Matthias's times. At the close of the last century the fountain was torn down, and the sculpture of Pallas Athene came temporarily into private hands. After its reinstallation on the Old Town Hall, the ravages of war and air pollution eventually necessitated its replacement by a copy in 1965 (the original statue is on view in the Central Town Hall [No. 63]).

24 Ruszwurm Pastry Shop

Ruszwurm cukrászda

Szentháromság utca 7

A venerable confectioner's and coffee shop, in business since 1827.

Szentháromság utca, which runs at a right angle to the longitudinal axis of the castle district and ends directly opposite the main entrance of the Matthias Church, provides a connection between the eastern and western fortifications of Castle Hill. Many of its buildings were severely damaged in the Second World War.

Opposite the Old Town Hall, two houses with unpretentious Baroque facades—Nos. 5 and 7—retain their medieval cores, including Gothic cellars, door frames, and vaulted entryways with seat niches. A gingerbread bakery was established in No. 7 as early as the Middle Ages. Today's little café and pastry shop is a period-piece of Buda Biedermeier, in operation continuously since 1827. In 1890 it was taken over by Vilmos Ruszwurm, who left behind not only a recipe for delicious cream cake but very cozy furnishings, including a tiled stove and Empire-style furniture by a Buda master of the art, Krautsiedler.

The showcase to the right of the cake buffet in the entrance conveys a lesson in period taste and the history of pastry packaging, illustrated by an endearing collection of gift tins, cake boxes, and china of the kind that once graced great-grandma's coffee table.

Empire-style furnishings of the Ruszwurm Pastry Shop

25 Hadik Monument

Hadik emlékmű

Úri utca / Szentháromság utca

Hussar on a high horse.

Úri utca widens toward the intersection with Szentháromság utca, by the west wing of the Old Town Hall. Since 1937 this site has been occupied by a monument that, as it were, divides the street into a northern and a southern section. The equestrian statue, a mature work of György Vastagh the Younger (1868-1946), commemorates the Third Austro-Hungarian Hussar Regiment of Arad. Former members of the regiment, which existed from 1702 to 1918, donated it in memory of comrades killed in action. Its design reflects the influence of Italian funerary sculpture, especially the equestrian monuments of the quattrocento. The rider is the renowned commandant of Buda, András Hadik (1710-90), whom Queen Maria Theresa promoted to field marshal for bravery. In 1756, planning to recapture Silesia, the queen sent troops into battle against King Frederick II of Prussia. In the ensuing Seven Years' War, the Hungarian regiment under Hadik distinguished itself, among other things, by pillaging Berlin. Later, Hadik became a reformer who attempted to improve the situation of the Hungarian peasantry by calling for the abolition of serfdom. He and his family resided in the Baroque mansion at Úri utca 58 (built 1720; now a registry office). His statue is a very naturalistic rendition of a moment of calm; man and horse seem one, and are treated as equally important. The sculptor obviously felt a great empathy with his subject, as evinced by the finely worked details of the bronze casting, from the historically accurate hussar's uniform and cap (shako) to the horse's magnificent tail and saddlecloth (the steed was modelled on a famous Hungarian stallion from the Bábolna stud).

Equestrian monument to András Hadik

26 Lord Street

Úri utca

The longest and most noble street in the castle district traverses the entire borough from north to south.

Remnants of old paving and masonry, vaulted cellars, and a number of well-preserved portals bear witness to the thirteenth-century origins of this narrow street. As postwar restoration was devoted to reviving its medieval character, it is not hard to imagine how Lord Street must have looked in its heyday. In the late fourteenth and early fifteenth centuries, when King Sigismund's continued presence in Buda lent the city the de facto character of capital of the Holy Roman Empire, Hungarian aristocrats, church dignitaries, and prosperous merchants built themselves mansions here. Many of the houses with ground-floor shops belonged to German drapers, who supplied the court with fine textiles from Verona, Nuremberg, and other centers.

The southern section of Úri utca runs from the Hadik Monument towards Buda Castle. Of the buildings on the west side of the street, Nos. 6 and 8 (a Neo-Gothic mansion designed by Alajos Hauszmann) and Nos. 14 to 24 are listed as historic monuments; on the east side, this status attaches to Nos. 5, 9, 13 (remnants of medieval murals in the interior), 17, and 19.

No. 19 was formerly the residence of one of Sigismund's magnates, the formidable ban (governor) of Temes, Filippo Scolari, alias Pipo of Ozora. In a biography of 1470, Jacopo di Poggi Bracciolini describes how the Italian's career began: "It came to pass that Pipo visited the bishop of Gran (Esztergom), at whose house the king also happened to be a guest at the time. When the table was cleared, the gentlemen began to consider how an army of twelve thousand cavalry could be raised in order to protect the country from the raids of the Turkish sultan.... And as there was no one

The entryways and courtyards on Úri utca harbor many architectural elements dating from the period prior to the Turkish occupation

among them who understood much about figures, who could calculate how much money was needed for the soldiers' pay, Filippo was called in. But he... finished his calculations so quickly that they all were astonished and heaped praise upon him.

A coat of arms crowns the facade at Úri utca 58

Sigismund,...who made a point of surrounding himself with men of high mental capacity..., saw the young man's eyes glowing with intelligence and immediately realized that he was called to higher tasks, instead of spending his life as a merchant.... The king therefore entrusted him with the management of the gold mines, the country's most important source of revenue." Four centuries later, this house was the birthplace of Baron József Eötvös (1813-71), scholar, writer, statesman, and author of an act introducing elementary public education in Hungary. As headquarters of the county council the building received a Neoclassical facade in 1829.

A bridge connects No. 19 with its neighbor to the south, **No. 17**. This is the sole surviving example of the bridges that were once typical features of medieval Buda. The narrow passageway is called Balta köz (Hatchet Alley), and the roughstone wall evinces two medieval window apertures and embrasures. Balta köz 4 is now occupied by a fine shop specializing in handcrafted leather goods. Visible at the corner of the passageway, on No. 17, are the delicately carved console of a bay and painted ashlarwork dating from the end of the fourteenth century. Access to the house is by way of a garden court. Near the outer wall, overgrown with ivy, stands a decorative fountain composed of Gothic and Renaissance marble fragments, a few details of which — such as the finely chiselled lions around the foot, or the putti spouting water — evoke the high quality and Florentine idiom of the Buda stonemasons' shop headed by Chimenti Camicia (1479-91).

27 Buda Castle Labyrinth and Panopticum

Budavári Labirintus és Panoptikum
Úri utca 9

A serio-comic museum in the depths of Castle Hill, devoted to the city's Golden Age.

A network of underground passageways, natural springs, limestone caves, and cellars dug over seven hundred years ago extends throughout Castle Hill at various depths, with a total length of some six miles. About an eighth of the labyrinth is open to visitors. During the tours, which begin every twenty minutes, information is provided about the life-saving function of the tunnels during periods of war and natural disaster and about their military use during the Ottoman era and during the hand-to-hand fighting that took place in Budapest at the end of the Second World War. The guides also enjoy telling a good horror story or two, such as the one about the female bones discovered in an underground well, revealing how Sultan Süleyman got rid of the ladies he had grown tired of. A considerable dose of black humor is also contained in the "waxworks," made of plastic, that illustrate episodes in Hungarian history, from mythical origins to King Matthias's splendid court, in a grotesque, macabre, often amusingly exaggerated or cloyingly sentimental way. To ensure that the approximately one-hour tour through the cold and dripping-wet tunnels (humidity 90%, temperature about 15°C, or 60°F) does not leave one with a case of the shivers, a cavern bar and cozy wine cellar at the entrance offer a chance to warm up.

28 Hölbling House

Úri utca 31

One of the best-preserved Gothic residences in the castle borough.

The building's name derives from its first registered owner following the Turkish occupation, Johannes Hölbling. The core of the fabric, the vaulted cellars, and the entrance to the latter date from the early fourteenth century. About 1440 two further floors were added to the single-story structure, and a new facade went up, featuring an interesting window treatment on the second floor. The effectiveness of the facade is heightened by the play of light and shadow, color contrasts, and a considered use of ornament and imitated materials. The white mortar lines are painted on the reddish stuccoed wall, and they are echoed in the ornamental red tracing in the white field of the window arch. Such use of color to emphasize window openings and doorways is a unique feature of medieval architecture in Buda.

Here, again, seat niches have survived in the entryway. As regards the interior plan, we know from the historical description of a similar aristocratic mansion of the period that the dining room was generally located on the first floor, stove-heated living room and bedrooms on the second floor, and a room decorated with murals and a chapel on the third floor. After 1945 the Hölbling House was partially reconstructed, which involved the removal of its severely damaged 1862 facade.

The Hölbling House originated in the 15th century

29 Lord Street north

Úri utca

Characteristic architectural elements in the unique style of medieval Buda.

We recommend a look into the entryway of **No. 40**, for it is one of the most spacious and beautiful in the district. Behind the Neoclassical facade (c. 1830) the architectural core of two fifteenth-century Gothic mansions with a long garden have survived. An idea of the rich erstwhile ornamentation can be gathered from the remains in the entryway: the ribs of the cross-vaulting are linked like a web with the superbly worked, complex tracery of the elaborate seat niches with their interweave of lancet, trefoil, and ogee arches. One of the middle arches (without bench) serves as a doorway.

More fine examples of seat niches are to be found in the northern section of Úri utca: on the east side at Nos. 31 and 47, and on the west side at Nos. 32, 34, 36, 38, 40, and 48-50.

Various attempts have been made to explain the presence of these unusual, throne-like **seat niches** (*sedilia*), which began to appear in Buda towards the end of the fourteenth century—63 have been counted in the castle district. Perhaps the drapers who lived on Úri utca, most of whom were of German descent, used the stone benches to display their wares. The ground floors of some buildings were no doubt leased by Sarmatian fur traders, or of course by the Hungarian merchants who specialized in gold brocades, handwoven carriage upholstery, and scarlet "de granato" fabrics. Not least the Turks, who were granted the right of free trade in 1488 by King Matthias, and who did business in carpets, leather goods, velvet, and Turkish silk, contributed to the lively multilingual bustle in the entryways of medieval Buda. Apart from the merchants, prosperous landlords originating from the peasantry are thought to have used the seat niches for the purveying of wine. When a reception was being held in one of the aristocratic mansions, servants and coachmen waited for their masters here while the horses were being attended to in the courtyard stables. One can even imagine a night watchman spending long hours in one of these niches. At any event, the *sedile* is an element borrowed from ecclesiastical architecture and adapted for profane use, reflecting a rising middle-class interest in status and display.

Engravings published in the period prior to the Turkish conquest show another typical architectural feature of old Buda: several **tower houses** rising high above the roofs north of St. Mary's Church, and easily distinguishable from church towers. Only one of these residences has survived, in the courtyard of **No. 37**. The two-story, 50-foot-high tower (measuring about 30×20 feet in area) is still distinguishable in the old wall complex. It was probably built in the fourteenth century, though some historians date it a century earlier. Like the seat niches, such towers had multiple uses, serving both for defense and for the needs of an opulent life-style. Presumably the quarrels and rivalry between noble Hungarian families and their foreign counterparts, who were in the majority in Buda in those days, led to the construction of such fortified towers on the Italian model, which offered protection in times of danger. Their owners apparently vied with one another in building the most modern, comfortable, secure, or perhaps merely the highest tower in town. The arcades in the courtyard of No. 37 were erected in the course of its Baroque conversion and the redesign of its facade in the same style as the neighboring No. 39.

More listed buildings are to be seen on the way to Kapisztrán tér: **No. 38**: The two-story bishop's palace evinces a Neoclassical corner resolution, designed by Hugo Máltás. It was built around a thirteenth- and fourteenth-century core, including barrel-vaulted rooms on the ground floor behind the entryway niches decorated with round and pointed arches. The Baroque arcades in the courtyard blend well with the Gothic blind arches on the south wall.

Nos. 33 and 35: Built around 1710 and subsequently converted, the two houses occupy the site of a fourteenth-century convent. Its sole surviving features are the Gothic second-floor windows on the courtyard side.

No. 48-50: This was originally two merchants' houses separated by a narrow passageway, with fifteenth-century shop windows and seat niches in the entryways. They were connected around 1600 by a vaulted roof and integrated around 1740 into a single Baroque building whose over-

Gothic seat niches at Úri utca 32

all effect is determined by the elaborate stonemason's work on the two portals and above the upper-floor windows.

No. 41: The present building contains the nucleus of a spacious corner mansion of the thirteenth century, which was several times rebuilt in later years. The original southern boundary of the lot is marked by the remnants of a wall with stone gateway on Dárda utca, a relic of the period of the Turkish occupation.

Detail of the door of the Hadik House, Úri utca 58

No. 49: Built around a large courtyard, the house forms an architectural unit with Országház utca 28. As mentioned in the description of this street [No. 20], the lot was occupied from 1718 by the Order of Poor Clares, whose convent was considerably enlarged from 1743 to 1748 and then closed down by order of Joseph II in 1782. Shortly thereafter, in 1784, major government offices were relocated from Pozsony to Buda, which had a population of about 22,000 at the time and had been the seat of the royal chancellery since 1723. The convent was converted for the use of parliament and the supreme court by Franz Anton Hillebrandt in 1784, in the Austrian late Baroque style. After the Compromise (1867) the proverbial spirit of the plodding and precise Austro-Hungarian bureaucracy continued to suffuse the official chambers. A few years ago, the humanities departments of the Hungarian Academy of Sciences moved into the building.

No. 58: Former mansion of Field Marshal András Hadik [see No. 25]; Neo-Baroque with Baroque and medieval elements.

No. 53: The grounds of the Baroque residence (1701–22) belonged to a Franciscan friary until the end of the eighteenth century.

30 St. Mary Magdalen's Church

Mária Magdolna templom

Úri utca 55

Imposing remains of the first parish church built for Buda's Hungarian community.

The church was severely damaged twice in the course of its seven-hundred-year history, when Buda was recaptured in 1686 and at the end of the Second World War. In 1952 it was decided to demolish the damaged Baroque nave and preserve the five-story west tower, which was reconstructed in 1984-86 when the remnants of the church were converted into a "ruin garden."

The original church of the mid thirteenth century (first mentioned in records of 1276) was a modest aisleless structure. Its proximity to St. Mary's touched off a generation-long conflict of hierarchy involving the question of paying dues to Buda's main church. Finally, in 1390, parish boundaries were drawn on Castle Hill: from that point on, a territorial and ethnic demarcation line divided the borough at the Dominican monastery (now the Hilton Hotel), assigning the Hungarian Christians living to the north to St. Mary Magdalen's. Still a minority of the city's population at the time, the Hungarians converted their church around 1400 into a Gothic hall church with choir.

Almost a century passed before the **tower** was completed, a massive square structure supported by buttresses and with octagonal upper ranges; sacristy chapels were built to the north and south. The delicate fillets in the pointed-arch windows of the tower and the effect of weightlessness they create, the wonderfully sculpted west portal, the doors leading to the two side chapels, and the finely chiselled ribs of the stellar vaulting on the ground floor mark an extremely ambitious architectural project.

That the interior of the church was decorated with frescoes in the late fifteenth century is evidenced by the fragments now on display in the Historical Museum. During the first third of the Turkish era, St. Mary Magdalen's was the only church in Buda not to be converted into a mosque; Protestants were permitted to hold services in the nave, Catholics in the choir, until 1596. In 1602, however, the Mohammedan community renamed the church Fethijje ("Victory") Mosque.

The severely damaged church was taken over in the late seventeenth century by the Franciscans, who retained it until the dissolution of their order in 1782. For a brief time the Hungarian National Archive occupied the now Baroque-style building, but in 1790, after the death of Joseph II, it was reconsecrated and designated the coronation church. As preparations were underway for the coronation of Francis I as king of the Hungarians (1792), a late Baroque/Neoclassical vestibule by Josef Tallherr was added to the west tower to facilitate the access of state coaches to the church. After Duke Ferdinand of Este appropriated it as a garrison church in 1817, it retained this name until its final demolition. In sum, the history of St. Mary Magdalen's is marked by many a dissonance. So it can really come as no surprise that enterprising young Hungarians now exploit the classical ambience of the surviving west tower for the purveyance to the tourist trade of fancy gifts, from toys via briefcases to stone Easter eggs. Art exhibitions have recently been added to the program.

31 Capistrano Square

Kapisztrán tér

Memories of the Turkish wars and the military exploits of Austria-Hungary.

Little remains of the medieval proportions that once gave the square in front of St. Mary Magdalen's its quaint atmosphere and, as intersection of the main streets of the castle district, made it the hub of Hungarian commercial and social life down through the centuries. The National Press (**No. 1**)—built by Lajos Kimnach as a Neoclassical residence in 1834 and enlarged and converted into a printing house in 1876—and the former Ferdinand Barracks (**No. 2-4**)—built in 1847, most recently converted in 1926-29 and used as a museum and archive of military history since 1938—mark the northwestern boundary of the castle district. Attempts to improve the aspects of the square included, in 1922, the erection of the **Kapisztrán Monument**, a sculpture by József Damkó (on a pedestal by Ernő Foerck), that gave the square its present name. Giovanni Capistrano, a Franciscan monk from Italy canonized in 1724, recruited mercenaries at the pope's behest for a crusade against

Ruins of St. Mary Magdalen's Church

the Turks, and in 1456 he personally fought alongside János Hunyadi at the battle of Belgrade. The victory temporarily stopped the Ottoman onslaught, and it is still celebrated today by the ringing of church bells at noon. Damkó's work stands in the tradition of French revolutionary monuments of the nineteenth century. With great naturalism and in an agitated pyramidal composition, he brings the banner-waving, rosary-girdled heroic monk to dramatic life.

The **Institute and Museum of Military History** (Hadtörténeti Intézet és Múzeum, entrance Tóth Árpád sétány 40) contains objects and historical documents relating to warfare since 1600, with special emphasis on the uprising of 1848/49, the Austro-Hungarian monarchy, and the First World War. Those interested in weapons of all varieties, from Turkish sabers via Spanish flintlock pistols to Sardinian cannon, are sure to enjoy the copious displays. Exam-

The ancient cannon on Tóth Árpád sétány no longer daunt invaders

ples of artillery and armored cars are displayed on Esztergom Bastion, the authentic site of the storming of Buda in 1686, 1849, and 1945, and in the museum courtyard, where a thirteenth-century bastion and portions of the ramparts came to light during excavations in 1987/88.

The showcases of the numismatic collection are filled with an array of commemorative medals, plaques, insignia, and military decorations (from the reign of Maria Theresa onwards). Pride of the flag collection are Honvéd banners from the 1848/49 uprising and regimental ensigns from the First World War. The collection of uniforms includes an example of the earliest standard army garb issued in the country, dating from the first third of the seventeenth century. Also on view are uniforms of the Royal Hungarian Militia (1868-1918). Researchers value the exhaustive photographic archive of the museum. Fine art is also collected here in the shape of paintings and prints on military themes, such as portraits of famous generals and representations of historical events (especially battle scenes).

This museum is perhaps the most interesting in Budapest at the moment, because it brings things into the public eye which long lay under lock and key. Its special exhibitions have been sensationally successful.

32 Anjou Bastion

Anjou bástya

Eloquent testimonies to Hungary's quest for freedom, and to her respect for worthy opponents.

The displays in the Museum of Military History are not the only records of the Hungarians' tenacious battle for self-determination and independence. The castle district abounds with plaques commemorating their love of freedom and their gratitude for every victory over foreign domination. "Here, on July 27, 1686, for the first time in one and one-half centuries, the Hungarian flag flew," proclaims the inscription on a stone atop the outer wall; at this point, where the Anjou Bastion ends at Vienna Gate, a metal fence also marks the spot where Hungarian mercenaries, heyducks, entered the castle district to reconquer Buda.

More or less in the middle of the ancient, tree-lined promenade, where the wall opens out into a roundel, there is also a monument to the enemy: a turban-crowned gravestone bordered by four pedestals bearing stone cannonballs, with an inscription in Hungarian and in Turkish Kuran characters reading: "The last governor of Buda during the 143-year Turkish rule, Vizier Abdurrahman Abdi Arnaut Pasha, fell near this spot on the afternoon

Monument to the last Ottoman governor of Buda

of the second day of the last summer month of 1686, in the seventieth year of his life. He was a heroic opponent; may peace be with him." The aging Turkish castle commandant gained the Hungarians' respect because, instead of accepting an offer to escape, he chose to hold his position to the death. The modest monument, designed by the painter Kálmán Zsille, was erected in 1936, the 250th anniversary of the battle. It was donated by descendants of a Veszprém infantryman, György Szabó, who also lost his life on September 2, 1686, and whose name is recorded on the horizontal plaque.

On Anjou Bastion, the section of fortifications between Vienna Gate and Esztergom Bastion, the Turks withstood the siege by troops of the Holy League for 75 days before finally succumbing in one of their worst ever defeats. The armies attacking Castle Hill from the north under commander-in-chief Charles of Lorraine included fifteen thousand Hungarians fighting for their country's freedom. With the royal palace in flames and the town of Buda devastated, one can imagine how the survivors of the united European forces received the news of the Turkish commander's death on that September night some three hundred years ago.

33 Árpád Tóth Promenade

Tóth Árpád sétány

Offers a fine view of the erstwhile Turkish bastions.

One striking remnant of Ottoman rule in Budapest is the well-preserved fortification system. Even though the wide promenade along the western wall is largely the product of late-nineteenth-century, and subsequent, reconstruction, many features still recall its seventeenth-century character and appearance. Projecting from the "Long Wall" are four bastions built on semicircular or three-quarter-circular plans: (from north to south) Esztergom, Veli Bey, "Sour Soup," and Fehérvár bastions (completed under Pasha Kasim, 1666/67). These bulwarks were the reply to the new and more formidable types of artillery then being developed in Europe.

Today peace reigns, and the bastions serve as vantage points offering a fine panoramic view. From the Esztergom Bastion we can see the distant lookout tower on the 1,734-foot-high János-hegy ("John Hill"), and further south, in succession, Sváb-hegy ("Swabian Hill"), Sas-hegy ("Eagle Hill"), Nap-hegy ("Sun Hill") with a transmitter of the Hungarian news service, MTI, and finally the citadel crown-

A mansion on Tóth Árpád sétány

Tóth Árpád sétány, in front of the Museum of Military History

ing Gellért Hill, which was covered with vineyards until the latter half of the nineteenth century. To the right of János-hegy the chain of the Buda Hills begins with Hárs-hegy ("Linden Hill") and continues to the north with Remete-hegy ("Hermit Hill"). At our feet is South station and the green belt of the park and historic "Jacobin" site, the Vérmező ("Blood Meadow"). This part of the city, Krisztinaváros ("Christinetown"), is accessible by a covered stairway leading down from the end of Szentháromság utca. Prominently sited at the edge of Veli Bey Bastion is the striking equestrian monument created in 1934 by Lajos Petri (1884-1963) to commemorate the Second Transylvanian Hussar Regiment of the Austro-Hungarian army; it was donated by officers of the regiment in memory of their comrades who fell in the First World War. At the south end of the promenade, between Fehérvár Bastion and Dísz tér, stands another hussar monument, a bronze statue by Zsigmond Kisfaludi Strobl (1926, erected 1932; illustration on p. 40). Consciously historical-revival, popular and rather sentimental in style, it adds a new accent to a district already rich in monuments and fountains. A miniature version of the statue in Herend porcelain sold in large numbers.

After touring the castle district (we can descend by bus, by elevator from wing F of the palace, by funicular, or by one of the many stairways), the experience may well lead us to agree with the UNESCO declaration of 1988: "The ensemble of Buda's castle district," it states, "is one of the world's most beautiful examples of a harmonious combination of landscape and townscape, of the works of nature and man, and thus deserves to be protected and preserved for posterity." Castle Hill is accordingly designated a World Cultural Heritage site.

34 Emperor's Baths

Császár fürdő

Frankel Leó út 31-33

A typical Budapest Turkish bath with a history extending back to Roman times.

The healing waters here were already prized by the ancient Romans. In the thirteenth century the northern city limits were drawn "inter Budam et calidas aquas" (between Buda and the hot waters).

But it was the Turks who raised bathing to an art and designed architecture to match. The Emperor's Baths were enlarged by Sultan Süleyman in the sixteenth century, and over the next two hundred years they became the most popular in Buda. The elaborate interiors, the bathing and massage facilities, and especially the therapeutic effects of the waters were extolled by travellers from far and wide. Edward Brown, famous physician to Her Majesty the Queen, wrote in 1763 that excellent baths were to be found in Buda—he had counted eight, in some of which he had bathed, but the loveliest of all was the "Veli Bég" steam bath, where much had been done in the way of external amenities as well.

The Neoclassical building to the west of Emperor's Baths was designed by József Hild and built in 1837-44. During the summer months Hild Court hosts concerts in keeping with its spa character.

35 Tomb of Gül Baba

Gül Baba türbéje

Mecset utca 14

A Turkish mausoleum on Rózsadomb ("Rose Hill"), which offers a beautiful view of the Danube.

The picturesque Gül Baba utca leads to the tomb of a Turkish governor of Hungary, Gül Baba, who was later revered as a holy man. The mausoleum (türbe) was erected in conjunction with a religious institution from 1543 to 1548. Gül Baba was one of the few Ottoman potentates who was loved and respected by the Hungarians during the occupation. Legend has it that he introduced rose growing into the country, which brought him the nickname

Hild Court, between Lukács and Emperor's baths, site of open-air concerts in summertime. The courtyard was named after its architect, József Hild, an outstanding representative of Hungarian Neoclassicism.

"Father of the Flowers." Until the Second World War the tomb was the goal of Muslim pilgrimages, and it remains as a testimony to Islamic culture in central Europe.

36 Watertown

Víziváros

Riverside quarter with reminiscences of the Turkish era.

An urban district had begun to form below Buda Castle in the Middle Ages. Known as "Watertown" (Víziváros), it extends from Fö utca (Király Baths) to Chain Bridge, and is demarcated inland by the curve of present-day Mártírok útja. Because of the floods that continually plagued the low-lying area, it ranked in terms of social status some way behind the castle district. The aristocrats and officials lived "up the hill," merchants, artisans, and fishermen "down the hill." River access favored trade and brought customs revenues. The soil of the surrounding hills was perfect for grape growing, and the wine made here enjoyed great popularity.

The earliest still visible architectural period is that of the Turks, who made use of already existing structures or built new ones over medieval or Renaissance foundations.

The **Király Baths** (Király fürdő) at Fő utca 82-86 are a well-preserved example. Comparatively small even by the standards of the day, they were built by the pashas in the Turkish residential area, directly adjoining the city wall, in 1566-70. In 1827 the then owners, the König family—who later assumed the Hungarian version of their name, Király—had Mátyás Schmidt design the adjacent guest house and spa. As befits such an establishment, the courtyard has a drinking fountain with mineral water.

The small bathhouse with octagonal central pool and reconstructed Turkish domes crouches modestly among the modern apartment buildings and the busy streets. Its warm, cozy atmosphere is particularly enjoyable on cold winter days, but bathing here is an experience at any season. Following the signs reading Gőzfürdő, you ascend a spiral staircase and proceed to the changing room. After

The oldest buildings on Batthyány tér, the White Cross and the Hikisch House (right), now stand below street level

Of the once numerous Turkish baths in Budapest, only the Király Baths have been preserved largely in their original state

donning the linen smock offered, you lock your cabinet door with the key found there — and don't forget to memorize the number! After bathing you can relax in the lounge. To open the changing cabinet a second key is required; just ask the attendant, who will expect a modest tip for his services.

The original lighting and ventilation openings are still visible in the cupola over the central pool

37 St. Anne's Church

Szent Anna templom

Batthyány tér 7

The slender towers with their elaborate spires are a good orientation point when exploring Buda.

Batthány tér is the hub of Víziváros, with its bustling market hall and subway interchange with the HÉV rail link to Aquincum and Szentendre. It also has some interesting examples of Baroque architecture, of which the finest is undoubtedly the

Castle Garden Bazaar

twin-spired St. Anne's on the south side. (The adjoining old rectory now houses a very pleasant café, the Angelika.)

The High Baroque church was erected in 1741-61 to plans by Matthäus Nepauer and Miklós Hamon, who based their design on Italian models. In the niche in the center of the facade is a statue of St. Anne with the Virgin; the pediment bears the Buda coat of arms and is crowned with the symbol of the Trinity flanked by kneeling angels. The interior is dominated by an opulent canopied altar, whose sculpture depicts St. Anne and the young Mary; it dates from about 1771-73 and, like the pulpit, is the work of Carlo Bebo.

The walls were faced with artificial stone in 1935, and the fresco on the ceiling of the nave—by C. Pál Molnár and Béla Kontuly—was also done around this time. A special feature of the church is its oval ground plan, which has rarely been employed in Hungarian ecclesiastical architecture.

Located at **Batthyány tér 4** is the former White Cross Inn (Fehér kereszt fogadó), built around 1770. Once famed for its masquerade balls and theater productions, it now houses a bar with the promising name of Casanova, who reputedly once visited the establishment.

The adjacent Hikisch House (**No. 3**) was built over medieval walls, and its ground floor lies a couple of feet below the level of the modern street. Four reliefs representing the seasons adorn its facade, which dates from about 1795.

◁ *St. Anne's reveals influences of southern German Baroque, especially in its oval ground plan*

The Church of the Elizabethine Sisters (**Fö utca 30-32**), which prior to the Turkish occupation was part of a Capuchin friary, still bears traces of the alterations made when it was converted into a mosque—see for example the south windows and door. After the expulsion of the Turks the archbishop of Esztergom had it restored as a Christian house of worship between 1703 and 1716. The adjacent hospital building was erected in the early nineteenth century.

38 Castle Garden Bazaar

Once-resplendent staircase to Buda Castle.

One of the most impressive achievements of the architect Miklós Ybl was certainly his Castle Garden Bazaar, erected between 1875 and 1882. The terraced stairways connecting the royal palace with the Danube embankment were originally intended to be flanked by shops, with a restaurant at the bottom. Ybl's design relied largely on Italian and French terrace layouts, but echoes of the Orangerie in Potsdam (1850-56) are also evident. Today the stairs are in such poor condition that their former Mediterranean character can only be imagined. The balustrade sculptures have disappeared, and the erstwhile shops at street level now serve as sculptors' studios.

Just across the road, fronted by a small garden with a statue of the architect, stands one of Ybl's finest Neo-Renaissance works, the Castle Garden Kiosk, originally designed (1874-79) as a pump house for the palace water supply. That it today radiates all of its pristine glory may have something to do with the fact that it has been converted into a gambling casino.

Empire-style pharmacy in the Semmelweis Museum of Medical History

39 Semmelweis Museum of Medical History

Semmelweis Orvostörténeti Múzeum

Apród utca 1-3

Memories of a famous physician.

This small house, renovated in the Rococo style in 1810, was the birthplace of Ignaz Semmelweis (July 1, 1818). A physician at St. Roch's Hospital (on Blaha Lujza tér), Semmelweis is famous for his 1847 discovery of the cause of puerperal fever, long a fatal post-childbirth affliction, and of the use of antiseptics for its prevention.

The museum gives a well-organized review of the history of therapeutic methods and the related implements. Among its rarities is a wax female figure—made in Florence in the eighteenth century—that was presented by Emperor Joseph II to the University of Pest in 1789. The finely crafted model of a reclining woman was used for anatomical studies; her male counterpart is in the Vienna Museum of Medical History.

The parks extending between the south slope of Castle Hill and Gerhardus Hill (Gellért-hegy) occupy the site of what was once a crowded and lively urban district, **Tabán**. It fell prey to a turn-of-the-century slum clearance program that spared only the parish church, the Rácz and Rudas baths, and a few residential buildings. For centuries Tabán had been a center of craftsmanship and trade, whose population structure was determined by the nearby Danube and its shipping; it also abounded in wine cellars and taverns.

The Rácz fürdő (Hadnagy utca 8-10) was King Matthias Corvinus's favorite thermal bath; there was allegedly a tunnel between the palace and the baths that permitted the monarch to visit them undisturbed whenever he wished. Matthias is credited with having greatly furthered the practice and art of bathing in Renaissance times. The **Rudas fürdő** (Döbrentei tér 9) still has its dome and other features from the Turkish period.

40 Gerhardus Monument

Gellért emlékmű

Gellért-hegy, above Döbrentei tér

Crucifix held high, the bishop glares down on the sinful metropolis.

According to tradition, Bishop Gerhardus of Venice, known to the Hungarians as Gellért, paid for his missionary zeal with his life on this very spot. He was nailed into a barrel by heathen Magyars and rolled down the hill into the river. The statue was realized with the financial aid of Kaiser Wilhelm II of Germany, who after a visit to Hungary in 1897 decided to sponsor the erection of monuments to historical personalities in Budapest. Gyula Jankovits received the commission, and the monument was ceremonially unveiled in 1904.

Rising above an artificial waterfall, the statue of St. Gerhardus (Gellért) is a landmark of the Hungarian capital

We recommend climbing past the statue to the top of Gellért Hill, where you will be rewarded with a fabulous view of the Danube, Parliament, and Castle Hill.

41 Citadel

Citadella

Citadella sétány

Has not always been the place for wining and dining that it is now.

Built by imperial decree in 1850, with the recent uprising very much in mind, this fortress in the medieval style initially served as a barracks. The walls, up to twelve feet high and ten feet thick, enclose an area about two hundred yards long, at the west end of which the troop quarters were located. The Citadel was expressly intended to demonstrate military strength and superiority, underscored by regular roll-calls and parades, and cannon shots fired in salute to passing ships.

In 1899 the Citadel became municipal property, but instead of razing it the city decided to convert it to peaceful uses; a ho-

Márta Lessenyei's Royal Couple *preside atop the reservoir on Gellért-hegy*

tel and restaurant now occupy the premises. The complex is a favorite resort of locals and tourists, who enjoy the superb view of the city from here — especially after dark, when downtown Pest is transformed into a glittering sea of lights.

The park with its Liberation Monument by Zsigmond Kisfaludi Strobl was laid out in 1947 as a reminder of the horrors of war and occupation. For forty years afterwards the monument played a key role in every national celebration, as a symbol of Hungarian postwar socialism. The Russian memorial has since been removed from the monument.

Playful putti in the Gellért Baths

42 Gellért Baths

Gellért gyógyfürdő

Szent Gellért tér

The most romantic and sensual bathhouse in town, designed in sinuous Viennese Jugendstil.

The first bathhouse on this site was erected in 1687 by Friedrich Illmer, court physician to King Leopold I. Like most such establishments in Buda, it changed owners several times over the years and became so dilapidated that it was torn down in 1904. The competition for a replacement was won by Sebestyén Hegedűs and Isidor Stark, but as their plans required revision, construction did not begin until 1911.

The design of the facility is based on the classic Roman model. It has a central domed hall from which the various bathing departments lead off; a wave pool outside is enclosed by white stuccoed walls in the Mediterranean tradition. The most popular feature of the baths is probably the indoor pool. The Art Nouveau hall is richly clad in marble, ornamented with ornate columns, and the pool is faced with turquoise tiles. The glass roof can be opened in fine weather.

By the time the baths and the adjoining hotel were opened in 1918, the Art Nouveau building was stylistically outmoded. That did not bother the Budapesters, however, who have made "the Gellért" into one of their most cherished institutions. Among the villas in the vicinity are other fine specimens of Hungarian Art Nouveau (e.g., Kelenhegyi út 11); unfortunately most of these are, however, not in very good condition.

Gellért Baths, large indoor pool

43 Technical University

Műszaki Egyetem

Műegyetem rakpart/Budafoki út

The university campus dominates the embankment between Liberty Bridge and Petőfi Bridge.

The introduction of technical colleges in Hungary goes back to an ordinance issued by Maria Theresa, which provided for the establishment of specialized institutions for higher education; the teachers were at first usually recruited from the religious orders. By 1782 Buda had its "Institutum Geometricum," which was transformed into a polytechnic in 1856 and raised to university rank in 1871 by Baron József Eötvös, the minister of education. The central building at the corner of Budafoki út and Műegyetem rakpart and the various pavilions between Szent Gellért tér and Bertalan Lajos utca were designed by Alajos Hauszmann at the beginning of the century; other institutes went up in the years prior to 1936.

The landscaping around the Roman Catholic church in Pasarét has a definitely Mediterranean air

44 Városmajor Roman Catholic Church

Maros utca/Csaba utca

Modern ecclesiastical architecture in a middle-class residential area.

Though Hungarian domestic and public architecture rapidly took up the functionalist ideas of the Bauhaus in the early 1930s, church construction remained largely traditional. Congregations had the right to give their opinion when a church was to be built, which generally led to the rejection of designs that were considered too modern.

At this period the Városmajor district was primarily populated by an educated upper middle class. This may partially explain why not only several modern secular buildings were erected here and in the adjoining Second District during the 1930s, but two functionally designed churches as well.

The small chapel to the right of the church, by Aladár Arkay, dates from 1923 and reveals the influence of the German Werkbund. Just under ten years later, Arkay and his son Bertalan completed the hall church with its two narrow aisles. Its rigorously cuboid design is gracefully offset by the soaring, free-standing bell tower.

45 Pasarét Roman Catholic Church

Pasaréti tér

An outstanding example of Hungarian architecture of the 1930s.

This small aisleless church with rectory was the first independent project by Gyula Rimanóczy, a pupil of Aladár Arkay, whose name is associated with the church in Városmajor [No. 44]. The freestanding bell tower, the finely articulated facade of church and rectory, and the unpretentious interior design evidence the architect's affinity with the German Bauhaus, but also his individual application of Bauhaus principles. In his layout of the entire plaza, including the bus station, Rimanóczy created an architectural ensemble that is beautifully integrated into the given landscape situation.

46 Elizabeth Bridge

Erzsébet híd

This graceful suspension bridge is a symbol of the city's reconstruction after the Second World War.

The first Elizabeth Bridge, which was the fourth permanent bridge over the Danube, was built in 1898-1903. Like the underground railway to City Park, it was considered a technological wonder. The world's hitherto longest chain-suspension structure, it bridged the 300-yard-wide river in a single span, with one pier on each bank. To add to the city fathers' pride, it was built entirely of domestic materials.

The bridge was heavily damaged during the last war, and reconstruction was delayed until the early 1960s. Designed by Pál Sávoly, who incorporated the still extant old piers, the new, white, futuristic-looking bridge connecting Gellért Hill with central Pest was completed in 1964.

47 Széchenyi Chain Bridge

Széchenyi lánchíd

The first permanent link between Buda and Pest, Chain Bridge was a masterpiece of nineteenth-century engineering.

The idea of connecting the two towns by a permanent bridge over the Danube emerged in the 1820s, when the reformer Count István Széchenyi (1791-1860) advanced the notion to the city's Beautification Commission. Twenty years were to pass before the project was finally realized. After devoting much study to bridge building throughout Europe, Széchenyi commissioned the man who had constructed the famous Thames bridge in Hammersmith, Tierney William Clark, to span the Danube. In 1836 an association to further the building of the bridge was founded, and four years later the first pier went into place. Supervisor of construction was a Scotsman, Adam Clark (not related to the English designer). The suspension bridge —a superb engineering achievement—was opened to regular traffic on November 20, 1849. A vital link had been established between Pest, center of political affairs and administration, and the castle district.

Adam Clark settled in Budapest and collaborated on many other engineering projects. Among them was the 350-yard-long tunnel that provided a convenient and rapid connection between Krisztinaváros and the bridge. With its Neoclassical portal at the east end, on Clark Ádám tér, and Romantic portal at the west, the tunnel was inaugurated in 1856. With these projects the development of Buda-Pest into a modern European metropolis began.

For the hundredth anniversary of the bridge's completion, in 1949, war damage was repaired and the structure was widened by about a yard.

Elizabeth Bridge and Pest by night

Open-air theater on Margaret Island, just one of the many entertainments offered there

48 Margaret Island

Margit-sziget

A place of recreation since ancient times.

Linked to both embankments in the north by Árpád Bridge and in the south by Margaret Bridge, the island is about a mile and a half long and a quarter of a mile wide. Over ten thousand plane trees determine the character of its extensive parks. Colorful flower beds, well-tended lawns, and shady trees invite the visitor to take a stroll or relax from an overdose of hard city pavements.

Foundations of the Dominican convent and remains of a well from the 14th century

When a hot spring with therapeutic properties was discovered in the northern part of the island in the nineteenth century, a spa was built on the site of the present Ramada Grand Hotel. This and the modern Hotel Thermal still attract cure-seekers from all over the world. The café terrace of the Ramada is a perfect spot to take a breather and recover from the noise and bustle of the big city. Automobile access is permitted by way of Árpád Bridge to the hotel parking lot, but the remainder of the island is free of motor vehicles.

For those looking for more active recreation, the island has a great deal to offer: tennis courts, an indoor swimming pool of Olympic standard (built 1935), and the popular Palatinus open-air baths (with thermal pool). Also very much worth a visit are the rose garden, the Japanese garden, and the sculpture park.

As early as the Roman era the island was linked to the Buda embankment by a pile bridge. In the Middle Ages it served as a royal hunting ground, which earned it the nickname "Hare Isle."

In the northeastern part, south of the Ramada Hotel, stands a small chapel built in 1931 over the foundations of a twelfth-century Premonstratensian monastery. In the center of the island, foundations remain of the Dominican convent erected by

◁ *A funicular railway (sikló) connects Clark Ádám tér at the end of the Chain Bridge with Buda Castle. The red star on the roundabout indicates that the photo was taken a few years back*

Liberty Bridge, originally named after EmperorFranz Joseph, was the third permanent link between Buda and Pest. Its designers were Aurél Czekélius, János Feketeházy, and Virgil Nagy

King Béla IV, where his daughter, St. Margaret, lived. Much has come down to posterity in the way of legends surrounding the life and good deeds of the saint to whom the island owes its name. Parts of the west facade and tower of a Franciscan church built in the thirteenth century are to be seen further south.

Margaret Bridge (Margit híd) was designed by the French engineer Ernest Gouin and erected in 1872-76. A small bridge leads to the island from the middle of the bridge. A fine view of both Danube banks is to be had from this point.

In November 1944 the German Wehrmacht detonated explosive charges installed under the bridge—in broad daylight and without the slightest warning. How many lives were lost in this monstrous act has never become known. Reconstruction of the bridge lasted into the 1960s.

Besides those already mentioned, two further bridges span the Danube in the southern part of the city: Liberty Bridge (Szabadság híd) and Petőfi Bridge (Petőfi híd). Liberty Bridge connects Szent Gellért tér in Buda with Vámház körút, the southern end of Pest's inner ring. Erected in 1894-96, the iron structure rests on two piers in the riverbed. It was originally named after Franz Joseph, and the emperor made a point of driving in the last, symbolic silver rivet himself. A replica of the stolen original with the initials F. J. is on display under glass. Perched on golden balls high above the iron bridge portals are four turul birds with outspread wings. Legend has it that the progenitress of the Árpáds (the Hungarian dynasty that ruled during the settlement period) bore a child by a turul, bronze sculptures of which have populated the entire country ever since the national Romantic period in the latter half of the nineteenth century.

Petőfi Bridge spans the Danube at the southern end of the outer ring (Ferenc körút). A girder bridge dating from 1937, it was modernized and widened in 1980.

49 University of Economic Sciences

Közgazdaságtudományi Egyetem

Fővám tér 8

The former customs headquarters was erected by order of Menyhért Lónyay, minister of the economy, in 1870-74.

The building, by Miklós Ybl, designer of the Opera House, proved highly influential on subsequent public construction in Budapest. Like all of his work, it is characterized by a harmonious blend of elements and design principles derived from various past styles.

The structure is 184 yards long and 60 yards deep. The tripartite plan — a feature borrowed from the Baroque — includes a spacious entry hall with elegant stairways (entrance in the middle of the river front). The Danube facade is articulated in 33 bays; the ornamentation relies on Greek and Roman models. The sculptures on the Danube frontage are allegorical depictions of the river, the railroad, steam shipping, painting, sculpture, etc. Reliefs above the doorways of the north and south facades symbolize the four parts of the world.

50 Central Market

Központi Vásárcsarnok

Vámház körút 1-3

A bustling marketplace under cast iron and glass.

A noisy and colorful place, its sights and smells are a relief to anyone who has grown tired of the regimented ranks of supermarket shelves. Located behind the former customhouse, the biggest market in Budapest was built in 1897, simultaneously with four others. The 160-yard-long steel and iron construction is divided basilica-style into a taller "nave" and two aisles. The galleries are largely the domain of the flower-sellers.

One of the nine courtyards of the huge University of Economic Sciences

Market on Vámház körút, the most popular of Budapest's nine market halls

51 Hungarian National Museum

Magyar Nemzeti Múzeum

Múzeum körút 14-16

A museum temple suffused with national sentiment, home of the legendary coronation insignia of Stephen I.

In 1802, Count Ferenc Széchényi donated to the city a portion of his collections — a superb library and a coin collection — which were later to form the museum's core. Palatine Joseph of Habsburg, who felt close ties with Hungary and unceasingly promoted her development, suggested the establishment of a national museum to the court board of works in Vienna in 1807. The following year an act was passed to this end, but construction was delayed by the Napoleonic wars, and did not get underway until 1836. Mihály Pollack's design exemplarily reflects the spirit of the Classical Revival in Europe. It is based on the ancient Greek temple, similar to Schinkel's Altes Museum in Berlin (1825-30) or Klenze's Glyptothek in Munich (1816-30). All of these museum buildings reflect a well-nigh reverent attitude towards the arts and sciences. The structure is arranged around two interior courts. A striking feature of the exterior is the markedly projecting portal with its eight Corinthian columns. The pediment relief, designed by the Munich sculptor Schaller, was executed by Raffaello Ponti of Milan. Behind the round colonnaded hall on the ground floor a broad, elegant staircase, decorated with frescoes by Mór Than and Károly Lotz, leads to the *bel étage*, which with its domed rotunda and adjacent grand hall is a typical example of Neoclassical museum design. Pollack's building, probably the finest accomplishment of Hungarian Neoclassicism, earned the architect honorary membership of the Vienna Academy.

On March 15, 1848, the museum witnessed the spark that set off Hungary's uprising against the Habsburgs. Standing on its steps, the young poet Sándor Petőfi declaimed his "Song of the Nation," and members of the "March Youth" spoke to the impassioned crowds.

The **collection**: The original stocks were soon enriched by private donations (Kubinyi, Marczibányi, Jankovich, and Pyrker collections). Towards the close of the century the natural science and ethnographic collections became independent departments, while the painting collection was transferred to the Museum of Fine Arts in 1906. The museum's rich collection of minerals was lost in the 1956 uprising.

Early medieval aquamanile, Hungarian National Museum

Ground floor: Archaeological department. Finds made on Hungarian territory dating from primeval times, the Neolithic and Bronze ages, the Roman era, and the Magyar settlement period.

Second floor: Middle Ages. From the Hungarian settlement through the eras of kings Sigismund and Matthias Corvinus to the period of Ottoman rule.

Eighteenth and nineteenth centuries. Ferenc Rákóczi and his times, the reform era, the struggle for independence.

The various departments display specimens of Hungarian decorative art, goldsmiths' work, ceramics, textiles, furniture, weapons, and religious relics. Highlight of a well-guarded chamber of honor are the insignia of Hungarian kingship — crown, scepter, and orb — which were in the United States from the end of the Second World War until 1978. The last king of Hungary to wear the crown was Charles IV of Habsburg, crowned in 1916.

The St. Stephen's Crown, probably created after King Stephen's reign, consists of two parts. The lower section, known as the corona graeca, *is Byzantine. The upper section, or* corona latina, *was added at a later date.*

The main altar of University Church with a sculpture of the Nativity of the Virgin dates from 1746. It is flanked by figures of the anchorite saints Paul and Anthony. All the sculptures are by Josef Hebenstreit

52 University Church

Egyetemi templom

Papnövelde utca/Egyetem tér

The finest, well preserved Baroque church in Budapest was founded by the Pauline order.

The order of St. Paul, Hungary's only congregation of hermit monks, existed until 1949. The Paulines, who had resumed activity in 1688 after the Ottoman period, erected their church on the site of a Turkish mosque (beginning of construction 1725, consecration 1742, towers 1771). The plans were probably drawn up by Andreas Mayerhoffer of Salzburg, a pupil of Johann Lukas von Hildebrandt and Anton Martinelli.

The ceiling fresco is the work of Johann Bergl (1776, signed on the right side of the choir). The wood carvings were done by the Pauline monks themselves. The Baroque pulpit is an outstanding piece by an anonymous Hungarian master. On the main altar with a figure group representing the Birth of the Virgin, there is a copy of the Black Virgin of Czestochowa (c. 1720).

In the late eighteenth and early nineteenth centuries the church was a bastion of the Hungarian reform movement, which demanded national independence from the Vienna court. The year 1831 saw the inauguration here of a "Practical School" devoted to the advancement of the Hungarian language.

The **Theological College** at Papnövelde utca 7 harbors the old library of the Pauline monastery, with magnificently carved bookcases from around 1770 and a frescoed ceiling by Pietro Rivetti (illustration p. 98).

53 University Library

Egyetemi Könyvtár

Ferenciek tere 6

Repository of eleven medieval manuscripts from the world-renowned collection of King Matthias Corvinus.

The library, along with the forerunner of the present University of Budapest, was founded in 1635 by Cardinal Péter Pázmány in Nagyszombat. During the reign of Maria Theresa, its stocks of books were transferred to Buda. A considerable portion of the volumes once belonged to the Jesuits, who had received them from noble families fleeing the Turks in the sixteenth century. Finally, the library moved from Buda to Pest in 1784, under Joseph II.

Its treasures include 11 Corvinas, and a further 160 medieval manuscripts and miniatures, among them a Dante codex written in Greek and the Abucasis Codex, which is especially interesting for the history of medicine. The library's almost two million volumes offer a rich repository for

University Library, main entrance

Library of the Theological College

studies, especially in the humanities. The Neo-Renaissance building was designed by Antal Szklaniczky and Henrik Koch and was built from 1873 to 1876. The frescoes in the reading room are by Károly Lotz, the sgraffiti by Mór Than, and the sculptures by Ágoston Sommer.

54 Serbian Church

Szerb templom

Szerb utca/Veres Pálné utca

Erected by the Serbian colony in Pest in 1688.

Presumbly designed by Andreas Mayerhoffer, the church was enlarged in 1733. The iconostasis is by Károly Sterio. On the garden wall there are a number of grave slabs with Cyrillic inscriptions dating from the eighteenth and nineteenth centuries. In the early nineteenth century Serbians made up nearly a quarter of Pest house owners.

Now an oasis of calm in the noisy downtown area, the church saw more exciting times in the last century. It was the focus of a reform movement led by Mihály Vitkovics, a lawyer of Serbian extraction who devoted himself to the advancement of the Hungarian language and of Hungarian journalism.

55 Franciscan Church

Pesti ferences templom

Ferenciek tere/Kossuth Lajos utca

Headquarters of the Franciscans in Hungary, with a checkered history.

After the Mongol invasion, in 1288, the Franciscans built a friary dedicated to St. Peter of Alcantara on the site of the present church. In 1298 the Hungarian constitution drawn up by the historic Diet of Rákos was proclaimed within its walls. The originally Gothic church was converted by the Turks into a mosque, which the Franciscans in turn used for their services when they returned in 1690. Between 1727 and 1758, finally, the present aisleless structure with vaulted roof was erected.

Paris Court arcade, lined with shops and a popular café. Moorish architectural forms and the suffused light lend it an inimitable atmosphere

The nave is very wide in accordance with Baroque practice. The six wall niches contain side altars, and an organ gallery extends over the entrance. The frescoes are by Károly Lotz (1894/95). The sculptures on the main altar date from 1741 and 1851. The side altars with paintings and the pulpit were created in 1851/52.

The tower on the south side of the choir, designed by Ferenc Wieser, was added in 1858. It is one of the finest specimens of Hungarian Romantic architecture, a style that did not bear much fruit in Budapest because of the political situation of the day.

A commemorative plaque of 1905 on the exterior wall on Kossuth Lajos utca recalls the great flood of 1838, in which Baron Miklós Wesselényi played a salient role in rescuing the people of Pest. Similar plaques expressing the citizens' gratitude to their past benefactors are found on many Budapest buildings.

The space in front of the church is graced by a pretty Naiad Fountain dating from 1835. The sculptures of the water nymphs are by Ferenc Uhrl, and the pedestals were designed by József Feszl. The art of fountain sculpture flourished in Budapest during the Neoclassical period. The city's spacious, atrium-style courtyard gardens and the warm summers created perfect conditions for a great number of delightful fountains, both freestanding and integrated as water-spouting sculptures in entryways and stairwells. Several fine specimens of the genre may still be seen along Váci utca and Andrássy út.

A relief by Barnabás Holló, installed on the north side of the Franciscan church to commemorate the great flood of 1838

56 Klothilde Mansions, Paris Court

Klotild paloták, Párisi udvar

Szabadsajtó út/Ferenciek tere

The twin mansions flank the street as an imposing gateway to Elizabeth Bridge.

The architects of the **Klothilde Mansions**, Kálmán Giergl and Flóris Korb, were among Hungary's greatest at the turn of the century; like most of their confrères, they trained abroad, spending some years in Berlin. They designed these grand tene-

Klothilde Mansions, erected in 1902 for Archduchess Klothilde, wife of the Hungarian Palatine Archduke Joseph. Designed by Flóris Kolb and Kálmán Giergl, the twin structures have always been apartment buildings

ment buildings in 1902, taking their inspiration from Spanish Baroque architecture. The ground floors originally featured shopping arcades, as at Paris Court.

Paris Court (Ferenciek tere 11) is an Art Nouveau apartment building designed by Henrik Schmal and built in 1911. Its most attractive feature is its arcade, where the twilight under the stained-glass vaulting gradually reveals richly articulated walls of almost Byzantine opulence. Elegant shops and bookstores with foreign literature invite window-shopping and more. The seats outside the Piccolo bistro are a popular rendezvous. In summertime many windows in the arcade display portraits of high-school graduating classes with their teachers.

57 Inner City Parish Church

Belvárosi plébániatemplom

Március 15. tér

In downtown Pest's main church, Gothic and Baroque blend unusally harmoniously.

Inner City Parish Church is an interesting example of the variety of stylistic influences in Budapest's architecture, and also of the changes made in key buildings to satisfy current tastes. The earliest church on this site was a late Romanesque structure built in the twelfth century over a Roman *castrum*. During the Mongol invasion of 1241/42 city and church suffered severe damage. The succeeding fourteenth-century Gothic building was also later destroyed, apart from its choir, which was

The excavations of Contra Aquincum, with Inner City Parish Church in the background

converted into a Turkish mosque in the seventeenth century. A still-extant prayer niche, or *mihrab*, dates from this period.

The present appearance of the hall church with its three chapels on each side goes back to the Baroque era, when the nave and twin-tower facade by György Paur were built in 1725-39. The result, still evident today, was a harmonious coexistence of Baroque western section with Gothic eastern section. Under the nave there is a crypt whose stones were once part of the ancient Roman stronghold; it houses a collection of architectural fragments unearthed in the course of reconstruction work. The church also contains twentieth-century art: the main altar by László Gerő (1947) with paintings by C. Pál Molnár, and a font by Béni Ferenczy, a major Hungarian sculptor. In a niche in the external wall of the south tower there is a figure of St. Florian, who is traditionally invoked for protection from fire; it was sculpted by Antal Hörger in 1723.

The 15th-century fresco in the choir of Inner City Parish Church, originally located in the cloister, reflects Italian influences

For centuries the Danube marked the eastern frontier of the Roman empire. The Buda side with the town of Aquincum belonged to the province of Pannonia; on the opposite bank, where Pest now stands, "barbarian country" began. Here the Romans erected a fortified bridgehead named after its location, **Contra Aquincum**. Today the site with its carefully preserved wall remnants and reconstructed watchtower is a favorite summer meeting point for students and visitors.

58 Hungarian Orthodox Church

Magyar ortodox templom

Petőfi tér 2

A symbol of the multinational character of the Danube metropolis.

For centuries a great variety of ethnic groups lived more or less peacefully together in Budapest. The colony of Greek merchants, who became prosperous in the eighteenth century, decided to build a church for themselves in the center of town. The building went up in 1790-94 to plans by József Jung. The architectural ornamentation and iconostasis are by Miklós Jankovich (1797-99), while the paintings are by Anton Kochmeister of Vienna. A fire badly damaged the towers in 1810, but sixty years were to pass before they were renewed by the architect Miklós Ybl, who combined the Baroque elements of the facade design with Neoclassical forms. The south tower, destroyed in the Second World War, has yet to be rebuilt.

The **Petőfi Monument** on the square was based on a miniature sculpture by Miklós Izsó. It was created in 1881 by Adolf Huszár, the master of Hungarian academic sculpture.

The Százéves restaurant

59 Péterffy Mansion

Péterffy palota

Pesti Barnabás utca 2

Baroque townhouse with a fine restaurant.

This fine Baroque residence—veritably dwarfed by its modern neighbors—gives a good impression of the architecture in this section of town in the eighteenth century, when Pest was still enclosed by a wall. Today the house stands a fair bit below street level, its ground floor on a level with the basements of the surrounding buildings. It was built in 1755 for the Péterffy family by Andreas Mayerhoffer. The family arms are still to be seen in the tympanum over the broad gateway.

The Százéves ("Hundred-Year") restaurant has been in continuous operation here since 1831. A traditional establishment with prices in the upper bracket, it offers fine Hungarian and international cuisine.

The Hungarian Orthodox church lost its south tower in an air raid during the Second World War

The Pest Assembly Rooms (Vigadó), main elevation

Sculptures by Károly Alexy on the Vigadó

60 Pest Assembly Rooms

Pesti Vigadó

Vigadó tér 2

Originally a ballroom, the Vigadó is one of the loveliest and most mature works of Hungarian Romantic architecture.

Frigyes Feszl's masterpiece was erected between 1859 and 1865. Its Neoclassical predecessor had been destroyed during the 1848 uprising; the city fathers wanted not only their ballroom back but the spoilt waterfront panorama restored. In the new building, Feszl anticipated the Hungarian National Style that was not to fully develop until about thirty years later. The opulent facade decor and interior design employ folklore elements and combine a diversity of stylistic influences into a marvellously romantic whole.

Since it reopened in 1980, the Vigadó has again been hosting concerts and exhibitions, and its Great Hall can be leased for balls and other festivities. On the ground floor there is a beer hall and an art gallery.

61 Gerbeaud Café

Gerbeaud cukrászda

Vörösmarty tér 7-8

One of Budapest's most venerable coffee shops, located at the hub of the finest shopping streets and where the Little Subway (Kis földalatti) begins.

Slicing his first cake here on October 14, 1858, pastrymaker Henrik Kugler set up to compete with Ruszwurm's in the castle district. His successor, the Swiss Emil Gerbeaud, installed the interior, which has survived largely intact. Its elaborate stuccowork, chandeliers, marble-top tables, panelling and brocade wall coverings emulate the famous coffeehouses of Vienna.

In contrast to the exclusive London clubs, such establishments in Budapest and Vienna were products of urban middle-class society from the beginning. Elegance combined with a certain degree of coziness ensured both the anonymity and feeling of belonging that city dwellers seem to crave. Accordingly, crowds throng Gerbeaud from morning to night (despite the lax service, which is no longer what it used to be).

Weather permitting, we recommend taking a seat outside, to enjoy the animated yet intimate atmosphere of Vörösmarty tér (illustration p. 167).

Váci utca, a popular shopping street

Downtown Budapest pulsates with life: gypsy violinists, Transylvanian women offering embroideries for sale, buskers from the plains of Asia and beyond

62 Deák Square Protestant Church

Déak téri evangélikus templom

Deák Ferenc tér 4-5

The austere headquarters of Hungary's Lutheran community.

In 1781 Joseph II issued the Edict of Tolerance, which legalized the activity of reformed churches in Hungarian communities. It stipulated that wherever more than a hundred Protestant families lived, they were to be permitted to establish their own congregations. In 1791 the Lutheran community of Pest entrusted János Krausz with the building of a church, a parsonage, and a school on what was then a farmers' market. After the architect's death, construction was continued by Mihály Pollack. By 1808 the church building had been completed; the Neoclassical portico with engaged Doric pillars was a later addition, designed in 1856 by József Hild. The **National Protestant Museum** (Evangélikus Országos Múzeum) illustrates the history of the Lutheran church in Hungary. During the Reformation period the new confession gained great numbers of adherents, but by the end of the sixteenth century, with the Counter-Reformation and mass expulsion of Protestant families (among the emigrants were the ancestors of Johann Sebastian Bach), the Roman Catholic church had regained its hegemony in those parts of Hungary not occupied by the Turks. At present, only about four percent of the Hungarian population are Lutherans (about 16% belong to the Calvinist Reformed church). One of the most interesting items in the museum's valuable collection is Martin Luther's last will and testament, written in Wittenberg in 1542; it was bought at auction in Helmstedt, Germany, in 1804 by the archaeologist Miklós Jankovich. The exhibition also includes the first Hungarian Bible translation, school books, chronicles, and portraits of the country's most famous Protestant personalities.

A commemorative plaque recalls the fact that the Romantic poet Sándor Petőfi (1823-49) was once a pupil at the Protestant school here. Perhaps his later career was shaped by the progressive education he enjoyed there. In 1816 the school's principal, Lajos Schedius, wrote an essay on the teachings of the renowned Swiss educator, Johann Heinrich Pestalozzi, which he adopted as the basis of his curriculum. The school continued to exist until its abolition by the Communist government in 1952. The grammar school was reopened in 1989.

Protestant stringency reflected in the church on Deák Ferenc tér

Atlas statue and allegorical female figures over the portal of the former war veterans' hospital, by the Viennese sculptor Johann Christoph Mader

63 Central Town Hall

Központi városháza

Városház utca 9-11

Budapest's municipal council convenes where veterans once recovered from their war injuries.

The most significant structure built in the reign of Charles III (1711-40), this former war veterans' hospital now serves as town hall. Originally a monumental freestanding building on the north edge of the inner city, it is now ensconced in narrow lanes and jostled by the high apartment houses that went up after Budapest's incorporation. Planning began in 1716, under Fortunato de Prati of Vienna, who was rapidly succeeded by another architect active there, Anton Erhard Martinelli. His design was based on the Italian Baroque palazzo, with a rectangular ground plan. Tuscan pilasters through the three upper stories provide vertical unity. The portals with their projecting pediments, the strongly modelled cornice, and the sculptures above the entrances are masterpieces of the epoch. The architectural beauty of the hospital was more than matched by its functional perfection. For almost half a century it was

Splendid Art Nouveau mosaic on the former Török Bank

Great Synagogue, detail of west facade

devoted largely to the treatment of disabled veterans, about two thousand of whom lived here at any one time. Besides living quarters, the building contained two clinics, a school, and a chapel with a capacity of three thousand (now used as a concert hall). There was also a butcher's shop, a bakery, and various other shops for daily needs, so that the inmates rarely had to leave the building. Later it was converted into a grenadier barracks, and in 1894 became the seat of Budapest's city government.

Just along the street, at **No. 7**, is Pest County Hall, a fine Neoclassical structure completed in 1838-41 by Matthias Zitterbarth Jr.

Walking back the other way, we emerge on **Szervita tér**, which boasts two interesting residential and commercial buildings from the early years of the century. The former Török Bank (**No. 3**), built in 1906, is crowned by an outstanding Art Nouveau gable, whose brilliantly colored glass mosaic represents the "Transfiguration of Hungaria." The Rózsavölgyi Building (**No. 5**) was erected in 1912 for a firm of tailors. Shop, office, and residential sections are clearly demarcated on the facade. In designing the decor, architect Béla Lajta was inspired by Viennese Jugendstil and German Werkbund architecture. The building's name derives from the music store that still exists here, but whose original furnishings were sadly destroyed by fire in 1955.

64 Great Synagogue

Nagy zsinagóga

Dohány utca 2-8

The spiritual center of Hungary's Reform Jewish community, and the second largest synagogue in the world.

After Óbuda and Pozsony, Pest became the third town in Hungary in which Jews were allowed to settle on the basis of Joseph II's Edict of Tolerance of 1781. As the inner city was still out of bounds, however, they established themselves just outside, in Erzsébetváros and Terézváros. By the beginning of the nineteenth century these quarters were almost exclusively Jewish,

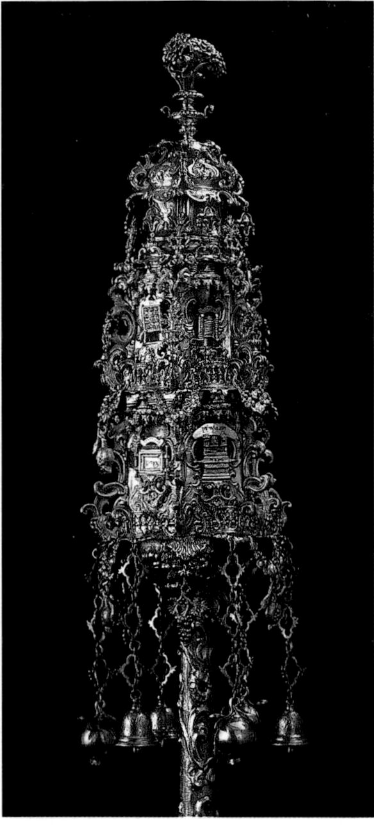

*Bell staff (*rimon*), preserved in the Jewish Museum adjacent to the Great Synagogue*

but until the Fascist period Pest never had a ghetto [regarding Buda, see No. 15]. After Vienna's Jews built a large synagogue in 1826, the Jewish community of Erzsébetváros decided to follow suit, but a number of years were to pass before the building was realized, its construction being delayed by the great flood, the 1848 uprising, and five cholera epidemics. In the meantime the community held prayers in schools and private apartments in the neighborhood.

Noted architects took part in the design competition for the new synagogue, which was won by Ludwig Förster, a German who had just finished a synagogue on Tempelgasse in Vienna (1854). The short time period between the two projects—the Pest synagogue went up in 1857—probably explains their stylistic similarity. Both are historical-revival buildings with a strong Moorish accent. The Great Synagogue is also influenced by Christian thinking, as the women's galleries that flank the nave over two stories create a space that definitely recalls the Christian basilica. Also, the 27-foot-high Torah cabinet (Arc of the Law), instead of standing in its customary position in the middle of the nave, is located in the "choir," where in Christian churches the altar stands. The synagogue has room for 1492 men and 1472 women. Cast-iron pillars and beams support the high roof, lending the spacious interior airiness and grace.

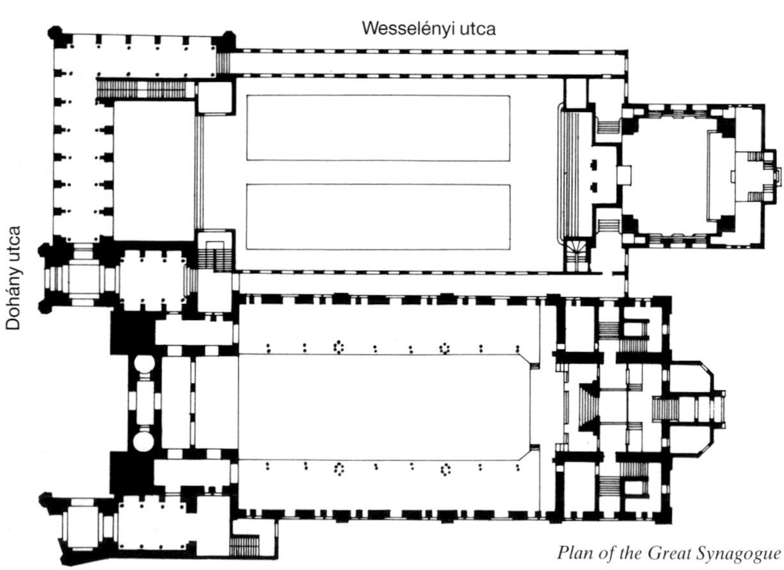

Plan of the Great Synagogue

Holocaust memorial by Imre Varga, behind the Heroes' Temple. Its thousands of silver leaves are dedicated to the victims of the 1944/45 German occupation

To the north of the synagogue there is an arcaded courtyard that calls to mind a cloister.

Europe's largest synagogue received two further annexes in 1929-31. **The Heroes' Temple** (Hősök temploma, Wesselényi utca 3) was erected in honor of Jewish soldiers who gave their lives in the First World War. Imre Varga's Holocaust Memorial was unveiled in the court behind it in 1990.

The National Jewish Religious and Historical Collection (Országos Zsidó Vallási és Történeti Gyűjtemény, Dohány utca 2), designed by László Vágó, is dedicated to the history of the Jewish community in Hungary from the ancient Roman era to the present day. The collection includes autographs by Theodor Herzl (1860-1904), Hungarian philosopher and founder of modern Zionism. He was born in a house that previously stood on this site, a fact recorded on a memorial plaque in the stairwell of the present corner building.

65 Orthodox Synagogue

Ortodox zsinagóga

Rumbach Sebestyén utca 11-13

An early work by the renowned Viennese architect Otto Wagner.

As Reform Judaism spread during the latter half of the nineteenth century and the influence of the Great Synagogue community grew ever stronger, the adherents of the Orthodox faith decided to build their own synagogue. They approached Otto Wagner of Vienna, who agreed to draw up the plans.

The oriental-looking tendril ornaments he designed for the facade anticipate Viennese Jugendstil. The interior is more traditional, with the vestibule clearly separated from the octagonal prayer hall with its central bema (lectern rustrum).

Heavily damaged in the Second World War, the synagogue is currently being restored.

66 Rákóczi Road

Rákóczi út

A busy shopping street dominated by buildings from the latter half of the nineteenth and the early twentieth centuries.

Leading eastward out of Pest, this street formerly ended at Hatvan Gate in the city wall; it received its present name in 1906, after the famous freedom fighter Prince Ferenc II Rákóczi (1657-1735). The oldest building here is St. Roch's Chapel (Szent Rókus kápolna, **No. 31**), which dates from the early eighteenth century (tower 1797). A votive church erected in memory of the plague victims of 1711, it was restored to its original state in 1958. **No. 18** is a work by Béla Lajta (1911), who was also the architect of the Rózsavölgyi House on Szervita tér [see No. 63]. The facade design he introduced, with arcades for business premises, proved influential on Budapest architecture down to the 1950s.

The facade of **No. 19** is graced by a bronze statue of King Matthias Corvinus, created in 1902.

No. 21, a historical-revival building erected in 1893, was the headquarters of the Hungarian Urania Society, which like its counterparts in Berlin and Vienna was devoted to the dissemination of scientific knowledge in a popular form.

The Palace Hotel (**No. 43**) is a typical specimen of Hungarian Art Nouveau, built in 1911.

We are now approaching East Station (Keleti pályaudvar), whose splendid Neo-Renaissance facade is visible from a distance. The large terminus, built in 1884, received a subway connection in 1969, when the plaza was redesigned, lowered considerably below street level, and made into a pedestrian precinct.

67 Museum of Applied Art

Iparművészeti Múzeum

Üllői út 33-37

The city's most beautiful and interesting museum building, completed in 1896 in the Hungarian National Style.

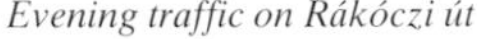

Evening traffic on Rákóczi út

Such "French" courtyards with circumambient galleries are characteristic of the large apartment buildings that went up in Pest in the late 19th century. They not only provide a refuge from street noise, but also encourage neighborly communication

The advocates of the National Style, putting behind them historical-revival modes, adopted the ornamental exuberance of folk art and absorbed influences from Islamic architecture and German and Austrian Jugendstil. The leader of the movement, Ödön Lechner, trained for almost ten years in several countries before beginning the present building. The facade is clad in glazed bricks ornamented with "pyrogranite" tiles, made by the Zsolnay Company in Pécs from a mixture of fire clay and clay kilned at a very high temperature. The metallic sheen of the tiles and the rich facade decor lend the exterior great fascination. Entering the snow-white interior, one feels spirited into the Orient: Moorish arches open off from the high central hall, and the vast foyer is over-arched by a cupola of brilliantly colored glass. The collection covers every major stylistic period. Domestic Haban ceramics are represented along with Meissen porcelain, oriental carpets, French goldsmith's work, and German Jugendstil jewelry.

68 New York Café

Erzsébet körút 11

The café's extravagant interior, largely preserved, is well worth seeing.

Reopened in 1954 as Café Hungaria, this erstwhile gathering place of the literary

View of the central hall of the Museum of Applied Art, by Ödön Lechner

world has been doing business under its original name again since the early 1990s. "New York" was the name of the life insurance company building in which the coffee shop with fin-de-siècle decor was installed in 1894. Its period interior still features the lamps and mirrors of the day, marble and bronze work by Gusztáv Magyar-Mannheimer and Ferenc Eisenhut, and frescoes by Károly Lotz. Displayed in the gallery with its theater-style boxes are caricatures of writers and artists who more or less successfully awaited fame here, and who often as not ran up huge coffee bills with the patient, poetry-loving waiters. The playwright Ferenc Molnár is said to have thrown the key to the café into the Danube on opening day, a symbolic gesture expressing the hope that its doors would remain forever open to writers and artists. Ernő Osvát, editor-in-chief of the literary journal *Nyugat* from 1908 to 1929, perused the manuscripts submitted to him at one of the tables. In addition to tourists, people associated with the arts in one form or another still congregate here in an ambience that puts many a movie set to shame.

Rich potpourri of period styles in the New York café

69 Music Academy

Zeneakadémia

Liszt Ferenc tér 8

Major work of the architects Kálmán Giergl and Flóris Korb, erected in 1904-07.

This concert hall with adjoining lecture and practice rooms is a fine example of the National Style, the Hungarian variant of Art Nouveau. The prime inspiration came from Assyrian ornament, stylized versions of which extend over both the facade and the interior. The foyer is clad with Zsolnay ceramic tiles made in Pécs. The frescoes are by the Art Nouveau master Aladár Körösfői-Kriesch, who also collaborated on the stained-glass windows of Parliament House. The concert hall of the Music

Upstairs foyer of the Music Academy, with Aladár Körösfői-Kriesch's Art Nouveau fresco The Fount of Youth

Academy is renowned for its fine acoustics. The building is usually accessible during the day by the side entrance on Király utca.

70 Hall of Fashion

Divatcsarnok

Andrássy út 39

Department store with tradition.

The original store, inspired by those in Paris, was built in 1882 by Gustav Petschacher. After being destroyed by fire around the turn of the century, in 1909 it received what was for the day a "modern" facade and interior layout designed by Zsigmond Sziklai. The building is a prime example of Hungarian reinforced-concrete architecture, technically masterminded by Gut & Gergely of Budapest, who also designed the watertower on Margaret Island.

At the rear of the second floor an old ballroom with frescoes by the Hungarian artist Károly Lotz has survived. The room was integrated into the reconstructed building in 1911.

71 Ernst Museum

Ernst Múzeum

Nagymező utca 8

Exhibitions focussing on contemporary Hungarian and foreign art.

Lajos Ernst, a well-known collector of the day, found this building to house his extensive collection in 1912. Primarily interested in progressive art, Ernst mounted a number of significant exhibitions in the 1920s. In 1932 the permanent collection was dispersed, works of earlier masters going to the National Museum and the Museum of Fine Arts and the music collection to the Opera House Museum.

Entryway and stairwell of this somewhat dilapidated Art Nouveau building were designed by Ödön Lechner.

72 János Arany Theater

Arany János Színház

Paulay Ede utca 35

Suffused with 1920s atmosphere, the interior is a wealth of fascinating Art Deco.

Before and after the First World War this section of town was the entertainment quarter. Clubs like the Arizona and the Parisiana were bywords for cultivated nightlife and modern trends in the performing arts. Today's János Arany Theater was originally the Parisiana, a 1909 building by Béla Lajta, who enriched Budapest with a number of structures in the Viennese Jugendstil style [see Nos. 63 and 66].

Since 1921 the premises have gone through several conversions and changes of proprietor, the result being a steady deterioration of the architectural substance. After being closed for restoration for many years, the building is now being used as a theater once more (illustration p. 173).

73 Hungarian State Opera House

Magyar Állami Operaház

Andrássy út 22

A dignified building reflecting the influence of both Tuscan and German Romantic architecture.

The latter half of the nineteenth century was a period of theater building in Hungary. Motive force was the bourgeoisie and their cultural aspirations, and also an increasing national awareness in the countries of the Habsburg monarchy accompanied by a desire to advance their native languages. This led to a furtherance of national music and the dramatic arts. Pest had had a German theater since 1812, and

Staircase in the opera house

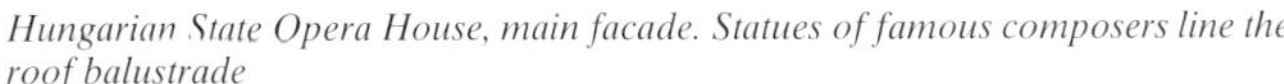

Hungarian State Opera House, main facade. Statues of famous composers line the roof balustrade

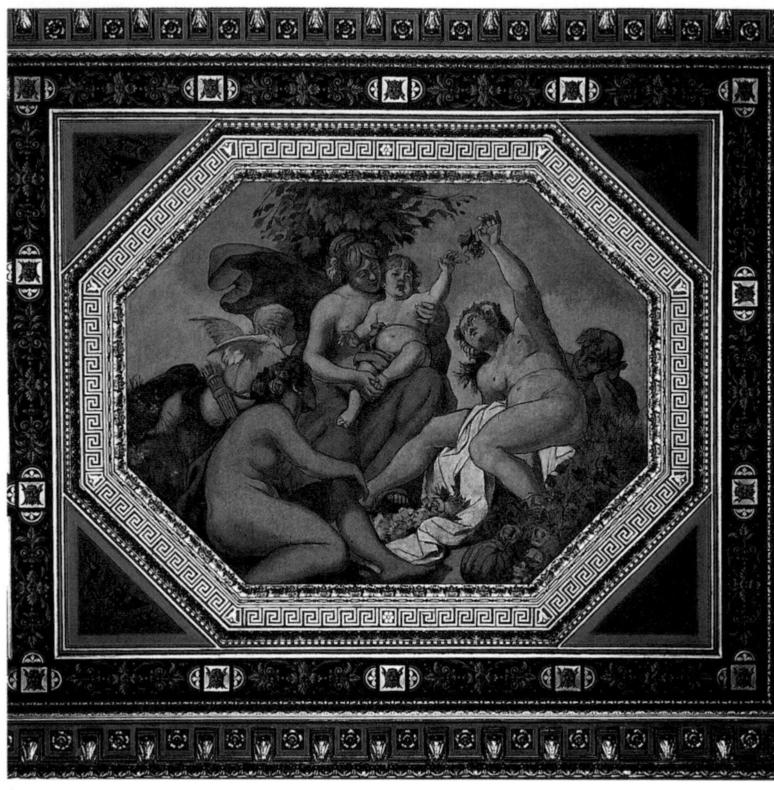

The ceiling paintings in the opera house create the illusion of cofferwork

the first Hungarian theater opened in 1837. The church schools also produced stage plays, but an opera house did not yet exist.

Two years before Buda, Pest, and Óbuda were united, the public works commission announced, in 1871, a competition for the design of an opera house. The project found the support of Emperor Franz Joseph, who wanted to see Buda-Pest follow the example of Paris, Vienna, and Dresden. Of the six designs submitted, that by Miklós Ybl took top honors. Construction of the opera lasted not quite ten years. It was ceremonially inaugurated on September 27, 1884, in the presence of the royal family and prime minister Kálmán Tisza, with a gala performance of the Hungarian national opera *Bánk bán*, by Ferenc Erkel.

The rigorously symmetrical facade relies strongly for articulation on elements of Renaissance architecture. In the niches flanking the main entrance stand Ferenc Erkel (left) and Franz Liszt (right). Figures of the muses grace the second-story niches, while those along the balustrade represent other famous composers.

The vestibule is a triumph of Neo-Renaissance ostentation. From the mosaics of the floor to the ornament in the vaulted ceiling, Ybl created a bravura achievement of interior design. The ceiling paintings were done by the major Hungarian artists of the period: Károly Lotz, Bertalan Székely, and Mór Than. The three-tier auditorium is overarched by a cupola decorated with frescoes by Károly Lotz. The Székely Room contains the opera house's art collection and archive, illustrating the history of the house in visual and documentary form.

Opposite the Opera House (**No. 25**) is an imposing building in the style of a French Renaissance chateau, the former Drechsler Palais, which is now occupied by the ballet school. An early design by Ödön Lechner, it was built in 1883 for the state railroad administration. Though revealing little of the great Hungarian Art Nouveau master's later originality, the building already evinces folk-art ornament on the ground floor, in what used to be a coffee shop. It also derives a special charm from the contradiction between its style and its site. Based on architectural forms intended for a rural setting, Lechner's chateau stands in an environment entirely metropolitan.

74 St. Stephen's Church

Szent István templom

Szent István tér

Budapest's largest church harbors a revered relic.

Because of its sheer size, not its architectural form, the former parish church of Leopoldtown (Lipótváros) is often called simply the "Bazilika." The building was commissioned in 1845 from József Hild, the outstanding representative of Hungarian Neoclassicism, who had designed the monumental cathedrals in Esztergom and Eger. He chose a Greek cross ground plan for St. Stephen's and supervised construc-

Neo-Gothic reliquary, Chapel of the Holy Right Hand, St. Stephen's Church

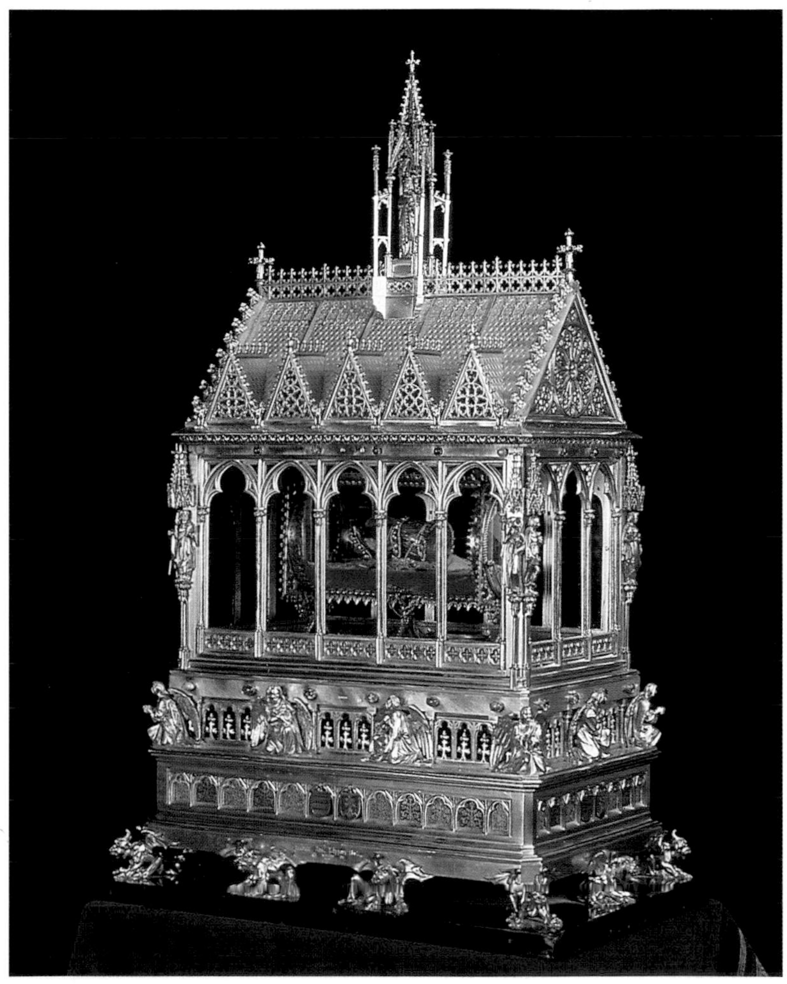

St. Stephen's Church, west facade

tion from 1851 until his death in 1867. A year later the central dome collapsed, and Hild's successor, Miklós Ybl, designed the present dome, which is effectively counterpointed by the two west towers. Ybl gradually diverged from his predecessor's Neoclassical approach in favor of Neo-Renaissance, which is especially in evidence in the church interior. Major artists of the period, Gyula Benczúr and Károly Lotz, contributed the mosaics and frescoes. Ybl died in 1891, leaving the project to Josef Kauser, who finally finished the church in 1905.

St. Stephen's is dedicated to the first Hungarian monarch to be baptized a Christian. The right hand of the holy king is preserved in a gilded reliquary in the northeast chapel, the Szent Jobb kápolna. Since the reign of Maria Theresa the relic has been carried through the streets with liturgical ceremony every August 20, the day on which King Ladislas (László) I is said to have found Stephen's hand miraculously intact.

The new, electrically operated bell was presented to the church by the city of Passau, Germany, on August 20, 1990, in memory of the opening of the Hungarian border the year before, which permitted thousands of East Germans to flee to Austria.

75 Gresham Palace

Gresham palota

Roosevelt tér 5-6

Art Nouveau enhancement of a corporate image.

A British insurance company, the Gresham, commissioned this office building from Zsigmond Quittner in 1907. Both fa-

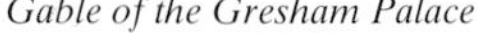

Gable of the Gresham Palace

Hall of ceremonies in the Academy of Sciences

cade decoration and technical installations (elevators, central heating) met the day's highest standards of quality and materials; the ground-floor arcade boasts wrought-iron gates, fine tiles, and stained glass. During the 1920s a café in the building attracted the Hungarian avant-garde, who formed a group known as the Gresham Circle.

76 Hungarian Academy of Sciences

Magyar Tudományos Akadémia

Roosevelt tér 9

The first Neo-Renaissance building in Budapest.

The Hungarian Academy of Sciences was founded during the reform period (1825), but it did not receive its own building until 1865. The design competition was won by a Berlin architect, Friedrich August Stüler; Miklós Ybl supervised construction. The frescoes in the auditorium were executed by Károly Lotz. When the building was inaugurated, the *Pest Sunday News* immediately noted its similarities with the Stockholm museum, another work of Stüler's.

In front of the academy stands a monument to its founder, István Széchenyi, and on the other side of the square a monument to Ferenc Deák (1803-76), a leading Hungarian politician who contributed materially to the historic Compromise with Austria.

The core of the academy's library was formed by the Teleki family collection, which was supplemented by important autographs after 1840. Towards the close of the century, György Ráth gave his valuable collection of rare Hungarian books to the library, and the Elisch bequest enriched it with manuscripts and books of the Goethe period. Perhaps its most significant department is the oriental collection, which includes the bequest of Sándor Kőrösi Csoma (1784-1842), who researched into the origins of the Hungarian people.

Roofline decoration on the Postal Savings Bank, a major work of Ödön Lechner's

77 Liberty Square

Szabadság tér

A horseshoe-shaped plaza with homogeneous architecture, one of the city's most beautiful.

The grim Lipótváros barracks used to stand on this site, scene of the execution on October 6, 1849, of Count Lajos Batthyány, prime minister of the first—short-lived — independent Hungarian government. An Eternal Flame in his memory has burnt continuously since 1926 (Hold utca/Báthory utca).

After the demolition of the barracks in 1886 the square was laid out and flanked with prestigious buildings to serve the world of finance. The former stock exchange on the west (No. 17) is now the headquarters of Hungarian Television. It was built in 1902-05 under the influence of Art Nouveau by Ignác Alpár, who also designed the fine Hungarian National Bank on the opposite side of the square (No. 9).

78 Postal Savings Bank

Postatakarékpénztár

Hold utca 4

Art Nouveau with interesting majolica ornamentation.

After completing the Museum of Applied Art (1896) and the Geological Institute (1899), Ödön Lechner continued his efforts to develop a Hungarian "National Style" with his Postal Savings Bank building (1899-1902). Whether the originality of his architecture permits one to classify it as a "national style" is debatable. Beyond a doubt, however, Lechner made a significant contribution to European Art Nouveau, and he succeeded in integrating the multifarious ornamental motifs of Hungarian folk art into architecture. This is compellingly evident here in the roof design of hexagonal colored tiles.

The interior decor of the bank once included depictions of bees and beehives in mosaics, on the columns, and on the etched glass windows. Today such motifs are visible only on the roof and in the gable area.

79 Parliament House

Országház

Kossuth Lajos tér

Imposing landmark of the Hungarian capital.

After the 1867 Compromise with Vienna, Hungary enjoyed enough political and economic independence to begin considering the construction of a parliament building. On December 4, 1880, Emperor Franz Joseph and prime minister Kálmán Tisza cemented the project by decree. Until 1847 the diet had met in Pozsony (Bratislava); it had moved at Széchenyi's suggestion to Pest, where it convened in the Vigadó assembly rooms. In 1866 Miklós Ybl was asked to design a provisional house of representatives; this building (Bródy Sándor utca 8) now belongs to the Italian Cultural Institute.

The competition for a new parliament building drew entries from a number of famous Hungarian and foreign architects, including Alajos Hauszmann, Albert Schickedanz, and Otto Wagner. All of the submissions were in a Neo-Renaissance style except for that of Imre Steindl, which was finally accepted. Steindl, a student of the Vienna architect Friedrich von Schmidt, took his inspiration from the famous London Houses of Parliament (Charles Barry, begun 1836), no doubt counting on the symbolic value of that venerable democratic institution.

Combining a Baroque ground plan with a Neo-Gothic superstructure, and employing modern iron technology, Steindl capped the building (1885-1902) with the huge, 315-foot-high dome that has become its hallmark. "As if somebody had grafted a Turkish bath onto a Gothic church,"

Parliament House, domed hall

mocked the poet Gyula Illyés. The wings of the building radiate symmetrically from the domed hall and enclose ten interior courtyards. The main entrance, known as Lion Door, is on Kossuth Lajos tér.

The best artists of the day were engaged to decorate the interior. Mihály Munkácsy's history painting *The Magyar Conquest* dominates one of the rooms of the presidential wing; the frescoes are by Károly Lotz; the stained-glass windows with motifs from Hungarian history are the work of Aladár Körösfői-Kriesch; and the wrought-iron grilles are by Gyula Jungfer, who was also involved in the decoration of the opera house and St. Stephen's around the same time. Architecture and fittings represent a superb latter-day adaptation of the English Decorated Style.

Steindl's decision to employ Neo-Gothic was not without its critics, some of whom flatly rejected the ecclesiastical character of the building, which stands in strong contrast to the Classical rigor of the Vienna Parliament. Budapest's capitol extends 293

Plan of Parliament House

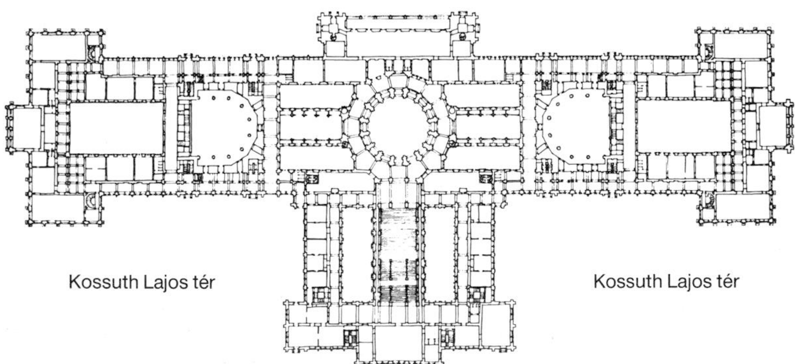

Seen from the Danube, the gigantic scale of Parliament House becomes impressively evident. The chamber of deputies is situated beneath the raised section of roof to the right of the dome; its counterpart to the north marks the now defunct upper house

Parliament House, deputies' foyer with sculptures by György Kiss

yards along the Danube embankment, a frontage length that fulfills two key criteria — it provides a counterweight to Buda Castle on the opposite bank, and it emphasizes the importance of the river for the city's aspect.

The parliamentary library (south end of the Danube side), which is particularly well stocked in the fields of law and history, is open to the public; tours of the rest of the building are organized by various agencies.

80 Ethnographic Museum

Néprajzi Múzeum

Kossuth Lajos tér 12

An interesting collection of cultural treasures from Hungary and other lands.

Opposite the main entrance to Parliament House stand two massive historical-revival structures: the ministry of agriculture and

Staircase in the Ethnographic Museum. Originally known as the Curia, the building was until 1945 seat of the supreme court

the former Curia, which now houses the Ethnographic Museum. The latter was designed by Alajos Hauszmann, a much-employed protagonist of the Eclectic school. The Curia, built from 1893 to 1896, initially served as the seat of the supreme court. Its exterior recalls such other buildings of the period as the Berlin Reichstag or the courts of justice in Munich. A dome, however, was precluded by the location directly across from Parliament House. The ostentatious interior, with huge vestibule and stairwell frescoed in pastel hues by Károly Lotz, is well worth seeing.

Shepherd's jacket, felt with flat-stitch embroidery

Mask from the Congo

The collections of the museum go back to János Xantus (1825-94), a diplomat and scholar of Far Eastern culture who collected valuable ethnological material in the course of his travels. They were considerably enriched by the acquisition of the exhibition of Hungarian folk art painstakingly assembled for the millennium celebrations of 1896. A third source of the museum's stocks were documents and objects collected in Siberia by a nineteenth-century expedition in quest of the origins of the Hungarian nation.

The second floor contains a collection of Hungarian folk art and culture, including an archive of folk music. The rooms with authentic furniture, household appliances, and clothing convey a realistic picture of prewar life in Hungarian towns and villages. Especially noteworthy are the specimens of elaborate embroidery dating back over five centuries.

Located on the third floor is a collection devoted to non-European cultures. Apart from archaeological finds from the Stone and Bronze ages, it includes implements and ritual objects of the American Indians, the Melanesian and Indonesian peoples, and various African tribes.

81 West Station

Nyugati pályaudvar

Teréz körút 55-57

An elegant iron and glass construction by the world-famous Eiffel firm.

On July 15, 1846, when the first train left the station here for Vác, forty miles north, the history of Hungarian railroads had begun. The initial, relatively primitive station was supplanted in 1877 by the present terminus. Its construction came at a propitious time, when Budapest was seeking to assert itself as the equal of Vienna both politically and in its urban aspect. The West Station was an important feature in an ambitious project launched by the Commission for Public Works headed by Count Gyula Andrássy: the laying out of a "Grand Boulevard." This outer ring (Ferenc körút to Szent István körút) was to be linked to Pest's inner ring (Vámház körút to Deák Ferenc utca) by broad radial avenues (e.g., Andrássy út, Rákóczi út).

The tender for the building of the station was won by the Eiffel company of Paris, later to gain world renown. Each of the

West Station, planned by the bureau of Gustave Eiffel, renowned French architect

station halls is 160 yards in length, with a 138-foot span; the central hall is 82 feet high. Though the first iron columns were supplied from Paris, a Hungarian company soon took over production, and a considerable proportion of the iron structural elements were manufactured in Hungary.

Superbly restored, West Station is an engineering and architectural feat of the first order, as evinced by the elegant glass facade that reveals the iron construction behind. The east wing contains a large hall of mirrors; built for the reception of Their Majesties at the 1896 millennium festivities, it displays on the ceiling the arms of the counties served by the station. The former restaurant is now a modern, American-style eating place. Budapest's first electric streetcar line, inaugurated in 1887, ran from West Station to Király utca.

82 Ferenc Hopp Eastern Asia Museum

Hopp Ferenc Kelet-Ázsiai Múzeum
Andrássy út 103

Exotic collection of a nineteenth-century traveller.

The museum originated from the collection of Ferenc Hopp (1833-1919), who travelled widely in eastern Asia; he was an employee of the Calderoni Optical Company, and later became its owner. His residence now houses the museum to which he bequeathed an interesting collection of

Replica of a Far Eastern garden gate in the courtyard of the Ferenc Hopp Museum

decorative art from various phases of the cultural history of India, including some fine erotic figurines. The museum contains about twenty thousand items all told.

The Japanese and Chinese departments are now located in the second Ráth György Múzeum not far away, at Városligeti fasor 12. Besides outstanding individual pieces, this collection includes a beautiful array of Japanese combs and Chinese fans. The museum's special charm probably derives from the fact that it was not so much scholarly interest as a connoisseur's predilections that guided its compilation.

83 Heroes' Square

Hősök tere

Historic plaza flanked by important museums, an attraction for Budapesters and tourists alike.

Budapest's most beautiful and architecturally elegant radial avenue, Andrássy út, culminates in a masterpiece of Hungarian Eclecticism. Heroes' Square, the Millennium Monument, and the flanking buildings were designed for the celebration of 1,000 years of Hungarian history by the architect Albert Schickedanz and the sculptor György Zala; a number of other artists collaborated in the realization. Between the two wings of the semicircular colonnade stands a 120-foot-tall Corinthian column bearing a figure of the archangel Gabriel, from whom personally, according to legend, St. Stephen received the Hungarian crown. Around the pedestal are equestrian figures of the seven Hungarian chieftains (Árpád, Előd, Ond, Kond, Tas, Huba, and Tétény). The statues in the left-hand wing represent Hungarian kings of the Árpád dynasty and the house of Anjou: from left to right, St. Stephen (István I), St. Ladislas (László I), Koloman the Booklover (Könyves Kálmán), Andrew (András) II, Béla IV, Charles Robert (Róbert Károly), and Louis (Lajos) I. The right-hand colonnade originally contained statues of the Habsburg monarchs, but these were replaced after 1945 with those of János Hunyadi, Matthias Corvinus, and various Hungarian freedom fighters. Bronze reliefs under each statue describe historical episodes associated with the persons represented.

Concurrently with the Millennium Monument, the Feszty Panorama, an enormous 393-foot-long and 49-foot-high painting depicting the Magyar conquest, was erected here; this is now being reconstructed in time for the 1996 World Expo.

As Budapest had neither a triumphal arch nor a hall of fame, the millennium was seen as a challenge to create some national monument of the kind. And, as elsewhere, a backward-looking style was judged the most suitable. The thousandth anniversary celebrations were not always viewed so positively by later generations: Marxist historians flatly rejected them and the associated architecture as foreshadowing Fascism, and chose to ignore the aesthetic and technological renewal that transformed Budapest into a modern European city and still contributes to its unique character today. Heroes' Square, now purged of the monuments to Communist greats, is again one of Budapest's most beautiful spaces. That it has become a favorite resort of skateboard and rollerblade fans, rather than detracting from its historical evocativeness, only makes the place more appealing and human.

Key figures in Hungarian history congregate on the Millennium Monument on Hősök tere

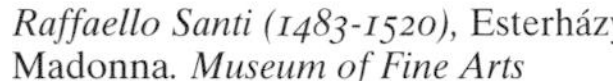

Raffaello Santi (1483-1520), Esterházy Madonna. *Museum of Fine Arts*

In keeping with its fin-de-siècle spirit, Heroes' Square received two temples of the muses: the Museum of Fine Arts (Szépművészeti Múzeum) to the left of the monument, and the Arts Hall (Műcsarnok) to its right. The **Museum of Fine Arts**, also a fruit of the Millennium Act, was completed in 1906. Borne on the last great wave of museum building in nineteenth-century Europe, it is comparable to the Kunsthistorisches Museum in Vienna. Its two architects, Albert Schickedanz and Fülöp Herzog, combined the Greek temple with Italian Renaissance architecture in their design. The main building is fronted by three temple-like pavilions connected by tracts with lower rooflines. The pediment relief above the eight Corinthian columns of the central portico represents the Battle of the Centaurs and Lapiths, a copy of the Centauromachia on the Temple of Zeus in Olympia.

The basis of the museum was the Esterházy Collection, which since its purchase in 1870 had been exhibited in the Academy of Sciences. Originally the museum possessed only paintings, drawings, and prints, but its first director, Károly Pulszky (1881-96), began to acquire sculptures as well. Further departments were founded after the new building was inaugurated. The department of antiquities began with the purchase of the Paul Arndt collection in 1908, and the Egyptian department opened in 1934. Both Graeco-Roman and Egyptian collections are on the ground floor right. The collection of nineteenth-century paintings and sculptures, in which French art is particularly well represented, is displayed in the rooms to the left of the entrance.

The gallery of old masters is on the second floor. Here we can admire a collection of Spanish painting that is considered the most comprehensive and highest-ranking in the world after the Prado in Madrid. It includes seven large-format El Grecos, and also fine specimens of Murillo, Velázquez, and Goya (*Girl with a Pitcher*). Italian painting is represented with major works by Ambrogio Lorenzetti, Titian, Guardi, and others. The collection of early German painting is also of great interest:

Central portico of the Museum of Fine Arts

The Arts Hall, where periodic exhibitions provide fascinating insights into contemporary trends in art

in addition to works by Altdorfer and Cranach, it has a *Portrait of a Young Man* by Dürer that attracts art-lovers from around the world. The third floor is devoted to sculpture.

Like other enterprising European cities, Budapest felt the need for an exhibition hall to display contemporary art in changing exhibitions. The first building devoted to this end, located at Andrássy út 69, was designed by Adolf Lang and completed in 1877. In the course of the next decade it proved too small, and the approaching millennium celebrations again offered a welcome chance to consider a new building on Hősök tere. Albert Schickedanz designed the Arts Hall to complement the Museum of Fine Arts across the square. The vestibule provides access to the exhibition rooms, including a sculpture room installed in the semicircular "apse" at the rear of the building. Efforts are now underway to restore the structure to its original state, including a renewal of the glass roof. The Arts Hall management also administers the Ernst Museum [No. 71] and galleries at Dorottya utca 8 and Olof Palme sétány 1.

84 Little Subway

Kis földalatti

An early direct connection from downtown to City Park, running beneath Andrássy út.

Between 1894 and 1896 the "Franz Joseph Underground Railway" was built to link Vörösmarty tér in the inner city with City Park (today it continues to Mexikói út). It was the first electrically powered subway on the entire Continent.

Although London already had its famous underground, the trains were pulled by steam locomotives, which posed considerable ventilation problems—every station had to be equipped with a steam and smoke exhaust vent. To avoid such difficulties, Budapest envisaged electric power from the start. The tunnel design was also more advanced than London's, the railbed running at a relatively shallow depth beneath street level, which facilitated excavation and construction work. Low cars with "inset" wheels further contributed to an effective use of space. For over sixty years the "Little Subway" operated virtually unaltered over the three-mile line, until new cars were substituted for the original ones in the 1960s. Some of the old rolling stock is on view in the Subway Museum, located in the underpass at Deák tér.

City Park (Városliget) and Outskirts of Pest

Towards the end of the eighteenth century, the chronicles record, "the conscience of the city cried out for vegetation, because the dust on the Pest side was reaching intolerable proportions." Until the beginning of that century Budapest's green lung, a park of about two hundred fifty acres, had been a royal hunting preserve. Once a swampy and desolate place, the park now offers a variety of sights and diversions that make it a popular recreation area. The oldest subway line on the Continent [see No. 84] takes us from the city center to the Széchenyi fürdő baths, and from there it is only a short walk to the other attractions of the park. Vajdahunyad Castle, made up of small-scale replicas of a number of historic Hungarian buildings, rises in the middle of an idyllic lake that offers boating in summer and ice-skating in winter. The park also boasts technological museum pieces, Hungarian Art Nouveau, and an attractive zoo. Relaxing in the thermal baths or enjoying Hungarian specialties in the venerable gourmet restaurant Gundel's are good ways to round off a pleasant day in City Park.

Vajdahunyad Castle, based on a Transylvanian prototype, one of the series of historical-revival buildings erected in City Park for the millennium celebrations

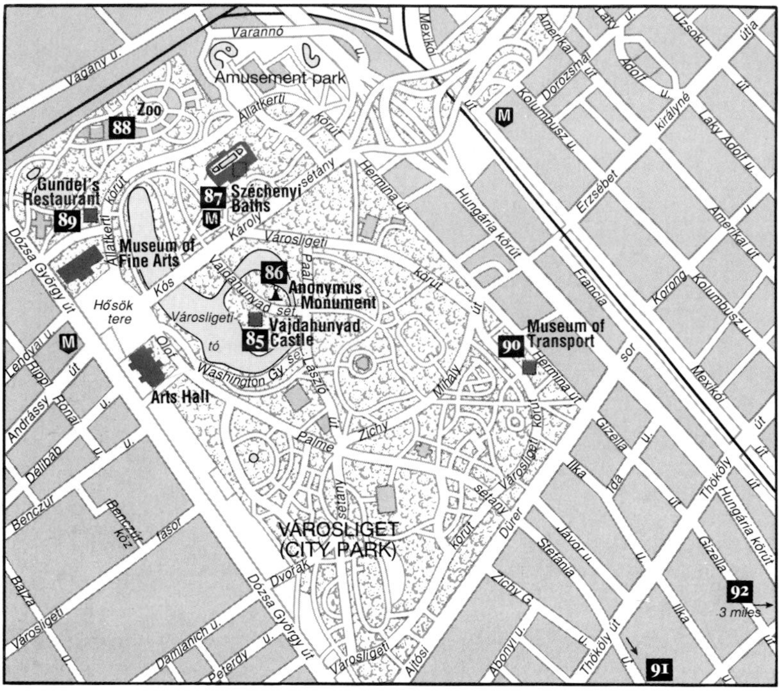

The Neo-Baroque Museum of Agriculture, an apotheosis of Vienna's Hofburg

85 Vajdahunyad Castle

Vajdahunyad vára

Széchenyi-sziget

Twenty-one Hungarian architectural styles assembled into a fairy-tale castle.

Vajdahunyad Castle was based largely on a castle of the same name in Transylvania, but, not satisfied with leaving it at that, its architect, Ignác Alpár, decided to create a compendium of the country's historic buildings in every style, from Romanesque to Rococo. His fantasy castle, which like so many other structures was built for the 1896 millennium celebrations, is like a Hungarian Disneyland of the fin-de-siècle.

The Neo-Baroque wing of the castle was designed to house the Museum of Agriculture (Mezőgazdasági Múzeum), which illustrates the history of farming, cattle-raising, fishing, hunting, and gardening, and also gives a detailed review of Hungarian horse-breeding, including the genealogy of the country's best stud- and racehorses.

The artificial lake is a favorite spot for boating and ice-skating, depending on the season. In 1870, Crown Prince Rudolf of Habsburg decided to have a skating rink with warm-up hall erected on the lake. Completed on December 11, 1875, the attractive domed building by Ödön Lechner contains a restaurant in addition to dressing and warm-up rooms. The artificial ice rink was installed in 1926.

Replica of the church in Ják, the most significant ecclesiastical building of the Romanesque era in Hungary

86 Anonymus Monument

Anonymus Emlékmű

Northeast forecourt of Vajdahunyad Castle

Monument to a nameless chronicler of the Middle Ages.

What is probably Budapest's most popular monument stands across from the entrance to the Museum of Agriculture. In contrast to the Eclectic sculptures on Hősök tere and most of the city's other public spaces, the figure of Anonymus evinces a refreshingly modern approach.

On his 1897 visit to Budapest, Kaiser Wilhelm II was struck by what seemed to him the city's paucity of monuments. He donated funds to remedy this; along with the Gerhardus Monument and others, the present sculpture, completed by Miklós Ligeti in 1903, was one of the fruits. It honors the anonymous chronicler of King Béla III in an original way, the scribe's face being completely obscured by his monk's cowl. Anonymus wrote the first history of the Hungarian people, the *Gesta Hungarorum* (c. 1204).

Anonymus, nameless court scribe to Béla III, comes to life in a sculpture that has won the country's affection

Aerial view of Széchenyi Baths, clearly revealing the influence of Baroque palace layouts on the design

87 Széchenyi Baths

Széchenyi fürdő

Állatkerti körút 11-13

A place where Budapesters take it easy, exchange the latest gossip, and play chess, immersed in 100°F water.

While on the Buda side residential growth centered around the hot springs, in Pest, which had no such natural baths, people tended to settle near the river. It was not until 1868 that drillings were undertaken in the City Park area and the engineer Vilmos Zsigmondy struck water. The resulting spring, 560 feet deep, produces nearly a hundred gallons of water a minute, with a temperature of 165°F. The first bathhouse with twenty pools was inaugurated in 1881. More recent drillings have tapped medicinal springs over three-quarters of a mile below ground.

Men enjoying only one of the many ways to relax in the warm waters of Széchenyi Baths

Today's facilities were built to plans by Győző Czigler. The symmetrical structure with domed central hall and lateral wings for medicinal baths was enlarged in 1927, and a Neo-Baroque vestibule was built on the north side. Also laid out at this time were the outdoor pools that are so popular with the Budapesters, where respectable gentlemen sit for hours in the warm water over their games of chess. The pools are also open in winter, when the steaming water is especially inviting.

88 Zoo

Állatkert

Állatkerti körút 6-12

Exotic flora and fauna in City Park.

Budapest's first zoo opened in August 1866. Its progressive-minded founders sought to create as natural a habitat as possible for animals living in captivity.

Initially run as a joint-stock corporation, the zoo entered municipal ownership in 1905, and four million crowns were earmarked for its modernization. Two stone elephants have since guarded its gates. The improvements included the installation of artificial cliffs in the enclosures of the mountain animals. The then director, Adolf Lendl, had reason for pride, for by 1910 the Budapest zoo ranked in Europe second only to that of Berlin. The architects of the new buildings belonged to a younger generation out to continue the reform efforts of turn-of-the-century European architecture. Besides employing folk-art idioms, they relied stylistically on the German Werkbund and Viennese Art Nouveau. The elephant house so closely resembled a mosque that the Islamic community objected, and it had to be redesigned.

Of the eleven animal houses built at the time, only seven remain. Károly Kós's aviary has been reconstructed and again houses a great variety of free-flying birds. Although the zoo's area is comparatively limited, good breeding results are now being obtained. The hot springs of the Széchenyi Baths, for instance, have proven very favorable for the raising of baby hippopotami.

The palm house has a fine collection of tropical plants; located in its wings are an aquarium and a terrarium. The "Cave Cinema" (Barlang mozi) offers non-stop screenings of popular scientific films.

Even pachyderms live in Art Nouveau houses at Budapest's zoo

Its reputation reestablished, Gundel's is again one of the finest and most expensive restaurants in town

89 Gundel's Restaurant

Allatkerti út 2

Superb Hungarian cuisine served in a homely atmosphere.

This City Park restaurant has been run by the Gundel family since 1869. After Károly Gundel took over in 1912 his cooking skills rapidly brought it Europe-wide fame. Not even the last war and its aftermath were able to shake Gundel's reputation. During the 1993 state visit of Queen Elizabeth II and Prince Philip the meals for the honored guests were prepared on these premises. Now once more in private ownership, the restaurant continues the Gundel gourmet tradition on two smoothly serviced floors.

90 Museum of Transport

Közlekedési Múzeum

Városligeti körút 11

Displays ranging from model trains to Danube steamers.

The millennium celebrations of 1896 included a transportation exhibition, which formed the basis of the present museum, established in 1899.

Heavily damaged during the Second World War, it was not reopened to the public until 1966. In 1987 it received a modern annex that increased the museum's total floor space to fifty thousand square feet—no match for the Deutsches Museum in Munich, the leading museum of technology on the Continent, but quite sufficient for an interesting and unwearying exhibition:

1. Survey of the history of Hungarian railroads, including equipment such as engines, examples of track construction, and switching and signalling equipment.
2. Road transport, with original Hungarian and foreign automobiles, and other vehicles and various types of urban transport.
3. Shipping, including freight transport, shipyards, and Danube steamers.
4. Road and bridge building, including archaeological finds made during survey work.

The permanent collection is regularly supplemented by temporary exhibitions, especially of works by professional modelbuilders in various technical fields. A model train layout operates daily. Among the museum's curiosities is a Swiss calculating machine dating from 1895, which was still used as late as 1970 in ship design projects. Also on display are rare Hungarian cars with four-stroke engines from the 1930s.

Outside the museum are busts of famous Hungarian scientists. Ányos Jedlik (1800-95), a Benedictine priest and university professor, was the greatest Hungarian physicist of the nineteenth century. He also invented such practical everyday things as the soda syphon (1825), which no modern Hungarian household can do

Evoking an abstract sculpture, technical equipment points the way to the Transport Museum

without. In 1830 he presented the first electromagnetic motor, and in 1867 his accumulator made of lead was shown at the Paris World's Fair. Tivadar Puskás (1845-93), an associate of Thomas Edison's, installed Europe's first telephone exchange in Paris. As his assistants were Hungarian, a word from their language—*hallod* ("Can you hear me?")—entered the world's vocabulary as "hallo." In Budapest, Puskás introduced a telephone information service in 1893. From 1897 to the end of the Second World War the service offered an all-day program from 9.30 a.m. to midnight.

To supplement the Museum of Transport there is a Postal Museum, now located at Andrássy út 3. It was established over a hundred years ago, and provides insight into telephone and radio communications as well. It has a branch at Hársfa utca 47 devoted to a stamp collection numbering about half a million specimens.

91 Geologic Institute

Földtani Intézet

Stefánia út 14

An Art Nouveau structure with blue ceramic decor.

Shortly after completing the Museum of Applied Art (1896), Ödön Lechner designed several other buildings that reflected his effort to create a Hungarian variant of Art Nouveau. The Geologic Institute is the best preserved of all, and it exhibits the full range of Lechner's typical decor and design elements. Especially characteristic are the roofing of colored Zsolnay tiles, the use of color to emphasize the load-bearing elements, and the idiosyncratic facade design. The building reflects the influence of Lechner's years in Berlin, where he was particularly impressed by the functionalism of the city's industrial architecture.

The institute's library has an interesting exhibition of minerals and geological rarities.

92 Jewish Cemetery

Zsidó temető

Kozma utca (trams 28 and 37 from Blaha Lújza tér)

Art Nouveau funerary architecture.

In the course of the nineteenth century the growth of Reform Judaism brought changes in the funeral liturgy, which ultimately led to the establishment of separate Orthodox and Reform cemeteries. The liberalization process also gave rise to new developments in Jewish funerary art. A salient example is the **Schmidl Mausoleum**, by architects Ödön Lechner and Béla Leitersdorfer (1875-1920), who later became famous under the name of Lajta. The mausoleum for the Schmidl family (1902/03)

The Schmidl mausoleum in the Jewish cemetery in Kőbánya makes a trip out to the erstwhile (c. 1900) city limits well worthwhile

was Lechner's third joint project with the young Lajta. The latter was proud to collaborate with Hungary's most famous Art Nouveau architect, with whom he also designed the chateau in Szirma (1901/02) and a postal and telegraph building in Bratislava, which, however, was never erected. The two architects saw the mausoleum project as a chance to create a work of art very much in the spirit of the fin-de-siècle, if modest in dimensions. It exhibits the idiom of Hungarian Art Nouveau in full flower—quite literally, with shimmering blue-green tiles undulating in blossom, tendril, and leaf ornament. The mosaic inside representing the tree of life also exemplifies Lechner's decorative exuberance. The formal diversity of the whole is matched by that of the materials, which range from majolica tiles and ceramic elements to cast glass and wrought iron.

As regards Lajta, the design of mausoleums and gravestones became an important focus of his work. The cemetery contains about twenty specimens thereof, including the Gries family vault immediately adjacent to the Schmidl mausoleum and the 1906 gravestone for Sándor Epstein. Even these less ambitious works clearly indicate the stylistic change that began in about 1904. Lajta went his own way, deriving inspiration from folk-art ornament and abandoning the oriental elements so favored by his mentor, Lechner.

93 Kiscelli Museum

Kiscelli Múzeum

Kiscelli utca 108

Fascinating review of the city's later history in a branch of the Historical Museum.

In 1724 the Zichy family, lords of Óbuda, laid the cornerstone of a chapel on the slopes of Hermit Hill (Remete-hegy). Intending it to become a place of pilgrimage like Mariazell in Styria, Austria, they named it Kiscell ("Little Zell"). For the consecration on September 8, 1733 (Nativity of the Virgin), a copy of the Mariazell madonna was unveiled. In 1744-48 the Zichy family endowed a Trinitarian monastery with an aisleless church, erected next to the chapel to designs by the Vienna architect Johann Entzenhoffer and consecrated in 1760.

The Trinitarians, whose mission included the redemption of Christians from Turkish captivity, were able to use the building for less than a quarter century. In 1783 Emperor Joseph II dissolved the order, and its scholarly library and mineral collection were given to the university. For over a hundred years thereafter the monastery was used as a barracks and military hospital. In 1912 it was acquired by Maximilian Schmidt, a Vienna furniture manufacturer, who altered the building by making various additions, including a Rococo portal salvaged from the demolished war ministry in Vienna. Schmidt, an avid art collector, converted the rooms into display spaces for the furniture he had restored.

On his death in 1935 the building came under municipal administration. Today's museum is based in large part on the portion of Schmidt's collection devoted to the history of Budapest. The city's life and times in the eighteenth and nineteenth centuries are illustrated by paintings and engravings, specimens of decorative art, architectural plans, and industrial products. A complete pharmacy, guild emblems, and weapons round off the picture. There is also a significant collection of photographs of the city, which is however accessible for research purposes only. The gallery on the second floor presents an informative survey of twentieth-century Hungarian art.

A former Trinitarian monastery now houses an interesting collection on the history of the city, the Kiscelli Museum

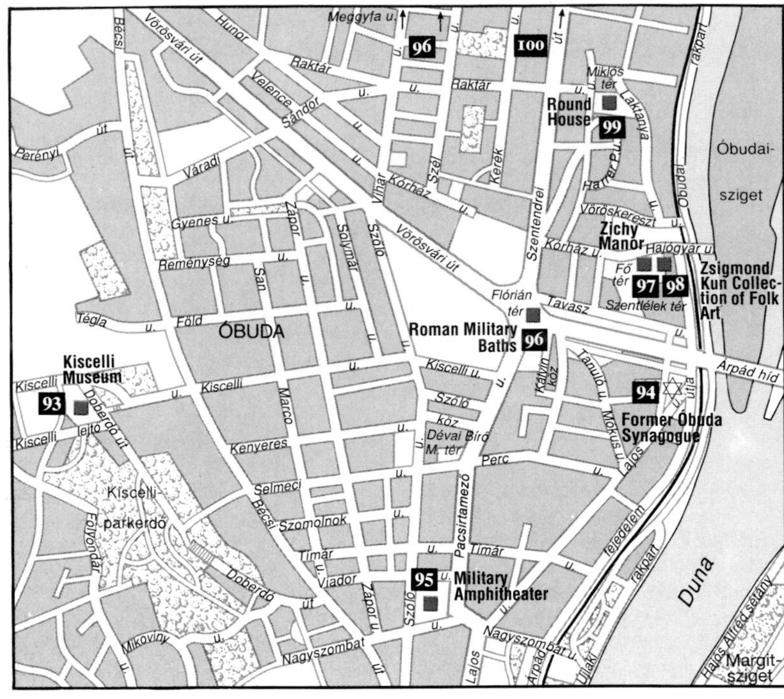

The cast-iron dragon outside the entrance, a bridgehead sculpture dating from the millennium festivities, came here from City Park. The recently renovated church is used for exhibitions and concerts.

94 Former Óbuda Synagogue

Lajos utca 163

Temple of the once large Jewish community of Óbuda.

In 1727 the noble Zichy family granted Jewish immigrants the right to settle in Óbuda, a right they enjoyed neither in Buda nor in Pest at that time. They began to establish trades and manufacturing businesses that were soon to have a material influence on the development of the local economy. By 1737 the town of Óbuda counted 24 Jewish families, and a synagogue already existed.

The present-day Lajos utca was Óbuda's main street and an important commercial center, lined with workshops run principally by Jews and German immigrants from Swabia. With the growth of the Jewish community a new, larger synagogue became necessary. The architect selected, Andreas Landherr, designed the grand building (1820-25) in the Neoclassical spirit. All that remains to testify to its beauty is the portico, with pediment resting on six Corinthian columns. The original interior is no more; it is now a studio of Hungarian Television.

95 Military Amphitheater

Katonai amfitéatrum

Nagyszombat utca/Pacsirtamező utca

Roman arena with a history shrouded in legend.

In past centuries these ruins inspired many and varied speculations. The royal scribe Anonymus wrote in his chronicle that chief Árpád, halting here, gazed with astonishment on the ruins of a castle, which he thought must have been built by Bleda, brother and co-regent of Attila, king of the Huns (the Etzelburg of the Nibelungenlied). This error remained in currency until excavations made for baths on nearby Flórián tér disproved the "castle

The Roman military amphitheater, excavated in the 1930s

theory" and confirmed that the ruins dated from Roman times.

The amphitheater was presumably built during the reign of Emperor Antoninus Pius (138-61), and served to entertain the legionaries stationed here with gladiator battles and animal baiting. It measures 142 yards in length and 116 yards in width; the inner wall of the arena, built to protect the spectators, was probably about twelve feet high. The tribunes seated about twelve thousand (by comparison, the entire town of Aquincum had a population of about twenty thousand at the time). The amphitheater continued to be used until the demise of the empire, and its oval shape still appeared on maps of the sixteenth and seventeenth centuries. Excavation of the site began in 1932, when the structures built over it were razed and the foundations laid bare.

Majolica tablet with Classical motifs, made in the 18th century

Portions of the excavated Roman military baths are now under cover

96 Roman Military Baths, Hercules Villa

Romai kori katonai fürdő, Hercules villa

Flórián tér 3-4, Meggyfa utca 21

The common soldier's life was not without its comforts, that of the patrician positively luxurious.

In 1778 István Schönwiesner, the father of Hungarian archaeology, discovered the extensive ruins of a Roman *hypocaustum*, or underfloor heating system, along with the remains of a **bathhouse** measuring 130 by 152 yards, with hot, warm, and cold pools (*caldarium*, *tepidarium*, and *frigidarium*). The baths originally had a roof supported by colonnades, and there were outdoor pools as well. Decorated with mosaics, fountains, sculptures, and reliefs, they were presumably built at the end of the first century and continued in use until the

The Hercules Villa harbors mosaics in various states of preservation, rare testimonies to the art of the reign of Caracalla (late 2nd century)

fourth century. A small museum on the site illustrates Roman bathing practice and medicine, and just down the road at Pacsirtamező utca 63 is the Táborvárosi Múzeum with more relics of the military camp.

The Roman garrison was located immediately adjacent to present-day Flórián tér. A shopping center now stands over the site of the *praetorium*, the most important building in the camp; still extant, crowded in by the modern buildings towards Vörösvári út, is a pylon from its gateway.

Another outstanding discovery was the ruined, once opulent third-century residence known as the **Hercules Villa**. Its special interest lies in the splendid mosaics depicting the heroic deeds of Hercules and scenes from the Bacchus legend. One of the finest shows Hercules rescuing his bride, the nymph Deianeira, from the clutches of the centaur Nessus.

97 Zichy Manor

Zichy kastély

Fő tér 1

The erstwhile seat of Óbuda's lord of the manor now houses two museums of modern art.

The Zichy counts, to whom Óbuda belonged, where responsible for much new building in the eighteenth century. The **Parish Church of Sts. Peter and Paul** (Lajos utca 170) was erected in 1744 to plans by Johann Georg Paur. One of the finest surviving examples of Hungarian late Baroque, it contains five side altars with sculptures of the apostles by Carlo Bebo, Italian court artist to the Zichys, who also created the magnificent Rococo pulpit. The painting representing St. Charles Borromeo is by Gregor Vogl; the high altar dates from 1774.

The **Reformed church** on Kálvin köz was built in 1785/86 on the site of, and partly with materials from, a medieval queen's palace (fragments of the old palace are displayed in the Flórián tér pedestrian underpass). The parsonage, an interesting Art Nouveau building by Károly Kós, dates from 1909.

Zichy Manor contains a small but superb Vasarely museum, and hosts changing shows of contemporary Hungarian artists living abroad

The group of statues off Fő tér remind us that just along Laktanya utca is a museum dedicated to the sculptor Imre Varga, well worth a visit not just on a rainy day

The **Zichy Manor** designed by Johann Heinrich Jäger, was erected from 1746 to 1757. It is a plain Baroque structure in which status-consciousness evidently played less of a role than functional design; it is protected by a walled courtyard lined with ancillary buildings.

Several rooms of the mansion are now home to the Lajos Kassák Memorial Museum, a branch of the Petőfi Museum of Literature. Kassák (1887-1967), Hungarian avant-garde artist and theoretician, lived in Óbuda from 1954 to his death. The museum displays works and documents relating to his life and career. Influenced by the German artists associated with the journal *Der Sturm*, by Russian Constructivism, and by the Bauhaus, Kassák became the leading protagonist of Hungarian Constructivism in the 1920s. Revolt, anarchy, and utopian ideas for a better society were the motive forces behind his achievement.

Located in the southeast wing of the mansion is a Vasarely Museum featuring selected works of the Hungarian representative of Op Art, who lives in France. From the mid 1950s onwards Victor Vasarely (b. 1908) developed an optical and kinetic approach that proved highly influential on the art of the younger generation in the sixties.

98 Zsigmond Kun Collection of Folk Art

Fő tér 4

A small but fondly compiled collection.

When, in the 1970s, people began to realize that the new high-rise estates were sadly lacking in urban atmosphere, the city belatedly tried to save what was left of its earlier architecture, including the town houses on Óbuda's main square. Some of these houses were well suited for the installation of small private collections, like that of Mr. and Mrs. Kun, now housed in an eighteenth-century building. Brought together with patience and loving care, this collection of popular art comprises utilitarian and decorative items of various eras from all over Hungary.

The nearby restaurants are old-fashioned, hospitable places where you can choose from a long list of Hungarian dishes while being serenaded by gypsy violins.

99 Round House

Kerek ház

Miklós tér 1

Monument of the early industrial age.

This little Rococo building is a testimony to the industrial history of Budapest. Constructed by József Tallherr in 1785, its unusual shape—an oval with twin access stairways—derives from its function as a silk spinning mill. (The mulberry trees in many an Óbuda yard are a reminder that the raising of silkworms was once a major activity hereabouts.) Nothing remains of the original furnishings and equipment, because the factory was converted into a

Rustic interior in the Zsigmond Kun Collection of Folk Art

The unusual ground plan of the Round House reflects its original function as a silk-spinning mill

private residence in the early nineteenth century. Since the early 1980s it has housed an institute for environmental research.

100 Aquincum

Szentendrei út 139

Traces of an ancient Roman town.

The first town established on the territory of present-day Budapest was a Roman settlement, Aquincum. A few years after the birth of Christ the Romans set up a military garrison [see Nos. 95, 96] in what is today Óbuda, which was soon supplemented by a civilian town to the north. It experienced its heyday in the second and third centuries, when it was a station on the Amber Road, the connection between the Baltic and Rome; it received the status of municipality in 124 under Emperor Hadrian and that of a colony in 194 under Septimius Severus. Until its demise in the fourth century Aquincum was capital of the Roman province of Pannonia Inferior. Excavation of the civilian town, begun in the last century, brought remarkable finds to light that revealed much about the town's layout and the lives of its inhabitants. A number of water conduits and parts of the sophisticated sewage and heating systems are still extant. Other amenities available to the inhabitants included public baths, a market hall, and an amphitheater, which was however much smaller than that of the military garrison (diagonally opposite the museum, on the other side of the bridge). Urban living here was very much in the Roman style; the remains of potter's studios, glass-blowing shops, and metalworking shops testify to a flourishing of the arts and crafts. Trade was ensured by the Rhine-Danube link, which also brought artisans from the West, e.g. Cologne, to settle in Aquincum.

The Neoclassical museum, built in the midst of the ruins in 1894, displays archaeological finds; gravestones and statues are installed in the colonnades. In addition to gems and cameos, coins and jewelry, there are writing utensils for wax tablets and parchment rolls on view. Even the name of a local potter of the second century has been preserved for posterity — Patacus, a few of whose molds for ceramic vessels have also survived. In the early third century Aquincum experienced an influx of immigrants, who came with the Roman legions. In terms of art, this led to a mingling of Italic characteristics and Eastern influ-

The museum at Aquincum, built in 1894. Ancient tombstones are displayed in the colonnades

ences. As the altar tablets exhibited in the *lapidarium* behind the museum indicate, a variety of gods were worshipped by the ethnically mixed community alongside Jupiter, the official Roman deity.

The museum's rarities include a small water organ found in the ruins of the fire brigade house, the *collegium centonarium*, along with a sarcophagus inscription relating that Aelius Sabena sang beautifully to the organ's strains; it is a unique piece, no other instrument of the kind having been found anywhere else. The sophisticated level of stoneworking here is evident from the shrine sculptures as well as from the statue of Jupiter on the votive column outside the museum and the abundance of bronze and terracotta miniatures.

Excavated walls of the ancient Roman town, some still standing to cornice height

Budapest
Practical Tips

Information

In advance

Hungarian Tourist Board and agents

Országos Idegenforgalmi Hivatal, Pf. 11, **Budapest,** H-1387, Tel. 118 5044, 118 0750, 118 4954, Fax 118 5241, 118 4846.

OIH Film and Video Library, Hajós utca 29, **Budapest,** H-1065, Tel. and Fax 111 1233.

Kompas YU/Ibusz, Suite 401, 115 Pitt Street, **Sydney,** NSW, Tel. (2) 223 4197.

Danube Travel Ltd., 6 Conduit Street, **London,** W1R 9TG, Tel. (71) 491 3588, Fax 493 6963.

Ibusz, Suite 1308, 233 N. Michigan Avenue, **Chicago,** IL 60601, Tel. (312) 819 3150.

Ibusz, Suite 1104, 1 Parker Plaza, **Fort Lee,** NJ 07024, Tel. (201) 592 8585, Fax 592 8736.

Kompas YU/Ibusz, M/C79/40, 5000 Airport Plaza Drive, **Long Beach,** CA 90846, Tel. (213) 593 2952.

Diplomatic representation

Australia

Embassy, 17 Beale Crescent, Deakin, **Canberra,** ACT 2600, Tel. (6) 282 3226, Fax 285 3012.

Consulate, Suite 405, 203–233 New South Head Road, **Edgecliffe,** NSW 2027, Tel. (2) 328 7860.

Canada

Embassy, 7 Delaware Avenue, **Ottawa,** Ontario, K2P 0Z2, Tel. (613) 232 1711.

Consulate, Suite 2030, 1200 McGill College Avenue, **Montreal,** Quebec, H3G 4G7, Tel. (514) 393 1555, Fax 393 3528.

Consulate, Suite 1001, 102 Bloor Street West, **Toronto,** Ontario, M5S 1M8, Tel. (416) 333 3302, Fax 393 8226.

Ireland

Embassy, 2 Fitzwilliam Place, **Dublin** 2, Tel. (1) 612 903, Fax 612 8800.

UK

Embassy, 35 Eaton Place, **London** SW1X 8BY, Tel. (71) 235 7191, Fax 823 1348.

Consulate, 35b Eaton Place, **London,** SW1X 8BY, Tel. (71) 235 2664.

USA

Embassy, 3910 Shoemaker Street N. W., **Washington,** DC 20008, Tel. (202) 362 6737, Fax 686 6412.

Consulate, Suite 410, 11766 Wilshire Boulevard, **Los Angeles,** CA, Tel. (213) 473 9344, Fax 479 6443.

Consulate, 227 East 52nd Street, **New York,** NY 10022, Tel. (212) 752 0661, Fax 755 5986.

Hungarian airlines

Malév, Suite 306, 111 East Wacker Drive, **Chicago,** IL 60601, Tel. (800) 877 5429, (312) 819 5353, Fax (312) 819 5355.

Malév, 10 Vigo Street, **London,** W1X 1AJ, Tel. (71) 439 0577, Fax 734 8116.

Malév, Suite 410, 1888 Century Park East, **Los Angeles,** CA 90967, Tel. (213) 286 7980, Fax 286 1921.

Malév, Suite 1900, 630 Fifth Avenue, **New York,** NY 10111, Tel. (212) 757 6480, Fax 459 0675.

Malév, Suite 712, 175 Bloor Street East, **Toronto,** Ontario, M4W 3R8, Tel. (416) 944 0093, Fax 944 0095.

Hotel chains

Hungarian Hotels Sales Office, Suite 670, 6033 West Century Boulevard, **Los Angeles,** CA 90045, Tel. (800) 448 4321, 231 8704, (213) 649 5960, Fax (213) 649 5852.

◁ *The bronze carnival boy on the Danube promenade always has his admirers*

Visa

Citizens of European countries (except Turkey and Albania) and of the USA and Canada do not require a visa to enter Hungary; other nationalities should inquire at a Hungarian embassy or consulate.

In Budapest

Information offices

Tourinform, V, Sütő utca 2, daily 8 a.m.–8 p.m., Tel. 117 9800.
American Express, V, Deák Ferenc utca 10, Tel. 251 0010.
M1/M7 Expressway, western approach to Budapest, at AGIP gas station.

Radio

Radio Bridge, 102.1 MHz. Entertainment and information in English.
Radio Budapest, 6110, 7220, 9385, 11 910 kHz. News and features in English daily at 11 p.m.

Accommodations

Hotel reservation services

Eravis, XI, Bartók Béla út 152, H-1113, Tel. 185 1188, Fax 186 9320.
HungarHotels, V, Petőfi Sándor utca 16, H-1052, Tel. 118 3018, Fax 118 0894.
Pannónia, V, Kígyó utca 4–6, H-1052, Tel. 118 3658.
Danubius, V, Szervita tér 8, H-1052, Tel. 117 3652.
Student hotels (valid student identification required), VIII, Harminckettesek tér 2, Tel. 133 4998.

***** hotels

Atrium Hyatt, V, Roosevelt tér 2, H-1051, Tel. 266 1234, Fax 266 8659.
Corvinus Kempinski, V, Erzsébet tér 7–8, H-1051, Tel. 266 1000, Fax 266 2000.
Mariott, V, Apáczai Csere János utca 4, H-1052, Tel. 266 7000, Fax 266 5000.
Hilton, I, Hess András tér 1–3, H-1014, Tel. 175 1000, Fax 156 0285.
Thermal Margitsziget, XIII, Margitsziget, H-1138, Tel. 132 1100, Fax 153 3029

**** hotels

Buda Penta, I, Krisztina körút 41–43, H-1013, Tel. 156 6333, Fax 155 6964.
Flamenco Occidental, XI, Tas vezér utca 7, H-1113, Tel. 161 2250, Fax 165 8007.
Forum, V, Apáczai Csere János utca 12–14, H-1052, Tel. 117 8088, Fax 117 9808.
Gellért, XI, Szent Gellért tér 1, H-1111, Tel. 185 2200, Fax 166 6631.
Hungária, VII, Rákóczi út 90, H-1074, Tel. 122 9050, Fax 122 8029.
Korona, V, Kecskeméti utca 14, H-1053, Tel. 117 4111, Fax 118 3867.
Nemzeti, VIII, Jozsef körút 4, H-1088, Tel. 133 9160, Fax 114 0019.
Novotel, XII, Alkotás utca 63–67, H-1121, Tel. 186 9588, Fax 166 5636.
Olympia, XII, Eötvös út 40, H-1121, Tel. 156 8011, Fax 156 8720.
Opera, VI, Révay utca 24, H-1065.
Radisson Béke, VI, Teréz körút 43, H-1067, Tel. 132 3300, Fax 153 3380.
Ramada, XIII, Margitsziget, H-1138, Tel. 131 7769, Fax 153 3029.
Royal, VII, Erzsébet körút 47–49, H-1073, Tel. 156 8011.
Thermal Helia, XIII, Kárpát utca 62–64, H-1133, Tel. 129 8650, Fax 120 1429.
Victoria, I, Bem rakpart 11, H-1011, Tel. 201 8644, Fax 201 5816.

*** hotels

Aero, IX, Ferde utca 1, H-1091, Tel. 127 4690, Fax 127 5825.
Alba, I, Apor Péter utca 3, H-1011, Tel. 175 9244, Fax 175 9899.
Astoria, V, Kossuth Lajos utca 19, H-1053, Tel. 117 3411, fax 118 6798.
Budapest, II, Szilágyi Erzsébet fasor 47, H-1026, Tel. 202 0044, Fax 115 0496.
Emke, VII, Akácfa utca 1–3, H-1072, Tel. 122 9230, Fax 122 9233.
Erzsébet, V, Károlyi Mihály utca 11–15, H-1053, Tel. 138 2111.
Expo, X, Albertirsai út 10, H-1101, Tel. 184 2130, Fax 163 0014.
Liget, VI, Dósza György út 106, H-1068, Tel. 111 3200, Fax 131 7153.
Normafa, XII, Eötvös út 52–54, H-1121, Tel. 156 3444, Fax 175 9583.
Palace, VIII, Rákóczi út 43, H-1088, Tel. 113 6000.

Panoráma, XII, Rege út 21, H-1121, Tel. 175 0522, Fax 175 9727.
Rege, II, Pálos utca 2, H-1021, Tel. 176 7311, Fax 176 7680.
Taverna, V, Váci utca 20, H-1056, Tel. 138 4999.
Volga, XIII, Dózsa György út 65, H-1134, Tel. 129 0200, Fax 140 8316.

** hotels (some rooms with private facilities)

Csalogány, II, Csalogány utca 23, H-1027, Tel. 201 6333, Fax 201 7843.
Ében, XIV, Nagy Lajos király útja 15–17, H-1148, Tel. 184 0677, Fax 252 3273.
Eravis, XI, Bartók Béla út 152, H-1113, Tel. and Fax 166 7276.
Metropol, VII, Rákóczi út 58, H-1074, Tel. 142 1171, Fax 142 6940.
Minol, III, Batthyány utca 45, H-1039, Tel. 180 0777, Fax 180 1977.
Park, VIII, Baross tér 10, H-1087, Tel. 113 1420, Fax 113 5619.
Platánus, VIII, Könyves Kálmán körút 44, H-1087, Tel. 133 6505, Fax 133 6057.
Sommer Panorama, XI, Ménesi út 5, H-1118, Tel. 185 2122, Fax 186 9429.
Sunlight, XII, Eötvös út 41, H-1121, Tel. and Fax 175 6211.
Wien, XI, Budaörsi út 88–90, H-1118, Tel. 166 5400, Fax 166 7922.

* hotels (often multi-bedded rooms, without private facilities)

Építők Sport Club, X, Vajda Péter utca 38–42, H-1101, Tel. 113 9035, Fax 113 6602.
Lido, III, Nánási út 67, H-1031, Tel. 188 6865, 180 5549, Fax 180 5576.
Citadella, XI, Citadella sétány, H-1118, Tel. 166 5794.
M-Zero, XXI, Tejút utca 1, H-1214, Tel. 277 5374, Fax 276 8371.
Reál, IV, Blaha Lujza utca 9–13, H-1046, Tel. 189 3494.

Cat. 1 guesthouses (panzió) (some rooms with private facilities)

Bara, XI, Hegyalja út 34–36, H-1112, Tel. 185 3445, Fax 185 0995.
Beatrix, II, Széher út 3, H-1021, Tel. and Fax 176 3730.
Cinege, XII, György Aladár utca 35–39, H-1125, Tel. 155 5122, Fax 156 8199.

The Hungarian coat of arms crowns Liberty Bridge (Szabadság híd)

Korona, XI, Sasadi út 127, H-1112, Tel. 181 2788.
Molnár, XII, Fodor utca 143, H-1124, Tel. and Fax 161 1167.

Cat. 2 guesthouses (no private facilities)

Aquincum, III, Szentendrei út 105, H-1035, Tel. 168 2426, Fax 180 5794.
Dunaparty, III, Kossuth Lajos üdülőpart 43–44, H-1039, Tel. 168 7029.
Marika, II, Napvirág utca 5, H-1025, Tel. 176 4564.
Unikum, XI, Bod Péter utca 13, H-1112, Tel. 186 1280.

Youth hostels

Ananda, XIV, Bonyhádi út 18b, H-1141.
Donáti, I, Donáti utca 46, H-1013, Tel. and Fax 135 8321.
Kandó, III, Bécsi út 104–108, H-1034, Tel. 168 2036, Fax 168 2032 (July/Aug., at other times for small groups).

Bookings also through:
Eper, VI, Weiner Leó utca 20, H-1066, Tel. 111 1780, Fax 131 7970 (July/Aug.).

The city's exclusive fashion shops are found on Váci utca

Expresz, V, Semmelweis utca 4, Tel. 117 6634, and at East Station (open 24 hrs.).
Express, V, Szabadság tér 16, H-1054, Tel. 131 7777, Fax 153 1715 (groups).

Private accommodations

Bookable at agencies at main stations, and at:
Ibusz (24-hr. opening), V, Petőfi Sándor tér 3, Tel. 118 4842.
Budapest Tourist, V, Roosevelt tér 5, Tel. 117 3555.
Cooptourist, V, Kossuth Lajos tér 13–15, H-1055, Tel. 112 1017, Fax 111 6683.

Camping

Information through:
Magyar Camping és Caravanning Club, IX, Kálvin tér 9, H-1091, Tel. 117 7208.

Campsites:
Hárshegyi, May 1 to Oct. 15, II, Hárshegyi út 5–7, Tel. 176 1921.
Római Fürdő, May 1 to Oct. 15, III, Szentendrei út 189, Tel. 168 6260.
Expo, July 1 to Aug. 31, X, Albertirsai út 10, Tel. 133 6536.

Arrival

Registering with the police

If remaining longer than thirty days, a tourist staying in private accommodations must register at the appropriate district police station. The necessary forms and stamps for the fee can be obtained at tobacconists' and post offices. Visas can be renewed at the main police station: Budapesti Rendőrfőkapitányság, VI, Andrássy út 12, Tel. 118 0800.

By car

Approaching from the west on the M1 or M7 expressway, follow the signs "Erzsébet híd" for the city center. The speed limit on expressways is 75 mph (120 km/h), on dual-carriageway highways 60 mph (100 km/h), on country roads 50 mph (80 km/h), and in built-up areas 30 mph (50 km/h). It is an offense to drive after the consumption of even a minimal amount of alcohol. All the usual types of fuel are available, though unleaded gasoline (95 octane) is not sold at all gas stations.

By bus

Regular bus lines operate between Budapest and several major European cities. For information on international travel: **Central Bus Station,** V, Erzsébet tér, daily 6 a.m.–6 p.m., Tel. 117 2562, 118 2122.

By train

Budapest has four international train stations:
East (Keleti), VIII, Baross tér.
South (Déli), I, Krisztina körút 37.
West (Nyugati), VI, Teréz körút 57.
Kelenföld, XI, Etele tér.
The first three stations are connected with the center of the city by subway (*metró*). The subway interchange is in the center of Pest, at Deák tér.

By plane

The Hungarian capital has two airports in close proximity to each other on the southeastern edge of the city, about 10 miles from the city center. Between the two airports, Ferihegy I and Ferihegy II, and downtown (Central Bus Station, V, Erzsébet tér), shuttle buses run every 30 minutes, on the hour and half hour. A more expensive minibus service operates between the airports and various hotels in Budapest. Interested parties can inquire at the LRI Shuttle Bus Service near the baggage claim area. Cheapest is the municipal bus 93 to Kőbánya-Kispest subway station.

By boat

A hydrofoil service operates on the Danube between Vienna and Budapest from the beginning of April to mid October, disembarking near the Elizabeth Bridge (Erzsébet híd); journey time approx. 5 hours.

Information **in Vienna:** Mahart Tours, Karlsplatz 2b, A-1010 Wien, Tel. 505 5644
Erste Donau-Dampf-Schiffahrts-Gesellschaft (DDSG), Handelskai 265, A-1020 Wien, Tel. 266 536.

Information **in Budapest:** Mahart Tours, V, Belgrád rakpart (international landing-stage), Tel. 118 1586, 118 1704.

Fine embroidery for all weathers

Banks, Post, Telephone

Changing money

Forints can be bought at banks, border stations, hotels, and other exchange offices; the receipt will be needed for re-exchange of forints for hard currency. Exchanging money on the black market is highly inadvisable. Banking hours are normally 9 a.m.–5 p.m., Mon.–Fri. Major credit cards and eurocheques are accepted at the higher-class establishments, and can be used to draw cash at some banks.

Post

The postcode for Budapest is H-1xxx; the second and third digits indicate the municipal district.
Post offices open day and night:
VI, Teréz körút 59, next to West Station.
VIII, Baross tér 11c, at East Station.
Head post office (poste restante address):
Posta 4, Petőfi Sándor utca 13–15, H-1052.

Telephone

From abroad, the code for Hungary is 36, for Budapest 1.

In Hungary (long-distance): Dial 06—wait for dial tone—dial area code and local phone number.
International: Dial 00—wait for dial tone—dial country code, area code, and local phone number.
International operator: 09.
Direct line to home-country operator (credit card and collect calls): Dial 00 and then

Australia		366111
Canada		361111
New Zealand		80006411
UK		80044011
USA	ATT	80001111
	MCI	80001411
	Sprint	80001877

International information: 117 2200.
Downtown telephone office (Belvárosi Telefonközpont): V, Petőfi Sándor utca 17–19, second floor, telephone books from all over the world.
Payphones operate with 5, 10, and 20 Ft coins and with phonecards; the more modern ones can be used for international calls.

Culture

Hungary established itself on the map of the musical world around the middle of the nineteenth century, with such pioneering personalities as the composer and piano virtuoso Franz Liszt (1811-86) and—no less popular in his own country—the "creator of Hungarian opera," Ferenc Erkel (1810-93). Their legacy found worthy successors in Béla Bartók (1881-1945) and Zoltán Kodály (1882-1967). The latter two musicians devoted themselves to the investigation and recording of Hungarian folk music and adopted its fundamental elements into their own compositions, seeking to achieve a synthesis of the specifically Hungarian and European music of the twentieth century. The teaching methods they developed found adherents all over Europe and in the USA and Japan.

Hungary's worldwide reputation in the field of music has also been built up by her conductors, for example Jenő Ormándy, György Széll, Antal Doráti, György Solti, and the Fischer brothers.

The Budapest piano school has also become internationally known with such representatives as Zoltán Kocsis, György Ránki, and András Schiff.

The country's biggest orchestra is the State Concert Orchestra (Állami Hangversenyzenekar). After the death of János Ferencsik, Kobayasi Ken Ichiro became its principal conductor.

The high quality of Hungarian chamber music is evident from the numerous recordings of pre-classical works and of Mozart by the Ferenc Liszt Chamber Orchestra, led by János Rolla.

Opera has always been a vital force in the capital, not just at the end of the last century, when Gustav Mahler was in charge of the Royal Opera House (1888–91) and Johannes Brahms liked to linger in Budapest, where he praised the performances of *Don Giovanni.* In the first days of the October uprising in 1956 the staging of Ferenc Erkel's *László Hunyadi* created a sensation because of its relevance to the current situation. There are of course several Hungarian operas in the repertoire every season. Famous voices of the past include Mária Gyurkovics, Julia Osvát, Mihály Székély, and Sándor Svéd, and among the internationally successful Hungarian singers of the present are Veronika Kincses, Ilona Tokody, Dénes Gulyás, and László Polgár; the soprano Éva Marton is often a guest in her familiar roles in *Turandot* and *Tosca* in the opera house where her great career began.

Despite enormous financial difficulties following the curtailment of state subsidies, the Hungarian tradition of classical music will undoubtedly be kept alive by future generations.

Rock operas on patriotic themes are big crowd pullers. The production of *Stephen, the King* by Levente Szörényi and János Bródy in the City Park during the summer of 1982 was highly effective visually and was also made into a film. Szörényi's latest offering, *Atilla, the Sword of God*, also looks set for a long run.

Ticket sales

Tourinform, V, Sütő utca 2, Tel. 117 9800.
Nemzeti Fílharmónia (concerts), V, Vörösmarty tér 1, Tel. 117 6222.
Színházak Központi Jegyírodája (theater), VI, Andrássy út 18, Tel. 112 0000.

Shopping for souvenirs on the bank of the Danube

Interart Fesztiválközpont (Spring Festival), P.O. Box 80, H-1366, Tel. 118 9570.
Szabad Tér Jegyiroda (Fall Festival, open-air theaters), XIII, Hollán Ernő utca 10, Tel. 111 4283.

Concert-halls

Bartók Béla Emlékház, II, Csalán út 29.
Budapest Kongresszusi Központ, XI, Jagelló út 1–3.
Fészek Művész Klub, VII, Kertész utca 36.
MTA Kongresszusi Terem, I, Országház utca 28.
MTA Kongresszusi Terem, I, Országház utca 28.
Óbudai Társaskör, III, Kiskorona utca 7.
Pesti Vigadó, V, Vigadó tér 2.
Zeneakadémia, VI, Liszt Ferenc tér 8.

Opera, operetta, ballet, musical

Hungarian State Opera House (Magyar Állami Operaház), VI, Andrássy út 22, Tel. 153 0170.
Erkel Theater (Erkel Színház) (opera, ballet), VIII, Köztársaság tér 30, Tel. 133 0540.
Capital Operetta Theater (Fővárosi Operettszínház), VI, Nagymező utca 17–19, Tel. 132 0535.
Víg Theater (musicals), XIII, Szent István körút 14, Tel. 111 0430.
Operetta concerts in the Pest Assembly-Rooms (Pesti Vigadó), V, Vigadó tér 2, Tel. 117 5067, Tues., Thurs., and Sat. at 8:30 p.m. May–Oct. (Operatic concerts Fri. 8:30 p.m. Aug.–Oct.)
Madách Theater (musicals), VIII, Erzsébet körút 29–33, Tel. 122 2015.
Arany János Theater (musicals), VI, Paulay Ede utca 35, Tel. 141 5626.

Folk music and dance

Folklore Center, XI, Fehérvári út 47, Tel. 181 1360.
Buda Assembly Rooms (Budai Vigadó), I, Corvin tér 8, Tel. 201 5928.

Jazz

On a Danube boat, in June on Tues., in July and Aug. on Tues. and Thurs. 7:30 p.m.–10 p.m. Departure from the Vigadó tér landing stage, tickets on board; information Tel. 165 3196.
Fregatt Söröző, with the Budapest Ragtime Band and the pianist Ernő Weszely, V, Molnár utca 26.
Kosztolányi House of Culture, I, Bem rakpart 6, Tel. 115 2430, Thurs. Benkó Dixieland Band.
Eötvös Club, V, Károlyi Mihály utca 9, Tel. 117 4967, Tues.
Jazz Club of the University of Economic Sciences, IX, Kinizsi utca 2–4, Tel. 118 0193.
Merlin Jazz Club, V, Gerlóczy utca 4, Fri.–Sun. 10 p.m.–2 a.m.; ticket reservations Tel. 267 3625; table reservations for the health-food restaurant Tel. 122 9282.

Cinema

Budapest cinemas often show movies in the original language. Cinemas worth a visit for their atmosphere:

One of the many folk-craft shops in the castle district

Átrium, II, Margit körút 55.
Puskin, V, Kossuth Lajos utca 18.
Horizont, VII, Erzsébet körút 13.
Graffiti, VIII, József körút 63.
Uránia, VIII, Rákóczi út 21.
Bartók, XI, Bartók Béla út 21.

Laser light show

Planetarium, IX, Népliget. Multivision show with music by Genesis, U2, Pink Floyd, Depeche Mode, Mike Oldfield, Dire Straits, Jean-Michel Jarre, and many others. Ticket reservations daily from 10 a.m., Tel. 134 1161.

Pop and rock

Petőfi Hall, XIV, Zichy Mihály út 14, Tel. 142 4327.
Budapest Sports Hall, XIV, Stefánia út 2, Tel. 164 3323.
Kosztolányi House of Culture, I, Bem rakpart 6, Tel. 115 2430.
Leisure Center, VII, Almássy tér 6, Tel. 142 0387.
Vörösmarty House of Culture, VIII, Golgota út 3, Tel. 113 0607.
KÉK-Klub, XI, Villányi út 35, Tel. 185 0666.
R-Klub, XI, Műegyetem rakpart 9, Tel. 166 4011.

Puppet theater

State Puppet Theater, VI, Andrássy út 69, Tel. 142 2702; VI, Jókai tér 10, Tel. 112 0622. Performances for children and adults; closed in July and Aug.

Theater

Merlin Theater, V, Gerlóczy utca 4, Tel. 267 3625. Performances of Hungarian plays in English.

Dance House

Hungarian folk dancing and instruction.
Leisure Center, VII, Almássy tér 6, Tel. 142 0387.
Folklore Center, XI, Fehérvári út 47, Tel. 181 1360.

Circus

Fővárosi Nagycirkusz, XIV, Állatkerti körút 12. Performances, sometimes with guest circuses, Wed. 7:30 p.m., Thurs. and Fri. 3:30 p.m. and 7:30 p.m., Sat. and Sun. 10 a.m., 3:30 p.m., and 7:30 p.m.

Emergencies

Emergency phone numbers

Police: 07 or 121 6216.
Fire: 05 or 122 0848.
Ambulance: 04 or 111 1666.
English-speaking physicians: 118 8288, 118 8012.
Breakdown: Hungarian Auto Club, 115 1220, 169 1831, 112 6218; Yellow Angels 169 1831, 160 3714.

Tourist police

English-speaking officers, V, Deák Ferenc utca 26/18, Tel. 118 0800.

Auto accidents

Inform police and insurance company: Hungária Biztosító, XIV, Gvadányi utca 69, Tel. 252 6333.

Szénássy's in Petőfi Sándor utca is one of Budapest's old-established purveyors of fabrics

Medical assistance

Dental emergencies, VIII, Mária utca 52, Tel. 133 0189.
Gynecology and obstetrics, VIII, Üllői út 78a, Tel. 113 5220.
Internal medicine, VIII, Szentkirály utca 46, Tel. 113 8688.
Ophthalmology, VIII, Tömő utca 25–27, Tel. 113 0820.
Pediatrics, VIII, Bókay János utca 53, Tel. 134 3186.
Stomatology, VIII, Mikszáth Kálmán tér 5, Tel. 113 1639.
Surgery, VIII, Üllői út 78, Tel. 113 5216.

Pharmacies

With all-night service:
II, Frankel Leó út 22;
III, Szentendrei út 2a;
IV, Pozsonyi utca 19;
VII, Rákóczi út 86.

Lost and found

V, Erzsébet tér 5, Tel. 117 4961.
Public transport: VII, Akácfa utca 18, Tel. 122 6613.
Credit-cards: Ibusz Bank, XIV, Ajtósi Dürer sor 10, Tel. 252 0333.

Embassies

Australia, VI, Délibáb utca 30, Tel. 153 4233.
Canada, XII, Budakeszi út 32, Tel. 176 7711.
United Kingdom, V, Harmincad utca 6, Tel. 118 2888.
United States of America, V, Szabadság tér 12, Tel. 112 6450.

Food and Drink

"Hundreds of things speak for Hungarian cuisine; the first: it tastes good. And four speak against it: few vegetables; exclusive use of lard; often lukewarm; and, the decisive reason, it tastes *too* good." That's how the author Franz Fühmann evaluated Hungarian cuisine in the seventies. Many other famous personalities have expressed their opinion of the eating, drinking, and table habits of the Hungarians. Some have claimed, with malicious irony, that the Magyars, who are descended from nomads, cook their meat under the saddle....

Both literary gourmets and prosaic nutritionists use the attributes "rich" (i.e., stodgy and fatty) and "highly spiced" (especially with paprika, caraway, and pepper)—in short: not exactly an Eldorado for those on a diet, which also applies to the quantities that are set before diners. In Hungary, the full table and the plentiful feast is more than just a traditional part of the Sunday program, it is a cherished feature of the way of life, forum of communication, a family ritual, and expression of national pride. The Hungarian chef does not skimp and save—Galeotto Marzio, the biographer of King Matthias, made this clear for posterity five hundred years ago, when he wrote: "It is only with the greatest difficulty that one can keep one's hands and clothes clean when eating the rich and abundant food of Hungary, because the saffron-tinged juices occasionally spray one from head to toe."

The basic recipe for the preparation of many of the dishes that are typical of the land begins with onions browned lightly in lard; this hardy, peasant-style, traditional Hungarian fare requires a robust stomach. Over the years, however, it has been "ennobled" and refined through various influences—especially that of French cuisine—and has added new flavors to its repertoire. The generous portions of sour cream (*tejföl*) are as important an ingredient of the national cuisine as **paprika**. The pimento from which the spice is made originally came from the Americas. It is called "red Turkish pepper" in a book of 1570, because it was introduced to Hungary by Turkish gardeners as an ornamental, medicinal, and spice plant. It was first cultivated on a large scale around 1800, when the Napoleonic wars made other spices such as pepper difficult to obtain. The areas around Szeged, Kalocsa, and also around Budapest have proven to be favorable for growing this spice-cum-vegetable, which is sown in spring, transplanted into the fields in May, and harvested in the early fall. Before grinding, the farmers hang the red pods out to dry, tied in decorative garlands, on the eaves of their homes.

If a dish is occasionally found to be too generously laced with hot paprika, eating a small piece of bread will help to make it more bearable.

The bread basket is never missing from the table at mealtime in Hungary. Just as with the sun and with water, the Magyars' relationship to **bread** as a staple food is a particularly personal, almost religious, one. They love its aroma fresh from the oven, with a pleasant, golden-brown, crispy crust, white on the inside, fluffy, soft, and spongy, so that it melts in your mouth. In the early fourteenth century the recipe for this yeast-leavened wheat bread was only known in northern Italy and France—outside of Hungary, that is. Even in the late twentieth century, every Budapester knows how well the wheat is doing this year. With the serious face of a true connoisseur, he or she carefully selects a loaf of bread and carries it lovingly home under one arm. Before holidays—one of which (August 20) is specially dedicated to the "new bread" baked with freshly harvested wheat—there are long lines in front of the bakeries and the campers parked in the street from which household bread and sweet pastry-breads, plaited or braided in wreath forms, are sold. Only during the past ten years or so have dark, whole wheat breads and breads made from a mixture of whole wheat and white flour been added to the offerings in Hungarian bakeries.

Many of the specialties of Hungarian cuisine are prepared from **fish**. Medieval sources praise the wealth of fish in the "blue" Danube and the "blonde" Tisza, which rivers are said to have consisted of one-third fish and two-thirds water.

Even in winter the fishing used to continue through holes knocked in the ice. Since the Hungarian rivers were regulated in the mid-nineteenth century, large fish—like the sturgeon, a royal delicacy—only rarely find their way upriver from the Black Sea (the last time was in 1989). A big fishing industry on lakes Balaton (central Europe's largest freshwater lake), Velencei, Fehér, and Fertő (Neusiedlersee) now helps to meet the demand from Budapest's markets and restaurants. By far the best-loved fish is a whitefish of the perch family; *fogas* (Balaton pike-perch), which is particularly recommended for health-conscious eaters (378 kilojoules per 100 grams, or 25 kilocalories per ounce). Catfish, carp, and trout are other domestic fish much sought-after for the pot, the frying-pan, the grill, or the smokehouse.

"Fish," says a Hungarian axiom, "likes to swim." And since alcohol is also known to break down fat, **wine**, which has been cultivated here since Roman times, is the perfect accompaniment to Hungarian cuisine. *Vinum regum rex vinorum*—wine of kings, king of wines—that is the honorific designation of the most famous of these wines, Tokay, which comes from northeastern Hungary and has been exported throughout the world for centuries. Hungary's highly developed wine culture reached its nadir under the rule of the

The Café Dubarry, on the embankment near the Pest Assembly rooms, offers its terrace patrons a fine view across the river

Turks, who abhorred alcohol. It suffered yet another blow in the 1870s when the vines of several regions—including the Buda Hills—were ruined by Phylloxera and Peronospora. Outstanding wines are produced today in Transdanubia (the part of the country west of the Danube): Móri Ezerjó ("Thousandgood" from Mór) grows near Székesfehérvár; Szürkebarát (Gray Monk) ripens in the volcanic soil around Badacsony on Lake Balaton. The ethnic Germans in Hungary have also proven themselves successful vintners: in the area around Sopron, Kékfrankos (Blue Frankish) flourishes, near Pécs it is Villányi Kadarka. The peculiar name of a dark, full-bodied red wine from Eger, Egri Bikavér (Bull's Blood of Eger), has for more than a century now been the subject of macabre speculation. The art of distilling **spirits** has also been known in Hungary for ages. A clear fruit schnaps, *pálinka*, is distilled from cherries, pears, plums, or apricots. How to produce the last-named and most famous of these, *barackpálinka*, is best understood in Kecskemét, a city between the Danube and the Tisza.

Coffee has become the national drink of Hungary—*eszpresszo*, served in glasses or mocha cups, is obligatory after a meal and is also drunk several times during the day. According to tradition, the first Hungarian to taste coffee was a famous general by the name of Bálint Török. On August 29, 1541, Süleyman II invited Török into his tent for a meal and meanwhile cunningly sent his elite troops to occupy Buda Castle—a bitter fact that was finally revealed to the Hungarian during his coffee. Even if drinking coffee had disastrous consequences for Bálint Török—he was carried off to Istanbul to spend the rest of his life in prison—the incident did not deter his countrymen from adopting it as their favorite vice. Nevertheless, since then a common Hungarian expression when something unpleasant is in the offing has been: "The black soup is still to come!"

To help you a little through the menu we will describe a few of the important dishes of Hungarian cuisine. As in many southern countries breakfast plays a minor role. The main meal of the day, which usually consists of several courses, is taken between noon and 1 p.m., or in the evening.

Unikum, a kind of bitters with the pungent aroma of over forty medicinal herbs, is frequently chosen as an **aperitif**.

Hungarian households still prefer fresh to frozen

A good choice for a starter would be Hortobágy crepes (hortobágyi palacsinta), an old herdsmen's recipe from the lowlands, with a creamy filling of veal and onions. Salad-lovers will perhaps prefer a chicken salad à la Szent-Györgyi: boiled chicken combined with a mix of mushrooms, asparagus, green beans, lettuce, and of course, red peppers, in which Albert Szent-Györgyi, a professor of biochemistry at Szeged university, discovered vitamin C, for which he obtained the Nobel Prize. *Halászlé* is probably the best-known Hungarian **soup**: fresh-water fish, especially carp, are boiled in a bouillabaisse prepared from fish heads, bones, lots of onions, green peppers, cherry peppers, and tomato pulp, and finally seasoned with milt. The Tisza style from Szeged differs from the Danube style from Baja, which calls for the addition of vermicelli. The peoples of the various regions have their own typical soups. The Matyó in northeastern Hungary, for example, love chicken broth with white cabbage, bits of potato, and peppers. The Palóc in the north, on the other hand, prefer a stew of green beans and mutton with onions, garlic, and sour cream. *Jókai-bableves*, a sweet-and-sour soup of large white, red, and blue-gray beans, thickened with roux and beefed up with sausage and smoked pig's knuckles, was created by the nineteenth-century novelist Mór Jókai. *Gulyás,* made from beef and highly seasoned with paprika, caraway, and onions, was originally cooked outdoors by cowherds on the Puszta and is actually a soup. The stewlike meat dish that is known in many countries under the name "goulash" is called *pörkölt* in Hungary. The recipe for *tarhonya*, a traditional accompaniment to *pörkölt*, has come down from Hungary's nomadic days: the dough of pearl barley and eggs was dried in the sun of the steppes before being crumbled.

Pork enjoys preeminence among the **main dishes**. It appears on the menu in many variations, e.g. as pork chop à la Bakony with smoked bacon (with mushrooms and peppers as accompaniment) or as "applemeat" à la Székely stewed with tarragon. A true Hungarian side-dish for steak (filet mignon) is the delicious *lecsó*: vegetables (onion rings, slices of tender yellow pepper and peeled tomato) stewed in their own juices, with beaten egg added at the end. Of the extensive repertoire of hearty, homely fare, at least two dishes should be mentioned: layered potatoes (a gratin of sliced potatoes, salami, bacon, ham, and hard-boiled eggs, over which is poured a sour-cream sauce) and paprika potatoes (*paprikáskrumpli*) with sausages (a thick stew that gets its appetizing red color from fresh tomatoes and plenty of paprika). If stuffed peppers (*töltött paprika*) can be one of the unforgettable taste experiences of summer, then the winter equivalent of this dish is *töltött káposzta,* cabbage stuffed with minced beef and pork (but be warned: it is cooked with plenty of lard!). Fried chicken is served as a breaded cutlet, while paprika chicken (*paprikáscsirke*) is a festive poultry dish cooked in a rich sauce, best accompanied by home-made dumplings (*galuska*). In Transdanubia, goose risotto is often eaten on festive occasions: besides meat and rice, this dish contains a variety of spices, green peas, chopped mushrooms, and peppers; on serving, it is crowned with fried goose liver.

Favorite **desserts** such as plum dumplings are a culinary treat thanks to the excellent quality of the fruit. The paper-thin Gundel crepes are distinguished by the intensive rum flavor of their creamy filling of nuts and raisins; they are covered with chocolate sauce and flambéed. Among the other deliciously sweet temptations of Hungarian cuisine are dumplings à la Somló (*somlói galuska*), made from whipped cream, nut sponge, rum, and thick apricot marmalade. In the twenties, when people still cheerfully indulged in high-calorie desserts with fewer guilty feelings, a kind of fondant was given the name of a notorious gypsy violinist who abducted—and later married—the wife of the Belgian prince de Chimay, the daughter of an American millionaire: Rigó Jancsi. The

A rich variety of fruit and vegetables is always available at the markets

Indispensable ingredients for many Hungarian dishes, braids of dried peppers and garlic decorate most of the fruit and vegetable stands

The Mátyás Pince (Matthias Cellar) is, unfortunately, beyond the pocket of most Budapesters these days

famous Dobos gateau was also created during the golden age of Budapest confectionery.

Fresh **fruit** of the season rounds off the meal. The beautiful colors and beguiling aromas of Hungarian grapes, apples, apricots, and peaches make them both an attractive table ornament and a pleasure for the palate. Watermelons are ripe in August, and huge mountains of them are on sale at all the markets. The Hungarian is an expert at identifying the sweet, ripe fruits just by rapping on the shell.

"**Music** While You Lunch" is the title of a Hungarian radio program. Anyone strolling through the empty streets at noontime during the summer will hear the wistful strains of the pseudo-folksongs emanating from wide-open windows and balconies everywhere. It is well-nigh impossible to think of Hungary without the image springing to mind of a candlelight dinner with wine and gypsy music. In the classical arrangement, the *prímás* (first violinist) is accompanied by three other violinists, a cimbalom player, a cellist, and a bassist, all of whom entertain the guests, preferably foreign tourists, with their virtuoso playing and improvisational talent. One finds again and again that Hungarians will fervently protest against equating this so-called gypsy music with Hungarian folk music. In fact, the type of music usually played at restaurant tables corresponds neither to the old folk melodies of the Hungarians nor to the original tradition of gypsy music. Rather, the repertoire is based mainly on art songs composed in the nineteenth century, into which the folk music of many lands and even the melodies of hit songs have found their way. Nevertheless, this widespread misunderstanding hardly detracts from the magic of masters of the genre, such as the members of the Lakatos family.

As a point of interest, the name of Hungary's famous national dance, the *csárdás*, comes from the word for a country inn, *csárda*. This pair and group dance quickly became fashionable in the early nineteenth century and has been practiced ever since at many a get-together.

Restaurants for gourmets and aficionados of local color

Of the roughly five thousand restaurants in Budapest, the following are just a few, arranged by district, that are particularly characteristic of the nation's culinary culture. Hotel restaurants are not included. Be warned that some restaurants add a 10% or higher service charge to the check, without this necessarily being indicated on the menu.

Alabárdos, I, Országház utca 2, daily except Sun., Nov.–April 7 p.m.–midnight, May–Oct. noon–midnight
An elegant restaurant with international cuisine and guitar music in a medieval mansion near Buda Castle. [No. 21]

Arany Hordó ("Golden Cask"), I, Tárnok utca 16, daily 11 a.m.–midnight
A historic restaurant on three floors of an old Buda trading house, with tap room, wine cellar, gypsy music, and traditional Hungarian cuisine.

Aranyszarvas ("Golden Stag"), I, Szarvas tér, daily 6 p.m.–2 a.m., Sun. noon–midnight
Restaurant specializing in game, located at the foot of Castle Hill.

Fehér Galamb ("White Dove"), I, Szentháromság utca 9–11, daily 7 a.m.–11 p.m. (wine cellar 6 p.m.–midnight)
A restaurant in the old castle quarter, favored by foreign guests. Specialties with squab, game, and fish, served up with candlelight and gypsy music.

Fortuna, I, Hess András tér 4, daily noon–4 p.m. and 7 p.m.–1 a.m.
First-class restaurant in the center of the castle quarter. Hungarian specialties with gypsy band and a famous wine cellar. [No. 11]

Márvány Menyasszony ("Marble Bride"), I, Márvány utca 6, daily 5 p.m.–midnight
Hungarian *csárda.* Furnishings and fare in the style typical of the Great Plain. Specialties from the area around Szeged. Folk-music program with song and dance; gypsy band.

Tabáni Kakas ("Tabán Rooster"), I, Attila út 27, Mon. to Fri. noon–midnight, Sat. and Sun. 1 p.m.–midnight
In what used to be a populous quarter of old Buda stands this establishment, which is run with a personal touch but is part of the "in" scene. Its reputation is primarily based on the superb quality of the homely fare, prepared using goose-dripping.

Margitkert, II, Margit utca 15, daily noon–midnight.
An exclusive and sophisticated restaurant specializing in Hungarian cuisine, patronized by men of state — a far cry from the lowly wine tavern it once was.

Náncsi Néni Vendéglője ("Aunt Náncsi's Eatery"), II, Ördögárok utca 80, Mon. to Sat. noon–9 p.m., Sun. noon–5 p.m.
A family restaurant, a bit out of the way in Hűvösvölgy, Buda's "Cool Valley," with rustic decorations, a pleasant garden, and accordion music; offers refined versions of peasant dishes and other homely fare.

Vadrózsa ("Wild Rose"), II, Pentelei Molnár utca 15, daily except Mon. 6 p.m.–midnight
This fine gourmet restaurant in the Neo-Baroque salon of a villa is frequented by the diplomats who live in the green hills of Buda. The garden is open during summer months.

Sipos Halászkert, III, Fő tér 6, daily 5 p.m.–midnight
Famous fish restaurant on the main square of Óbuda, with garden and gypsy music.

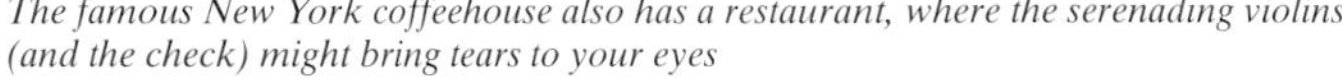
The famous New York coffeehouse also has a restaurant, where the serenading violins (and the check) might bring tears to your eyes

Apostolok, V, Kígyó utca 4–6, daily 10 a.m.–midnight
This restaurant, rich in tradition, is located in the pedestrian zone of downtown Pest and has a wood-paneled interior in the Neo-Gothic style with sculptures of the twelve apostles (listed for preservation); international and Hungarian cuisine.
Aranybárány ("Golden Lamb"), V, Harmincad utca 4, daily noon–midnight
Original Hungarian cuisine with lamb specialties in a rustic *csárda* atmosphere.
Kárpátia, V, Ferenciek tere 7, daily 11 a.m.–11 p.m.
The wood paneling, draperies, and paintings all contribute to the old-world atmosphere of this restaurant. International cuisine is offered along with gypsy music.
Légrádi Testverek ("Légrádi Brothers"), V, Magyar utca 23, Mon. to Fri. 5 p.m.–midnight
Leading gourmet restaurant in a cellar in Pest's downtown, whose excellent food and professional service have made it an insider's tip; primarily frequented by foreign businessmen.
Mátyás Pince ("Matthias Cellar"), V, Március 15. tér 7.
Restaurant specializing in traditional Hungarian cuisine. In 1904 Mátyás Baldauf opened a beer pub in what was then a tenement belonging to the Dreher brewery. It soon became a favorite spot where lawyers, industrialists, and artists had their regular tables. It was renovated and refurnished in 1937 and decorated with murals by Jenő Haranghy and painted glass windows depicting scenes from the life of King Matthias. Paintings and murals by Gyula Bozó were added between 1968 and 1971.
Ménes Csárda, V, Apáczai Csere János utca 15.
An elegant *csárda* in Pest near the waterfront. Flambéed specialties in the Hungarian style, prepared at one's table, can be enjoyed to the accompaniment of cimbalom music.
Százéves ("Hundred-year-old"), V, Pesti Barnabás utca 2, daily noon–midnight
This renowned traditional establishment offers international specialties; it has a garden and a gypsy band. [No. 58]
Lila Akác, VI, Nagymező utca 30, daily 10 a.m.–1 a.m.
Theatergoers like to end their evenings here, experiencing Hungarian specialties prepared from poultry, game, and fish.
Fészek Klub, VII, Kertész utca 36, daily noon–1 a.m.
This jewel of the run-down VIIth district was long an insiders' club for professional artists and has only recently become accessible to those without a membership card. The fin-de-siècle restaurant on the ground floor offers fine international cuisine with courteous service. A bar in the palatial building opens at 10 p.m. The courtyard is particularly attractive.
Kispipa ("Little Pipe"), VII, Akácfa utca 38, daily noon–1 a.m., closed Sundays and holidays.
The carp swimming in the display window are a living advertisement for the fine fish soup this restaurant serves to its regular public of elegant diners, who usually appear at a late hour. The famous songwriter Rezső Seress played the piano here every night until 1958. His song *Sad Sunday*, also sung by Ray Charles and Louis Armstrong, was written here.
Kalocsai Paprika Csárda, VIII, Bláthy Ottó utca 13, daily 4 p.m.–11 p.m.
Folk art combined with Eat art in the traditional Kalocsa manner.
Paradiso, XII, Istenhegyi út 40a, daily noon–3 p.m. and 7 p.m.–midnight
In this old villa furnished with antiques, in the green part of Buda, you can spoil yourself with piano music and gourmet dishes. A discotheque on the ground floor is open from 10 p.m.–4 a.m.
Hangulat ("Mood"), XIII, Népfürdő utca 17e, daily except Tues. 11 a.m.–10 p.m.
This restaurant near Árpád Bridge offers homely Hungarian fare and gypsy music.
Kis Kakukk ("Little Cuckoo"), XIII, Pozsonyi út 12, daily noon – 11 p.m., Sun. noon–4 p.m.
This restaurant in Újlipótváros near the Pest end of Margit Bridge is especially praised for its game dishes.
Gundel, XIV, Állatkerti út 2, daily noon–4 p.m. and 7 p.m.–midnight
A renowned traditional restaurant with international food, gypsy music, and a garden. [No. 89]
Robinson, XIV, off Állatkerti körút, daily noon–3 p.m. and 6 p.m.–midnight
An original island location on the lake in City Park; international cuisine.

A rich repertoire of fantastic creatures decorates Budapest's historicist facades, as that of the New York café

Beer pubs

The Hungarians, traditionally wine-drinkers, are by no means averse to a pint or two. More and more pubs have been opening up in recent years.

Kaltenberg, IX, Kinizsi utca 30–32, daily except Sun. noon–midnight
The beer is brewed on the premises. You can enjoy traditional Bavarian pub grub along with "oompah" music.
Prágai Venzel Sörház ("Prague Wenceslas Beerhall"), VIII, Rákóczi út 57a, 11 a.m.–11:30 p.m., Sun. noon–11:30 p.m.
Radebergi Söröző, III, Hídfő utca 16, daily noon–midnight
Pils from Radeberg in Saxony can be enjoyed in the heart of Óbuda to the sounds of accordion music.
Tuborg Viking Sörbár, VII, Károly körút 5, daily 9 a.m.–11 p.m.
The guest is transported back to the days of the Vikings in this pub established with Danish participation; accordion music.

Ethnic and other specialist restaurants

Arabic

Aladdin, VIII, Bérkocsis utca 23a, daily noon–midnight

Bulgarian

Szofia, V, Kossuth Lajos tér 13–15, daily noon–1 a.m.

Chinese

Szecsuan, V, Roosevelt tér 5, daily except Sun. and holidays noon–midnight, Fri. and Sat. noon–1 a.m.
Vörös Sárkány, VI, Andrássy út 80, daily except Sun. noon–midnight
China Palace, VIII, Üllői út 6, daily 11:30 a.m.–2:30 p.m. and 6 p.m.–midnight

Cuban

Habana, VI, Bajcsy-Zsilinszky út 21, daily noon–3 a.m.

Czech

Prágai Svejk Vendéglő, VII, Károly utca 59b, daily noon–midnight

French

Le Jardin de Paris, I, Fő utca 20, daily 11 a.m.–2 a.m.
Étoile, XIII, Pozsonyi út 4, daily noon–3 p.m. and 6 p.m.–1 a.m.

Georgian

Tbiliszi, VII, Bajza utca 1, daily 5 p.m.–midnight

German

Berlin, V, Szent István körút 13, Mon. to Thurs. 9 a.m.–midnight, Fri. and Sat. 9 a.m.–1 a.m.
Berliner Rathauskeller, VII, Dob utca 31 (entrance on Kazinczy utca), Mon. to Sat. noon–11 p.m., Sun. noon–4 p.m., in summer 6 p.m.–11 p.m.

Greek

Görög Taverna, VI, Csengery utca 24, daily noon–2 a.m.

Italian

Marco Polo, V, Vigadó tér 3, daily noon–3 p.m. and 7:30 p.m.–midnight

Napoletana, V, Petőfi tér 3, daily 11 a.m.–midnight
Don Alfredo, XIV, Hungária körút 53–55, daily 11 a.m.–midnight

Japanese

Japan, VIII, Luther utca 4–6, daily 10 a.m.–1 a.m.

Korean

Senara, VII, Dohány utca 5, daily except Sun. 11:30 a.m.–2:30 p.m. and 6 p.m.–11 p.m.

Polish

Kaczma Polska, XII, Márvány utca 19, daily 4 p.m.–midnight

Russian

Arany Kaviar, I, Ostrom utca 19, daily noon–midnight
Bajkal, V, Semmelweis utca 1–3, daily except Sun. 10 a.m.–10 p.m.

Serbian

Kislugas, II, Szilágyi Erzsébet fasor 72, daily noon–11 p.m., in summer noon–midnight
Szerb Étterem, V, Nagy Ignác utca 16, daily 10 a.m.–10 p.m.

Slovakian

Szlovák Söröző, V, Bihari János utca 15, Mon. to Sat. 10 a.m.–midnight

Kosher

Shalom, VII, Klauzál tér 2, Sun. to Fri. noon–11 p.m., Sat. noon–3 p.m.

Vegetarian

Vegetárium, V, Cukor utca 3
Vegetáriánus Étterem, XIII, Visegrádi utca 50a

Coffeehouses and pastry shops

Angelika, I, Batthyány tér 7, summer 9 a.m.–10 p.m., winter 10 a.m.–10 p.m.
Pleasant coffeehouse atmosphere; also a "literary café" for musical performances, podium discussions, and writers reading from their work.
Café Pierrot, I, Fortuna utca 14, 11 a.m.–1 a.m.
Piano music, specialty coffees, cocktails.
Korona, I, Dísz tér 16, daily 10 a.m.–9 p.m.
Coffeehouse atmosphere and a venue of musical and literary events in the evenings.
Ruszwurm, I, Szentháromság utca 7, daily except Wed. 10 a.m.–8 p.m.
Extremely popular small pastry shop with Empire furniture. [No. 24]
Auguszt, II, Fény utca 6, Tues. to Fri. 10 a.m.–6 p.m., Sat. 10 a.m.–2 p.m.
In the year it opened, 1896, this pastry shop was awarded a certificate of merit in conjunction with the millennium exhibition. Patrons praise the fine ice cream.
Anna Eszpresszo, V, Váci utca 7, Mon. to Sat. 8 a.m.–10 p.m., Sun. 10 a.m.–10 p.m.
Is particularly inviting in summer as a street café.
Galéria, V, Vitkovics Mihály utca 7, daily 11 a.m.–midnight
Café and cocktail-bar, sale of works of art.
Gerbeaud, V, Vörösmarty tér 7, daily 9 a.m.–9 p.m., closed holidays
A trendy meeting-place for visitors from all over the world, including many artists. Unfortunately, the culinary quality and friendliness of the service no longer consistently live up to the reputation of its legendary owner, Emil Gerbeaud. [No. 61]
Narcisz, V, Váci utca 32, Mon. to Sat. 9 a.m.–1 a.m., Sun. 2 p.m.–1 a.m.
Bistro with coffee specialties.
Spartakus-Presso, V, Aulich utca 8, daily 8 a.m.–10:30 p.m.
A meeting-place for artists because of the proximity of the Academy of Art; good breakfasts can be had here.
Lukács, VI, Andrássy út 70, daily 9 a.m.–8 p.m.
Typical coffeehouse atmosphere surrounds the guest in a palatial building with historic interior furnishings. The marble-clad ground floor has a stand-up coffee bar, a broad staircase leads to the decorative salons upstairs. Meeting-place primarily for the young intelligentsia and foreigners.
Művész, VI, Andrássy út 29, Mon. to Fri. 8 a.m.–8 p.m., Sat. 10 a.m.–8 p.m.
Silk carpets, cherrywood, small marble tables, candelabra, and old paintings lend a touch of genuine festiveness to this coffeehouse near the opera; a fair share of artists among the patrons.
New York, VII, Erzsébet körút 11, daily 9 a.m.–midnight
Splendid coffeehouse with fin-de-siécle decor. Then and now a meeting-place for Hungarian literati and artists. [No. 68]
Hauer, VII, Rákóczi út 49, daily 9 a.m.–8 p.m.

The best-known Budapest café is undoubtedly Gerbeaud's

This pastry shop in Józsefváros, near East Station, has been restored to its original condition, with white lacquer furnishings from 1890. Etched glass in the doors and windows, stylish furniture, and Herend porcelain set the tone of the establishment, which also has a garden court. The marble tables are primarily occupied by elderly ladies sitting alone in front of old-fashioned pastries with lots of whipped cream, enormous chocolate desserts, chestnut specialties, parfaits, and marzipan figures. A pianist tinkles away the afternoon hours.

Inteam, XII, Németvölgyi út 17, daily 4 p.m.–4 a.m.
Coffee in the garden and a bar in a turn-of-the-century villa surrounded by fir trees; music in the summer.

In several Budapest hotels there are equally atmospheric cafés, as for example the Viennese Coffeehouse in the **Forum**, V, Apáczai Csere János utca 12–14, the Café Pietro in the arcade of the **Taverna**, V, Váci utca 49, the Stefánia pastry shop in the Grand Hotel **Hungária**, VII, Rákóczi út 90, and the Ybl Café in the **Ramada** Grand Hotel on Margaret Island. The **Astoria** café gives one a feeling of being transported back to a more elegant age in surroundings of marble columns, chandeliers, and gilded stucco (V, Kossuth Lajos utca 19–21). The musicians' gallery displays charcoal drawings of Budapest's famous pastry chefs, restaurateurs, and gypsy violinists (Emil Gerbeaud, József Dobos, Károly Gundel, Henrik Kugler). In contrast, the art-nouveau-like white and gold furnishings of the Zsolnay Kávéház in the **Radisson Béke** (VI, Teréz körút 43) make for a vibrant, cheerful impression. Coffee specialties, the more old-fashioned pastries, and newer low-calorie creations, including sugar-free ice cream and cakes, are served on original hand-painted tableware from the Zsolnay porcelain factory. The specialties of the house include Lúdláb ("Goosefoot") gateau, Esterházi gateau with nuts, Alexander gateau with kiwis, and carrot-and-caramel-covered Dobos gateau. Ladies meet here to chat, and on Sundays families gather to drink coffee. The pastry chefs conjure up, from colored caramelized sugar, translucent garlands of flowers and baskets of fruit, which make popular souvenirs.

Holidays and Festivals

Public holidays are: January 1, March 15 (1848 uprising), Easter Monday, May 1, Whit Monday, August 20 (St. Stephen), October 23 (Republic Day), December 25 and 26.

A **calendar of events** in English is obtainable free of charge every month from Tourinform. Budapest's several English-language weeklies also publish listings.

January – February – March

On **New Year's Day** even the most sophisticated city dweller will refuse to eat poultry, since — according to an old saying — a chicken "scratches good luck away," while a pig "roots good luck into the house." Along with a bowl of Bohemian cabbage soup to cure the hangover, the culturally aware Budapester's program will also include the New Year's Day concert in the Pest Vigadó.

January 6 is called "Water Consecration Day" in Hungary. In the old days the itinerant mendicant monks blessed the water and the homes on this day.

After January 6 the **ball season** begins, lasting until Ash Wednesday. The most famous balls are the Gypsy, Swabian, Jurists', Doctors', and Journalists' balls. Although **carnival** festivities have a long tradition in the capital — going back as far as the Renaissance by way of King Matthias's second wife, Beatrix — fancy-dress parties nowadays are mainly private events. The Carnival of the Women and processions with carved animal masks still take place in villages in some parts of the country.

In **February** the Hungarians recall the old weather rule that results in record numbers of visitors to the Budapest zoo on February 2: If the brown bear comes out of his cave on a sunny day, sees his own shadow, then turns around and goes back inside, it will remain cold for a long time; if, on the other hand, he doesn't see his shadow because the sky is overcast, he stays outside and winter will soon depart. A similar significance is attributed to St. Matthias's Day, February 24: the proverb states that Matthias "breaks the ice if he finds any, but if he doesn't he makes some."

No other holiday expresses the Hungarian people's tremendous desire for freedom as clearly and deeply as **March 15**. Long before this day was reinstated as an official national holiday in 1989, every year thousands wearing the red, white, and green cockade would proudly march to the memorial sites of the revolution of 1848 against the Habsburg oppression: to the Petőfi Memorial (V, Petőfi tér); to the steps of the National Museum, where the poet recited his patriotic "Song of the Nation"; to the Lajos Kossuth Memorial in front of Parliament House; to the statue of a general of Polish descent, József Bem (erected by János Istok in 1934, I, Bem József tér); and to the Honvéd Memorial on Dísz tér.

The **Budapest Spring Festival** begins in mid March. Lovers of classical music can choose from among a variety of concerts in the Congress Center, the Congress Hall of the Hungarian Academy of Sciences, the Academy of Music, the Bartók Memorial House, the Pest Vigadó, and many churches throughout the capital. Appearances by world-class stars and foreign ensembles turn opera, operetta, and ballet performances into unforgettable experiences. Jazz and pop groups of international rank appear in the Petőfi Hall and at the Horticultural University. Museums schedule the openings of special exhibits in the final days of March, and the cultural institutes of other countries also contribute to the diversity of Budapest's spring.

April – May – June

Easter is primarily celebrated in Hungary as a festival in the tradition of the Roman Catholic Church. Easter Monday is an important holiday, a day for boiled ham and colored Easter eggs. One of the folk customs to have survived in Budapest is the sprinkling of the girls with Easter water, originally connected with the ideas of fertility and ritual cleansing, though today eau de cologne is used instead. Until midday of Easter Monday, Hungarian men wander the streets visiting their circle of female friends to wish them eternal youth with a fragrant greeting, for which they receive a red egg and usually a wee dram too, in return.

May 1 is another national holiday that has recently been revived in Hungary as a

Homemade kalács, *a kind of pastry, is a favorite treat on high days and holidays*

genuine people's holiday with colorful activities and games for the children in City Park, folk-craft markets, song and dance, and sporting competitions. The public pools with thermal baths are open, and agile youths try to prove themselves to their sweethearts by climbing up a maypole—a symbol of nature's eternal regeneration and of life reborn—decorated with wine bottles or scarves.

On **Corpus Christi** carpets of flowers are laid out in the churchyards for the processions at the Marian shrines in the vicinity of Budapest, e.g. in Máriaremete, Városmajor, and Pilisvörösvár.

As with St. Swithin, if it rains on **St.-Medárd's Day** (June 8th), rain can be counted on for the next forty days.

The long **summer vacation** in Hungary begins in the second week of June and lasts until August 31. The graduates of the eighth grade (primary school) and twelfth grade (secondary school) are bid farewell with the song "Gaudeamus Igitur," speeches, and mountains of flowers. The downtown shop windows display tableaux with photos of the secondary-school graduates and their teachers.

On the evening of June 23, the **summer solstice**, old pagan rituals of the fire-worshipping Magyars are recalled. Young people gather in the caves of Buda or at the Rózsika Spring in Hűvösvölgy to sing songs well into the night, to dance around the midsummer fire, or to jump over the blazing flames. It is interesting to note that throughout Hungary, these fires have the Slavic-Byzantine name "Saint Iván's Fires." Not only are they alleged to be powerful potentiators of love, but apples baked in the fire, herbs and flowers picked during the Saint Iván's celebration, and the wreaths made therefrom are all said to possess magical powers of healing and protection.

June 30, the anniversary of the departure from Hungary of the last Red Army troops in 1991, is celebrated across the country with the ringing of church bells, general merrymaking, and a country music festival.

July – August – September

Budapest is flooded with tourists in the summer. Street theater and the **open-air stages** on Margaret Island, in Buda Park, and in Városmajor now come into their own. Other romantic venues for open-air concerts and operas are the Dominican Court of the Hilton Hotel and the Carmelite Court next to the Castle Theater. Around July 10 the International Jazz Festival in the Kameraerdő youth park finds a large audience.

An important summer event for punters and other fans of equestrian **sports** is the Hungarian Derby which is run in mid July at the racecourse in the Xth district. The Hungarians are also great aficionados of sulky-racing, which in Budapest takes place on the track in the VIIIth district. Incidentally, the coach is demonstrably a Hungarian invention, the word deriving from the Hungarian *kocsi*: a four-wheeled horse-drawn vehicle with a covered area for passengers and baggage, built in Kocs ("Kocsi wagon"), is first mentioned in 1267. A lot more horsepower is involved in the Formula I race for the Hungarian Grand Prix, held in August at the Hungaroring in Mogyoród near Budapest. Athletes compete for the Budapest Grand Prix during the same month.

August 20, **St. Stephen's Day**, is a national holiday in memory of the first Christian king, István I (1000-38), who founded Hungary as a state. The saint's right hand is carried through the streets in a jubilant procession. In 1991 Pope John Paul II scheduled his first visit to Hungary on this special holiday and celebrated mass on Hősök tere. August 20 is also a nationwide celebration of the "Day of the New Bread," with church and harvest festivals. The festive mood reaches its climax in Budapest between 9 and 10 p.m., when a giant fireworks display illuminates the city from Gellért-hegy.

The fall celebrations in honor of the Virgin Mary have once again become an occasion to make a **pilgrimage** to the shrines in the vicinity of Budapest, where religious services are usually combined with a fair.

September 25, the birthday of the composer and musicologist Béla Bartók, marks the beginning of the **Budapest Fall Festival** with an ambitious program of music (including the concert series "Music of Our Time"), theater, and fine arts.

October – November – December

October 23 is a national holiday commemorating the declaration of the republic in 1989 and, thirty-three years before, the outbreak of the ill-fated uprising.

On **All Saints' Day**, November 1, thousands of candles burn to honor the dead in all the Budapest cemeteries. The choir festival Vox Pacis is presented in November.

On the evening of **December 5**, St. Nicholas comes to give sweets to the good children; his assistant carries a switch to punish the bad ones. Since December 13 was the shortest day of the year before the calendar reform, Luca (St. Lucia) Day is associated with a number of old folk customs connected with the festival of the winter solstice. Thus, it is said that the demonic Luca (from the Latin *lux*, light) punishes all those who work on her name day; hence, a "Luca chair" is a piece of furniture that is never finished. On Luca Day girls write ten male names on separate slips of paper, throwing one into the fire on each of the following nights; the last one will reveal the name of their future husband....

On Easter Monday, in rural Hungary, the boys pour water over the girls so that they will remain beautiful for the entire year; in the city nowadays they spray them with cologne

In the carols and nativity plays of **Christmas time** the episode with the shepherds is particularly popular. The Christmas tree has been known in Hungary since the middle of the nineteenth century; it is decorated with candles, sparklers, and chocolate-covered candies wrapped in silver or gold paper. On Christmas Eve the tree spreads its branches over the gifts for the family and their friends. On the two Christmas holidays, December 25 and 26, the Hungarians eat carp, turkey, stuffed cabbage, chestnut purée, and the traditional Christmas pastry, *beigli*, a roll made of flaky pastry with a nut or poppy seed filling. Since December 26 is also the feast of the other St. Stephen, and since this is one of the most common names in Hungary (István, with the diminutives Pista and Pisti), many families have a further excuse for indulging themselves. Name days are celebrated with more gusto and with a larger circle of friends than birthdays are (in earlier times, the two were usually the same).

On **New Year's Eve** Budapest bids farewell to the old year with a great deal of noise. The street celebrations along the Outer Ring are accompanied by rattles, paper trumpets, and confetti; the people, some wearing masks, shout "búék" to one another (*Boldog új évet kívánok*, "Happy New Year") and wish each other "Wine, wheat, and peace."

A musical clown on Vörösmarty tér

Language

Pronunciation

Hungarian words are stressed on the first syllable. The acute or double acute accent indicates a long vowel. Double consonants are pronounced double, as in Italian ("An-na"). Unvoiced consonants are voiced when they stand immediately before a voiced consonant, and vice versa, e.g. *István* is pronounced *Izsdván*, *országház* is pronounced *országkház*.

Hungarian letters, phonetic symbols, and approximate English equivalents:

a	[a]	more as in "hot" than in "hat"
á	[aː]	as in "father"
e	[æ]	more as in "bag" (affected British pronunciation) than in "beg"
é	[eː]	as in "say"
i	[i]	"sit"
í	[iː]	"suite"
o	[o]	"hotel"
ó	[oː]	"note"
ö	[ø]	"ton"
ő	[øː]	"hers"
u	[u]	"bull"
ú	[uː]	"rule"
ü	[y]	"Müller" (German) or "buffet" (French)
ű	[yː]	"führer" (German) or "fondue" (French)
c	[ts]	"hats"
cs	[tʃ]	"chop"
gy	[ȡ]	"d'you"
j	[j]	"yes"
ly	[j]	"yes"
ny	[ȵ]	"canyon"
s	[ʃ]	"shop"
sz	[s]	"sit"
ty	[ȶ]	"last year"
zs	[ʒ]	"measure"

Other consonants are pronounced as in English.

Old spellings still found in personal names:

ch = **cs**	**th** = **t**
cz = **c**	**thy** = **ty**
eö = **ö**	**y** = **i**

Numbers

0 nulla
1 egy
2 kettő/két
3 három
4 négy
5 öt
6 hat
7 hét
8 nyolc
9 kilenc
10 tíz
20 húsz
30 harminc
40 negyven
50 ötven
60 hatvan
70 hetven
80 nyolcvan
90 kilencven
100 száz
200 kétszáz
300 háromszáz
400 négyszáz
500 ötszáz
1000 ezer

Useful words and expressions

good morning	jó reggelt
good day	jó napot
good evening	jó estét
good night	jó éjszakát, jó éjt
goodbye	viszontlátásra
hello	szervusz, szia

(only used with those with whom one is on familiar terms)

yes	igen
no	nem
thank you	köszönöm
please	kérem
excuse me	bocsánat
Where is ...?	Hol van ...?
left	balra
right	jobbra
straight on	egyenesen
entrance	bejárat
exit	kijárat
closed	zárva
open	nyitva
How much does it cost?	Mennyibe kerül?
too expensive	túl drága
cheap	olcsó
Hungary	Magyarország
Hungarian (adjective, language)	magyar, magyarul
I don't speak Hungarian	Nem tudok magyarul
Hungarian (person)	magyar
street	utca
road	út, útja
square	tér, tere
church	templom
theater	színház
cinema	mozi
train station	pályaudvar
East Station	Keleti pályaudvar
South Station	Déli pályaudvar
West Station	Nyugati pályaudvar
airport	repülőtér
streetcar	villamos
subway	metró
railway	vasút
police	rendőrség
hospital	kórház
doctor	orvos
it hurts	fáj
forbidden	tilos
out of order	nem működik
large	nagy
small	kicsi/kis
beautiful	szép
wonderful	gyönyörű
warm	meleg
cold	hideg
Boy, is it hot!	Jaj de meleg van!
I love you!	Szeretlek!
restaurant	étterem (vendéglő)
café	eszpresszó
waiter	pincér
menu	étlap
We would like ...	Szeretnénk ...
... lunch	... ebédelni
... dinner	... vacsorázni
I would like a glass of...	Kérek egy pohár...
... water	... vizet
... beer	... sört
... wine	... bort
I would like a coffee	Kérek egy kávét
Check, please!	Fizetni szeretnék!

A popular tongue twister:

kedves megegészségesedésedre	(roughly) to your dear health!

The János Arany Theater [No. 72] stages musicals as well as Hungarian-language plays

Museums, Galleries, Libraries

The numbers in brackets refer to articles in the main guide.

Museums and permanent collections

Opening hours, unless otherwise indicated, Tues.–Sun. 10 a.m.–6 p.m.

Ady Endre, V, Veres Pálné utca 4–6.
Aeronautics, XIV, Zichy Mihály út 14, April–Oct.
Aeronautics, XIII, Mohács utca 16c (by appointment, Tel. 122 5779).
Agriculture, XIV, Vajdahunyad sétány. [85]
Applied art, IX, Üllői út 33–37. [67]
Aquincum, III, Szentendrei út 139, May–Aug. Tues.–Sun. 10 a.m.–6 p.m., Sept.–Oct. Tues.–Sun. 10 a.m.–4 p.m. (call ahead, Tel. 180 4650). [100]
Architecture, I, Táncsics Mihály utca 1.
Banknotes and coins, V, Szabadság tér 8, Thurs. 9 a.m.–2 p.m.
Bartók Béla, II, Csalán út 29 (call ahead, Tel. 176 2100).
Bible, IX, Ráday utca 28, Tues.–Sun. 10 a.m.–5 p.m.
Budapest history, I, Szent György tér 2, wing E, Wed.–Mon. 10 a.m.–5:30 p.m. (Nov., Dec. to 5 p.m., Jan., Feb. to 4 p.m.) [1]
Chinese and Japanese art, see **Ráth**.
Commerce and catering, I, Fortuna utca 4. [19]
Eastern Asia, see **Hopp**.
Ecclesiastical treasures, I, Szentháromság tér 2 (Matthias Church), 9 a.m.–6 p.m. [8]
Ecclesiastical treasures, V, Szent István tér (St. Stephen's), Mon.–Sat. 10 a.m.–4 p.m., Sun. 1 p.m.–4 p.m.
Electrotechnology, VII, Kazinczy utca 21.
Ethnography, V, Kossuth Lajos tér 12, Tues.–Sun. 10 a.m.–5:30 p.m. [80]
Fine arts, XIV, Dózsa György út 41, Tues.–Sun. 10 a.m.–5:30 p.m. (mid Nov.–mid Mar. to 4:30 p.m.) [83]
Firefighting, X, Martinovics tér 12, Tues.–Fri. 9 a.m.–4 p.m., Sat./Sun. 9 a.m.–1 p.m.
Folk art, see **Kun, Laki**.
Foundry, II, Bem József utca 20.
Furniture, see **Nagytétény**.
Geology, XIV, Stefánia út 14. [91]
Gül Baba mausoleum, II, Mecset utca 14, as for **Aquincum**. [35]
Hercules Villa, III, Meggyfa utca 19–21, April 15–Oct., by appointment only (Tel. 180 4650). [96]
Hopp, VI, Andrássy út 103. [82]
Jewish, VII, Dohány utca 2, Mon./Thurs. 2 p.m.–6 p.m., Tues./Wed./Fri./Sun. 9 a.m.–1 p.m. [64]
Jewish prayerhouse, I, Táncsics Mihály utca 26, May–Oct. Tues.–Fri. 10 a.m.–2 p.m., Sat./Sun./hol. 10 a.m.–6 p.m. [15]

Jókai Mór, XII, Költő utca 21, Tues.–Sun. 10 a.m.–2 p.m.
Kassák Lajos, III, Fő tér 1. [97]
Kiscelli, III, Kiscelli utca 108 (Nov.–March to 4 p.m. only). [93]
Kodály Zoltán, VI, Kodály körönd 1, Wed. 10 a.m.–4 p.m., Thurs.–Sat. 10 a.m.–6 p.m., Sun. 10 a.m.–2 p.m.
Kossuth Lajos, V, Széchenyi lánchíd (ship at Pest end), April 15–Oct. 31.
Kun, III, Fő tér 4, Tue.–Fri. 2–6 p.m., Sat., Sun. 10 a.m.–6 p.m. [98]
Labyrinth, I, Úri utca 9, 10 a.m.–6 p.m. [27]
Laki, XVI, Kalitka utca 1 (by appointment, Tel. 183 8083).
Lawyers, V, Szalay utca 7, Mon.–Fri. 10 a.m.–1 p.m., closed Aug.
Liszt Ferenc, VI, Vörösmarty utca 35, Mon.–Fri. 10 a.m.–6 p.m., Sat. 11 a.m.–5 p.m.
Liszt Ferenc, VI, Andrássy út 67, Mon.–Fri. noon–5 p.m., Sat. 9 a.m.–1 p.m.
Literature, see **Nyugat, Petőfi.**
Ludwig, I, Szent György tér 2, wing A, Tues.–Sun. 10 a.m.–5:30 p.m. [3]
Meat industry, IX, Gubacsi út 6b.
Medicine, see **Semmelweis.**
Military history, I, Tóth Árpád sétány 40, Tues.–Sat. 9 a.m.–5 p.m., Sun./hol. 10 a.m.–6 p.m. [31]
Modern history, I, Szent György tér 2, wing A, Tues.–Sun. 10 a.m.–5:30 p.m.
Music, I, Táncsics Mihály utca 7, Mon. 4 p.m.–9 p.m., Wed.–Sun. 10 a.m.–6 p.m. [13]
Nagytétény Manor, XXII, Kastélypark utca 9–11.
Napoleon, XX, Ady Endre utca 82.
National Gallery, I, Szent György tér 2, wings B/C/D [3]
National Museum, VIII, Múzeum körút 14–16, Tues.–Sun. 10 a.m.–5:30 p.m. [51]
Nyugat, XII, Városmajor utca 48b, Tues.–Sun. 10 a.m.–2 p.m.
Óbuda, III, Fő tér 1.
Petőfi, V, Károlyi Mihály utca 16.
Pharmacy, I, Tárnok utca 18, Tues.–Sun. 10:30 a.m.–5:30 p.m. [7]
Philately, VII, Hársfa utca 47. [90]
Post, VI, Andrássy út 3. [90]
Protestant, V, Deák Ferenc tér 4, Tues.–Sun. 10 a.m.–5:30 p.m. [62]
Ráth, VI, Városligeti fasor 12, 10 a.m.–6 p.m. [82]
Rescue services, V, Markó utca 22, Thurs. 8 a.m.–2 p.m.

The entrance to Vidámpark, Budapest's largest amusement park

Roman baths, III, under Flórián tér, Sept./Oct. to 4 p.m. only, closed Nov.–April 15; by appointment only (Tel. 180 4650). [96]
Roman camp, III, Pacsirtamező utca 63, May–Oct. Tues.–Fri. 10 a.m.–2 p.m., Sat./Sun. 10 a.m.–6 p.m.
Semmelweis, II, Apród utca 1–3, Tues.–Sun. 10:30 a.m.–6 p.m. [39]
Sport, XIV, Dózsa György út 3.
Subway, V, Deák Ferenc tér (subway passage), 9 a.m.–5 p.m., closed Mon. [84]
Synagogue, VII, Dohány utca 2–8, Mon.–Fri. 10 a.m.–1 p.m. [64]
Telephony, I, Úri utca 49.
Textiles and clothing, XIII, Gogol utca 9–11.
Theater, I, Krisztina körút 57.
Transport, XIV, Városligeti körút 11, Tues.–Fri. 10 a.m.–4 p.m., Sat./Sun. 10 a.m.–6 p.m. [90]
Vajdahunyad Castle, XIV, Vajdahunyad sétány, Tues.–Sat. 10 a.m.–5 p.m., Sun. 10 a.m.–6 p.m. [85]
Varga Imre, III, Laktanya utca 7.
Vasarely Victor, III, Szentlélek tér 6, Tues.–Sun. 10 a.m.–5 p.m. [97]

The art scene

Hungary began to emerge from the backwoods of the art world in 1968/69, when two Budapest exhibitions presented the efforts of young artists to introduce to the domestic repertoire such international currents as Pop Art (Konkoly), Hard Edge (Bak, Hencze, Nádler), Environments

(Jovánovics), or Conceptual Art (Szentjóby). The cultural commissars felt distinctly uneasy at the way things were going, and they closed down the 1970 exhibition of Conceptual Art shortly after it opened—this was the legendary show at which Miklós Erdély presented his drawing *Electric Policeman*, a combination of the Hungarian flag with a traffic-light. The metaphor all too clearly reflected Hungarian cultural policy in the sixties and seventies, when artists were classified according to the principle of the "three T's:" *tiltott* (red)—prohibited, *tűrt* (white)—tolerated, and *támogatott* (green)—encouraged.

The art scene has of course since become more liberal —perhaps not entirely for its own good. The avant-garde artists who formerly fell into the first of the above categories began in the early eighties to be admitted to the official temples of art, and since then many have complained of the lack of "friction," the lost excitement of working underground, and especially the lack of interest in their work on the part of the broader public; they nostalgically recall the good old days of the officially frowned-upon "self-help" exhibitions and the sensational shows at the Fészek Artists' Club or the Ernst Museum. But the new climate has also fostered art of lasting significance, as reflected in such exhibition series as "Tendencies" (from 1980 on) and "New Sensitivity" (from 1981 on) and the shows "Wet Paint" (1984) and "Eclectica" (1986), in which the Hungarian art of past decades was reappraised and new work was presented. Budapest's Arts Hall (Műcsarnok) has long been in touch with the international art market and has organized well-received exhibitions of the works of foreign artists.

There are today a host of private galleries in Budapest, ranging from the conventional to the highly unconventional, occupying opulent premises or crowded into the tiniest of spaces. The classic schools of modern art are represented, and current trends also find a showcase: violent, Neo-Expressionist painting, gestural meditation, the surreal and the grotesque (e.g., Roczkov Gallery), the sensitive creations of individual mythicism, concrete art, and installations (e.g., NA-NE Gallery). A focus of interest within this lively scene is the Knoll Gallery (with a second showroom in Vienna): opened in the fall of 1989 with an exhibition of the prints and neon installations of the prominent Hungarian émigré Joseph Kosuth (New York), it has become a forum for eastern European artists and the young Austrian avant-garde. The success of Art Expo, the market for eastern European art that since 1991 has been held annually in March, also bodes well for the continuing vitality of the Budapest art scene.

Galleries and exhibition halls

Hours, unless otherwise stated: daily except Mon. 10 a.m.–6 p.m.

Art Gallery, I, Táncsics Mihály utca 5; V, Petőfi Sándor utca 18.
Arts Hall (Műcsarnok), XIV, Dózsa György út 35. [83]
Barcsay Exhibition Hall (Gallery of the Hungarian Academy of Visual Arts), VI, Andrássy út 69–71, Mon. to Fri. 10 a.m.–6 p.m., Sat. 10 a.m.–1 p.m.
Bartók 32 Gallery, XI, Bartók Béla út 32, daily except Mon. 2 p.m.–6 p.m.
Blitz Gallery, V, Falk Miksa utca 30.
Budapest Galéria, V, Szabadsajtó út 5; III, Lajos utca 158; III, Laktanya utca 7.
Budatétényi Gallery, XXII, Nagytétényi út 35, daily 2 p.m.–7 p.m.
Chagall Gallery, VII, Garay utca 48, Mon. to Sat. 3 p.m.–6 p.m.
Csók István Gallery, V, Váci utca 25, Mon. to Fri. 10 a.m.–6 p.m., Sat. 9 a.m.–1 p.m.
Dorottya Utcai Exhibition Hall (dependency of the Arts Hall), V, Dorottya utca 8.
Duna Gallery, XIII, Pannónia utca 95.
Éri Gallery, V, Ferenciek tere 5.
Ernst Museum, VI, Nagymező utca 8. [71]
Fészek Club Gallery, VII, Kertész utca 36, Mon. to Fri. 2 p.m.–8 p.m.
Fortuna 11 G, I, Fortuna utca 11, Tues. to Fri. 11 a.m.–6 p.m., Sat. and Sun. 10 a.m.–4 p.m.
Gaál Imre Gallery, XX, Kossuth Lajos utca 39.
Gallery II, XI, Irinyi utca 1, daily 11 a.m.–11 p.m.
Gallery 56, V, Falk Miksa utca 7.
Gulácsy Galéria, V, Károly körút 6, Mon. to Fri. 10 a.m.–6 p.m., Sat. 10 a.m.–1 p.m.
Inart Gallery, XII, Maros utca 28/1/9, Mon. to Fri. 9 a.m.–5 p.m.
Józsefváros Exhibition Hall, VII, József körút 70.

Knoll Gallery, VI, Liszt Ferenc tér 10, Mon. to Fri. 11 a.m.–6 p.m., Sat. 10 a.m.–1 p.m.
Liget Gallery, XIV, Ajtósi Dürer sor 5, Mon. and Tues. 3 p.m.–7 p.m.
Luttár Gallery, XIII, Hegedűs Gyula utca 24, Mon. to Fri. 10 a.m.–6 p.m., Sat. 10 a.m.–2 p.m.
Molnár C. Pál Studio Gallery, XI, Ménesi út 65, Tues., Wed., Thurs. 3 p.m.–6 p.m., Nov. to April also Sun. 10 a.m.–1 p.m.; also by appointment (Eva Csillag, Tel. 186 1718).
Művész Gallery, VIII, Rákóczi út 7, Mon.–Fri. 2 p.m.–5 p.m.
NA-NE Gallery, IX, Lónyay utca 41, daily 10 a.m.–5:30 p.m.
Óbuda Cellar Gallery, III, Fő tér 1, Tues. to Fri. 2 p.m.–6 p.m., Sat. and Sun. 10 a.m.–6 p.m.
Óbudai Társaskör Galéria, III, Kiskorona utca 7, Tues. to Fri. 2 p.m.–6 p.m., Sat. and Sun. 10 a.m.–6 p.m.
Palme-ház, XIV, Olof Palme sétány 1.
Pandora Gallery, VIII, Népszínház utca 42, Mon. to Fri. 10 a.m.–6 p.m., Sat. 10 a.m.–1 p.m.
Pataky Gallery, X, Pataki tér 7–14.
Piktura Gallery, V, Vitkovics Mihály utca 10, Mon. to Fri. 10 a.m.–6 p.m., Sat. 10 a.m.–1 p.m.
Qualitas Gallery, V, Bécsi utca 2, Mon. to Fri. 11 a.m.–6 p.m., Sat. 10 a.m.–1 p.m.
Roczkov Gallery, VI, Andrássy út 1, Mon. to Fri. 11 a.m.–6 p.m., Sat. 11 a.m.–3 p.m.
Sztár Gallery, XIII, Poszonyi út 22, Mon. to Fri. 11 a.m.–6 p.m., Sat. 11 a.m.–2 p.m.
Stúdió Gallery, V, Bajcsy-Zsilinszky út 52.
T-Art Studio Gallery, III, Rózsa utca 12, Sat. and Sun. 10 a.m.–6 p.m.
Tölgyfa Gallery (exhibition hall of the Academy of Applied Art), II, Henger utca 2.
Vár Gallery, I, Táncsics Mihály utca 17, Mon. to Fri. 10 a.m.–4 p.m., Sat. 10 a.m.–1 p.m.
Várfok 14, I, Várfok utca 14, Wed. to Sun. 10 a.m.–6 p.m.
Vigadó Gallery, V, Vigadó tér 2.
Young Artists' Club (Fiatal Művészek Klubja), VI, Andrássy út 112, Mon. to Fri. 10 a.m.–10 p.m.

Libraries

National Library (Órszágos Széchényi Konyvtár), I, Szent György tér 2 (in wing F of Buda Castle). [2]
Municipal Library (Fővárosi Szabó Ervin Könyvtár), VIII, Szabó Ervin tér 1, closed Wed.
University Library (Egyetemi Könyvtár), V, Ferenciek tere 6. [53]
Art Library in the Museum of Fine Arts, XIV, Dózsa György út 41 (appointments Tel. 142 9759).

Nightlife

Bars

Miniatür, II, Buday László utca 10, Mon. to Sat. 10 p.m.–3 a.m.
Moulin Rouge, VI, Nagymező utca 17, daily 10 p.m.–3 a.m.
Maxim Varieté, VII, Akácfa utca 3, Mon. to Sat. 8 p.m.–3 p.m.
Rózsaszín Cicák ("Pink Pussycats"), VII, Wesselényi utca 58, daily 5 p.m.–6 a.m.
Fekete Lyuk ("Black Hole"), VIII, Golgota út 3, Wed. to Sun. 10 p.m.–4 a.m.

Discotheques

Cadillac Club, III, Szépvölgyi út 15, daily 8 p.m.–4 a.m.
Vén Diák, V, Egyetem tér 5, daily 10 p.m.–5 a.m.
Levi's 501 Dancing Club, VI, Nagymező utca 41, daily 8 p.m.–2 a.m.
Rock Café, VII, Dohány utca 18, daily 6 p.m.–2 a.m.
Blue Box, IX, Kinizsi utca 28, daily 8 p.m.–2 a.m.
Starlight Disco (in Petőfi Csarnok), XIV, Zichy Mihály út 14.

Gambling casinos

Hilton, I, Hess András tér, 5 p.m.–4 a.m.
Várkert, I, Ybl Myklós tér 9–11, 2 p.m.–5 a.m.
Gresham, V, Roosevelt tér 5, 2 p.m.–4 a.m.
Las Vegas, V, Roosevelt tér 2 (in the Hotel Atrium Hyatt), 5 p.m.–2 a.m.
Schönbrunn, V, Széchenyi lánchíd (boat moored at Pest end), 4 p.m.–4 a.m., open summers only.

Shopping

The addresses under each heading are grouped in order of municipal district.

Mihály Munkácsy's The Condemned Cell *(1870) is one of the best-known paintings of the Hungarian Realists in the National Gallery*

Antiques

Antique stores are open as a rule Mon. to Fri. 10 a.m.–6 p.m., Sat. 10 a.m.–1 p.m.

Antikvitás, I, Hess András tér 1.
Parti Antikvitás, I, Országház utca 2.
Relikvia, I, Fortuna utca 14.
Antiquity, V, Falk Miksa utca 19.
BÁV, V, Szent István körút 3;
V, Ferenciek tere 12;
V, Bécsi utca 1–3;
VI, Andrássy út 27.
Antiquitet, VI, Ó utca 17.

Bookstores, new and second-hand

Business hours as a rule Mon. to Fri. 8 a.m.–6 p.m., Sat. 10 a.m.–1 p.m.

Vörös Sün, I, Hess András tér 3.
Budai Krónika (second-hand), I, Várfok utca 8.
Budavár (second-hand), I, Országház utca 8.
Litea (with café), I, Hess András tér 4.
A Bagolyhoz (second-hand), V, Váci utca 28.
Kodály Zoltan (new and second-hand sheet music and records), V, Múzeum körút 17–21.
Könyvértéka, V, Honvéd utca 5.
Központi Antikvárium (second-hand), V, Múzeum körút 13–15.
Libri (books and music), V, Kossuth Lajos utca 4.
Libri (international), V, Váci utca 32.
Studium, V, Váci utca 22.
Erkel Ferenc (books and music), VII, Erzsébet körút 52.
Fókusz, VII, Rákóczi út 14.

Folk crafts

In the castle district and in downtown Pest there is no shortage of shops offering a wide variety of more or less genuine handcrafted articles. And there is always the chance of picking up an interesting bargain at one of the open-air markets held in the castle district, City Park, Óbuda (Fő tér), and other parts of town, often on public holidays, or from one of the street vendors who travel up to the capital from as far away as Transylvania to tout their homemade wares.

Embroidery from Kalocsa

In the 1860s peasant women in the villages around Kalocsa in southern Hungary began embroidering table-cloths, bedclothes, and garments to order for customers among the urban bourgeoisie. In keeping with the fashion of the time, the most favored type was *broderie anglaise* (white openwork embroidery) done from patterns. By the turn of the century this had developed into a veritable folk art. Through variation, the invention of new decorative elements and embroidering techniques, and the use of colored thread (initially black, then blue or red, and later a mixture of colors), a distinctive repertoire of forms and motifs arose, which the peasant women also used to decorate their own regional dress. Today, the traditional embroidered costume is virtually only worn as an attraction for tourists.

Lace from Halas

Lace from Halas is among the finest products of Hungary's textile arts. As a rule, a lacemaker requires two years to learn the more than forty techniques for stitches, working with the thinnest needles and the finest English thread or extremely fine silk. These techniques go back to Maria Markovics, who in 1902 created the first specimens of a lacework that was to win international awards and is now protected by trademark. A drawing teacher from Kiskunhalas, Árpád Dékáni, prepared the designs for her; distinguished by a beautiful clarity of line, they were inspired by motifs from old Hungarian textile art, and in turn strongly influenced the Secessionist (Art Nouveau) movement. The lacemaker's patternbook includes animal, vegetable, and anthropomorphic motifs (such as budding branches, roses, swans, peacocks, and deer) and also provides ornamentation for the bridges between the motifs (dewdrop, bell, and heart shapes). Halas lace has always been prized in the highest circles: the last queen of Hungary, Zita von Habsburg, carried a purse made thereof at her coronation in the Matthias church in 1916.

Indigo prints

Available by the yard or already made up as clothing and household linen, printed fabrics with white patterns on an indigo-blue background from the few remaining workshops of the indigo-dyers are sold mainly at market stalls. Linen cloth is dyed using the wax or "resist" technique of printing, and decorated with ornamental, often scenic, patterns. The wood blocks are sometimes engraved by the dyers themselves. It is generally presumed that textile printing spread in Hungary via German craftsmen: in the week before Easter the main altars of the churches would be hung with Lenten cloths printed with biblical scenes. The indigo technique was developed in the seventeenth century, with the introduction of the new dyestuff from India.

Leather apparel

Leather apparel has a long tradition in Hungary. King Matthias, in his palace in Buda, liked to wear as a "housecoat" the *suba*, a usually ankle-length, sleeveless garment of tanned sheepskin. The warm fleece side is turned inward and the outer side decorated—with regional variations—with leather trimmings and leather embroidery in flower and scroll patterns. Similarly decorated are the *ködmön*—a sleeveless fitted jacket with short skirt—and the vest that is part of traditional dress. Particularly around 1870, after the abolition of serfdom and of the laws prescribing the clothing to be worn by each estate, country people vied with each other as to who could boast the most lavishly decorated sheepskin garment.

Haban faience

After being driven from Swabia and Italy during the Counter-Reformation, some of the Habans, or Hutterites (members of an Anabaptist sect founded by Jakob Hutter, who was executed in Innsbruck in 1536), settled in Hungary. In the early seventeenth century they became known primarily for their talents in making white earthenware. They painted white-glazed ceramics with pale yellow, green, and blue colors from oxides of manganese, cobalt, copper, and antimony. In addition to Italianate, oriental, and Dutch stylistic elements, native Hungarian ornaments and scenes of rural life began to decorate their products in the early eighteenth century: plates with openwork filigree, pitchers, hexagonal or octagonal bottles and jars with pewter lids, apothecary's jars, dishes and plates embellished with coats of arms for the Hungarian and Austrian nobility. The folk-craft shops usually offer copies of this unique Hungarian earthenware art of the sixteenth to eighteenth centuries.

Miska jugs

Although the tradition of the *miska* jug is not all that old, it is one of the best-loved Hungarian folk-art objects. The first of these humorous decorative pitchers in the form of a pot-bellied hussar with shako and handlebar mustache appeared in the Tisza region near Szeged around 1830. By the turn of the century, when it went out of fashion, it had many imitators in Hódmezővásárhely, Debrecen, and Mezőcsát. It served as a wine-flagon and festive table decoration. Skilled potters gave portraitlike features to their pitchers and inscribed them with toasts. In the 1930s the tradition was revived by the potter Sándor Kántor from Karcag in southern Hungary.

In the vicinity of the Chain Bridge (Széchenyi lánchid) there is now a floating casino

Gingerbread

Gingerbread has always been a favorite item to bring back from the fair. Hearts, plates, dolls, and hussars are formed in molds carved of wood from a dough of flour, honey, and molasses, then baked, and finally decorated with icing, sprinkles, and colored foil. A historical curiosity are the molds in the likeness of famous politicians and other personalities. The colorful sweets should only be considered souvenirs and decorations, eating them is not recommended due to the preservatives that are added. The golden-brown gingerbread, on the other hand, which is sold in some shops and at folk-art fairs, can be safely enjoyed as a Hungarian specialty.

Carvings and basketwork

Woodcarving has a long tradition in Hungary. Its chief practitioners were the herdsmen, who used to while away the long hours in the open ornamenting the tools of their trade, such as crooks and whipstocks, and fashioning gifts for their brides (trinket boxes, mirror frames, mangle rollers). The making of baskets and other articles of wickerwork was another typical peasant pastime. These arts are still kept alive by rural craftsmen and cooperatives, and a good assortment of such wares is available in the souvenir shops of Budapest.

Easter eggs

Hungarian folk art has also developed its own methods for decorating the egg, that ancient fertility symbol and Easter present. For example, the egg is wrapped in a leaf, whose veins then show up prettily after the egg is dyed in a liquid made with onion skins, green walnut skins, and the peel of sour apples. Patterns are scratched into the shells after dyeing, or a horn is used to apply decorations in hot wax, the shell is then dyed red, and the wax is removed. The decorations vary from region to region, with such typical motifs as frog's feet, pumpkin seeds, butterflies on rushes, etc. It requires very sensitive fingers to fit the decorations of embossed tinplate, e.g., tiny horseshoes, onto the Easter eggs without breaking the shell.

Tulip chests

The construction of brides' chests made of spruce, part of the dowry of every peasant bride since the sixteenth century, was the specialty of a workshop in Komárom. The base coat of paint varies between black, green, brown, and dark blue; light blue also came to be used in the late nineteenth century, and white in the early twentieth century. The name, which soon became famous outside of Hungary, derives from the bouquet of tulips painted on the front of the chest. By the middle of the eighteenth century the tulip chests, whose motifs had become more and more elaborate and detailed, with flowers and pairs of birds—some were also carved—were in such high demand that their production was no longer limited to the Komárom center.

Shops where crafts are sold:

Judit Folklor, I, Országház utca 12; I, Tárnok utca 1 and 8.
Pántlikás Souvenir, I, Országház utca 16.
Piroska, I, Szentháromság utca 4.
Folkart Centrum, V, Váci utca 14.
Holló (furniture, woodwork, glass paintings, ceramics), V, Vitkovics Mihály utca 12.
Lux Folklor, V, Váci utca 6.
Bazaar, V, Régi posta utca 7–9.
Folk art, V, Kálvin tér 5.
Folk art, VII, Erzsébet körút 5.
Folk art, VII, Rákóczi út 32.
Muskátli, XII, Böszörményi út 16.

Herend porcelain

Domestic porcelain production began in Hungary in the early nineteenth century. The most successful enterprise was a porcelain factory founded in 1826 by Moricz Fischer in Herend in the Bakony Hills. Its delicate, fragile creations are still exclusively handmade and handpainted. In Herend they were soon able to imitate with perfection Bohemian porcelain and the styles of Meissen, Sèvres, Capodimonte, Ming *famille rose,* and Japanese Imari porcelain. In 1843 Fischer's company was granted the royal seal. They promoted their wares abroad: at the World's Fair in London, for example, Queen Victoria ordered a tea service decorated with an abundance of butterflies and flowers. This has since become famous, and is a sought-after collector's item, sold under the name "Queen Victoria" and bearing the trademark "Herend Hungary," the Hungarian coat of arms, and the year of manufacture.

Other famous Hungarian porcelain trademarks include Zsolnay and Hollóháza.

Herend, I, Szentháromság utca 5.
Károly Richter, I, Országház utca 12.
Amfora Studio (also Ajka lead crystal), V, Kossuth Lajos utca 4.
Herend, V, József nádor tér 11.
Zsolnay Márkabolt, V, Kígyó utca 4.
Haas & Czjzek, VI, Bajcsy-Zsilinszky út 23.
BÁV, VI, Andrássy út 27.

Markets

Auto markets

XIX, Nagykőrösi út (next to the flea market)

Flea markets

IX, along Zsil utca, Mon. to Fri. 8 a.m.–6 p.m., Sat. 8 a.m.–3 p.m., Sun. 8 a.m.–1 p.m.
XIV, Zichy Mihály utca 14, Petőfi Csarnok, Sat. and Sun. 9 a.m.–2 p.m.
XIX, Nagykőrösi út 156, Mon. to Fri. 8 a.m.–4 p.m., Sat. 8 a.m.–3 p.m.

Second-hand goods

XIII, Katona József utca 22.

Fruit and vegetables

II, Fény utca.
XIII, Lehel tér, Mon. to Fri. 6 a.m.–6 p.m. (winter 6 a.m.–5 p.m.), Sat. 6 a.m.–noon.

Markethalls

IX, Vámház körút 1–3. [No. 50]
II, Batthyány tér 2–6, also open Sun. 7 a.m.–1 p.m.

Fashion

If Budapest is occasionally called the "Paris of the East," the analogy also applies to the women of Budapest, who have a reputation for being prepared to give their last forint for clothes, hair styling, manicures, and cosmetics. On a stroll downtown one will notice women of all ages who are not simply well-groomed, but dressed "with flair" in an outfit in the latest style. At home, slippers (*papucs*) and the floor-length velvet-and-silk housecoat (*pongyola*) are the most important items of apparel, an outfit highly appropriate for the pose of the woman of the world, smoking a cigarette in the stairwell or in the courtyard of a Budapest apartment house and exchanging the latest gossip; it is even sanctioned as streetwear, on a quick trip to fetch the Sunday paper. The women of Budapest dress up all the more consciously however, for special occasions — evenings at the opera or the theater, visiting relatives, meeting in a café, weddings, funerals, leisure-time sports; they attach great importance to choosing the appropriate style for the occasion.

Suits of all kinds are very popular, and not only among career women. While Western trends are usually taken up quickly, Hungarian designers have had little success in their attempts to introduce native folk elements on the international scene.

Alongside their classy womenfolk most males over thirty are very conservatively, not to say indifferently, dressed.

One of the consequences of the great political changes in the country is that new shops bearing the great international names of fashion and cosmetics are opening up all the time in downtown Pest (the area bordered by Váci utca and Károly körút, Vörösmarty tér and Kossuth Lajos utca). The many boutiques of Budapest's traditional high-class shopping district are thus facing serious foreign competition.

A second shopping district has been evolving organically over the years along the "Grand Boulevard," the outer ring of *körúts* that describes a semicircle between Margit and Petőfi bridges. Neon signs and crammed display cases in the entryways attempt to lure shoppers into the salesrooms, usually no larger than a few square yards, in the courtyards, basements, and sometimes even on the upper floors. The effort of seeking out, stair-climbing, and choosing, are usually rewarded in the end, since the suits, handbags, knitwear, jewelry, and custom shoes obtainable here often cost only half the price of items of comparable quality downtown.

The majority of stores are open Mon. to Fri. 10 a.m.–6 p.m., Sat. 10 a.m.–1 p.m.

Zala Zia, I, Iskola utca 29. Walking from Batthyany tér to Buda Castle one passes a small store that offers everyday wear for the discriminating woman in her thirties or forties. The well-manufactured apparel is versatile, wearable, smart, and combines well. Friendly assistants, good materials, up-to-the-minute colors and designs are the keynotes of the establishment.

Fontana, V, Váci utca 16. Multilevel department store with mostly imported women's, men's, and children's fashions; also lingerie, shoes, cosmetics, and gifts.

Luxus, V, Vörösmarty tér 3. International ready-to-wear clothes, Hungarian designer fashions, perfume, brand-name cosmetics, lingerie, and leather goods.

Clara, V, Váci utca 12. One of the leading and oldest-established salons of Budapest, specializing in haute couture made to order.

Ékes Kesztyű, V, Régi posta utca 14. This glove shop with its own workshop has a long tradition going back to 1884. Original Hungarian handknit gloves can also be purchased here.

Glori, V, Párizsi utca 3. Expensive one-of-a-kind pieces of the finest material, predominantly of pure eggshell silk with flowing, very feminine lines and handmade lace trimmings.

Greti, V, Bárczy István utca 3. Arty apparel for the discriminating and for festive occasions.

Kaláka, V, Haris köz 2; I, Szentháromság utca 5; II, Áldás utca 12. Clothing from natural fibers of an original and sophisticated cut, also eyecatching shoes and purses.

Mente, V, Petőfi Sándor utca 11. Everything for the man.

Made in World, V, Kígyó utca 2. The basement boutique stocks a wide range of up-to-the-minute sports and leisure wear.

Pierre Cardin, V, Károly körút 8. Original couture from Paris alongside ready-to-wear fashions from Hungary.

Piri, V, Váci utca 10. To purchase one of the extravagant, handmade hats sold here, be prepared to reach deep into your pocket. The offerings range from saucy little caps by way of modish velvet berets and sporty peaked caps of atlas silk to wagon-wheel-sized hats and broad-brimmed straw hats to wear with a summer dress. Headgear for the bride can also be made to order, and old hats can be repressed into up-to-date forms. The Budapest theaters have their hats made here.

Prima Donna, V, Fehér Hajó utca 8–10. The clothiers for the young are guided by the example of Italian youth fashion. As tempting as many of these articles might seem at first glance, it is a good idea to test the material to see if it will survive the first cleaning.

Soho, V, Párizsi utca 6. Avant-garde fashions in the style of Madonna.

V, Váci utca 10. The name of this boutique in a much frequented courtyard in Pest is also its address. Cheeky, sporty, a bit crazy; leather accessories.

Arissimeoni, VII, Rákóczi út 4–6; V, Petőfi Sándor utca 3. The Greek entrepreneur has found his main customers among the teens and twenties crowd. It is well worth carefully examining the quality of some of the showy fabrics before making a purchase.

Páva, VII, Dob utca 1. At the back of an out-of-the-way courtyard is the retail outlet of the Páva factory, which offers blouses of beautiful materials ranging from the tried-and-true to the fashionable, suitable for a variety of occasions.

Sightseeing

City tours

By bus

Budatours, daily 10:30 a.m. and 1:30 p.m., May 15 to Oct. 15 also 3:30 p.m., departure from buspark, I, Dísz tér, Tel. 153 0558.
Budapest Tourist, departure from V, Roosevelt tér 5, Tel. 118 6866.
City Bus, Tel. 118 1453.
Ibusz, departure from V, Erzsébet tér (stops 1 and 2), Tel. 118 1139; also tours of Parliament House, Buda Castle, etc.

By boat

Mid April to mid October, short daytime and evening cruises along the Danube, departure from Vigadó tér and Petőfi tér moorings.

Ibusz, Tel. 118 1139.
Legenda, Tel. 117 2203.
BKV, Tel. 129 5844.

By air

Moteam, XIV, Rona utca 171, Tel. 252 9922 (balloon).
Wagons-Lits Tourisme, V, Dorottya utca 3, Tel. 118 5090 (plane).

Guides

Euroguide, Tel. 142 3735, 122 3412.

Vantage points

From the paths around Castle Hill (Várhegy) and Gerhardus Hill (Gellérthegy), and particularly from the Citadel atop the latter, fine views of the cityscape are to be had by day and by night. There are also a number of observation towers, e.g. that on János-hegy (1,740 feet, accessible by bus 190 or by chairlift), the Józsefhegyi Tower in Rózsadomb (buses 91 or 191), or the Árpád Tower on Látóhegy (bus 11). Also recommended for an enjoyable visual experience are the trails high above the city on Sváb-hegy in the area of Normafa.

Other places of interest

Amusement park

Vidámpark, XIV, Állatkerti körút 14–16, daily 10 a.m.–8 p.m., 6 p.m. in winter.

Botanical garden

Opened in 1847, with palm house by József Drescher, VIII, Illés utca 25, Mon. to Sat. 9 a.m.–4 p.m., Sun. 9 a.m.–1 p.m., Tel. 133 4333.

Multivision show

Budapest Experience, I, Buda Castle, wing A, 10 a.m.–6 p.m.

Planetarium

X, Népliget, Tel. 134 4513.

Pumproom

Between Elizabeth Bridge (Erzsébet híd) and the Rudas Baths, with mineral waters from the Hungaria, Attila, and Juventus springs.

Stalactite caves

Pálvölgyi barlang, II, Szépvölgyi út 162, daily except Mon. 9 a.m.–4 p.m., hourly tours, Tel. 188 9537.
Szemlőhegyi barlang, II, Pusztaszeri út 35, daily except Tues. 9 a.m.–4 p.m., group tours only, Tel. 115 9271.

Zoo

Zoological and Botanical Garden, XIV, Állatkerti körút 6–12, daily except Mon. 9 a.m.–6 p.m., in winter 9 a.m.–4 p.m.
Aquarium-Terrarium, V, Párizsi utca 1.

Excursions

To **Szentendre** and the **Danube Bend** by boat, April–Sept.

Ibusz, Tel. 118 1139.
Mahart, Tel. 118 1704.

Into the **Buda Hills**: Subway to Moszkva tér, half-mile walk along Szilágyi Erzsébet fasor to cogwheel railway station, ride to terminus Széchenyi-hegy. Transfer to the "children's railway," get off at János-hegy (observation tower) and with the chairlift to Zugliget; or continue on the children's

The excursion boats for short and full-day cruises moor along the Pest embankment

railway to Hűvösvölgy terminus. Bus or tram back to Moszkva tér.

To **Szentendre** with the suburban railway HÉV from Batthyány tér (travel time approximately 40 mins.).

To **Sas-hegy** (Eagle Hill) nature reserve: Bus 8 or 8a from Március 15. tér to Kompai utca, short walk to warden's office at Tájék utca 26. Guided tours only, Sat. and Sun. 10 a.m.–5 p.m., inquiries and bookings Tel. 115 9467.

Sports

Fishing

Information available from Magyar Országos Horgász Szövetség (MOHOSZ), VI, Mozsár utca 8, Tel. 132 5315, Mon. and Thurs. 8 a.m.–5 p.m., Fri. 8 a.m.–4 p.m.

Spas and swimming pools

Rác spa, I, Hadnagy utca 8–10.
Rudas spa, I, Döbrentei tér 9.
Császár spa, II, Frankel Leó út 35.
Király spa and open-air pool, II, Fő utca 84.
Lukács spa and open-air pool, II, Frankel Leó út 25–29.
Csillaghegy open-air pool, III, Pusztakúti út 3.
Gellért spa, swimming, and wave pool, XI, Kelenhegyi út 4.
Hélia thermal spa, XIII, Kárpát utca 62–64.
Palatinus thermal and open-air pool, XIII, Margit-sziget.
Szabadság (Dagály) thermal, open-air, and indoor pool, XIII, Népfürdő utca 36.
Hotel Thermal, XIII, Margit-sziget.
Széchenyi spa and open-air pool, XIV, Állatkerti körút 11.

Hunting

Information from:
Huntours, II, Retek utca 34, Tel. 135 2313.
Mavad, I, Úri utca 39, Tel. 175 9611.
Vadex, I, Krisztina körút 41–43 (Hotel Buda Penta), Tel. 166 7652.
Pegazus Tours/Vadcoop, V, Apaczai Csere János utca 4 (Hotel Duna), Tel. 117 5122.

Some 45 miles north of Budapest the cathedral of Esztergom rises above the bank of the Danube

Bicycling

An information brochure "Cycling in Hungary" is available from tourist offices and from the Hungarian Bicycling Association, XIV, Szabó József utca 3. Bicycles, including those for two or more riders, and tape-recorded guided tours in five languages can be rented year round at the cycling center near the Hotel Thermal on Margaret Island.

Horseback riding

Riding tours can be booked at the Budapest Riding Club, VIII, Kerepesi út 7, Tel. 113 1349.
Riding demonstrations, coach rides, riding instruction, and cross-country rides: Budapest Riding Club, II, Feketefej utca, Tel. 116 4267.

Főtér, the main square of Szentendre, a quaint town of artists and museums, with churches and other reminiscences of a variety of ethnic groups

Venues of sporting events

Népstadion, XIV, Stefánia út/Dózsa György út.
National Pool, XIII, Margit-sziget.
Budapest Sports Hall, XIV, Stefánia út/Hungária körút.
Millennium Cyclodrome and Ice Rink, XIV, Szabó József utca 3.
Racecourse (flat), X, Albertirsai út 2, Thurs. 4 p.m., Sun. 1 p.m., Tel. 163 6895.
Racecourse (sulky), VIII, Kerepesi út 9–11, Wed. 4 p.m., Sat. 2 p.m., Tel. 134 2958.

Tennis

In addition to the tennis courts at hotels there are the following opportunities for tennis (with instructors, if desired):

Flamenco Tennis Center, XI, Villányi út 14–16.
Budapest Vasutas Sports Club, XIV, Szőnyi út 2.
Budapest Sports Association, XVIII, Városház utca 9–11.

Water sports

Programs with trained leaders and equipment rental:
Flotta Tours, VIII, Práter utca 60, Tel. 117 7217.

Rental of rowing boats, canoes, and kayaks also at the following locations:

Ezermester, III, Hajógyári sziget.
Béke, III, Nánási út 97, Tel. 118 9303.
Budapest Sports, II, Frankel Leó út 35, Tel. 115 0639.

Trade Fairs

February

Boat show
Fashion fair

March

Travel and tourism exhibition
Budapest Art Expo
Press
Baking and pastry industry

April

Agromasexpo — machines and equipment for the agricultural and food industries
Construma — construction industry
Ifabo — electronic data-processing, office organization, and communications technology
Hungaroplast — plastics and rubber industry
Limexpo — machines and light industry
Aqua-Term — heating, ventilation, climatization, sanitary, and environmental technologies

May

Budapest International Fair (spring fair) — technology, capital goods

September

Budapest International Fair (fall fair) — consumer goods
Hoventa — commerce and catering
Interplayexpo — toys
Auto — cars and trucks

October

Budatranspack — packaging and transport industries
Compfair — computer technology
Hungarokorr — corrosion protection
Hung Tech — supply industry and industrial technology
i e e — industrial electronics and electrical engineering
Ikal + Dental — medical supplies and technology
Information: the Budapest International Fairground is at X, Albertirsai út 10, mailing address: Hungexpo, P. O. Box 444, H-1441, Tel. 263 6105, Fax 263 6104.

Fairs and conventions also at: Budapest Kongresszusi Központ, XI, Jagelló út 1–3, H-1118, Tel. 166 6756, 186 9588.

Transport

Municipal transport

The sensible motorist will leave his car parked. For getting around town there is an extensive public transport system, with frequent services operating between about

4:30 a.m. and 11 p.m.; special bus and tram routes operate during the night.

The **subway** (*metró*) is especially useful for covering longer distances. Of the three lines, the M1 (yellow line) is the oldest, running between Vörösmarty tér and Mexikói út; it is the fastest connection between downtown and City Park. The M2 (red line) forms the east-west connection between Örs vezér tere in Pest and South Station (Déli pályaudvar) in Buda. The longest line is the north-south link M3 (blue line) from Újpest-Központ to Kőbánya-Kispest. All three subway lines cross in the center of the city at Deák tér.

The entire city is also covered by an extensive network of **bus, trolleybus, and streetcar** lines, which link up with the subway lines.

Tickets for all public transportation must be purchased before travelling and punched in the machine in the vehicle or at the entrance to subway stations. The ordinary flat-fare ticket (*vonaljegy*) is good for one journey without change of vehicle by subway, tram, bus, trolleybus, cogwheel railway, or HÉV suburban railway up to the city boundary; a book of ten tickets (*gyűjtőjegy*) is available at a discount. The one-day (*napijegy*) and three-day (*turistajegy*) go-as-you-please tickets only represent a saving for the intensive traveller; better value are the passes for 7 days (*hetibérlet*), 14 days (*kéthetibérlet*), or one calendar month (*havibérlet*), in price-categories with or without diesel-bus travel (photo required). Tickets and route maps can be bought at BKV sales points (head office VII, Akácfa utca 15 and 22, Tel. 142 2335, 117 5166) and subway stations; single tickets also at tobacco kiosks and vending machines. Children under 6 travel free, others pay full fare.

Car

Parking

Downtown garages:
V, Aranykéz utca 4.
V, Szervita tér 8.

Information for motorists

Magyar Autóclub, II, Rómer Flóris utca 4a, Tel. 115 2040.

Road conditions (24-hr. information)

Útinform, Tel. 122 2238, 122 7052, 122 7643.
Fővinform, Tel. 117 1173.

Car hire

Shell/Interag, I, Alkotás utca 20–24, Tel. 156 3485.
Hertz, VII, Kertész utca 24, Tel. 111 6116, and V, Aranykéz utca 4–8, Tel. 117 7533.
Budget, I, Krisztina körút 41–43, Tel. 156 6333.
Europcar, VIII, Üllői út 60–62, Tel. 113 1492.

Taxi

You are advised to use an established firm such as the following. All cabs are required to display their rates on the nearside passenger window (basic charge/km charge/waiting minute). Complaints to City Hall (Városház utca 9–11).

Főtaxi, Tel. 122 2222.
Volántaxi, Tel. 166 6666.
Budataxi, Tel. 129 4000.
Citytaxi, Tel. 153 3633.

Air

International flight information

Tel. 157 7155, 157 7695, 157 2122.

Airport bus

To Ferihegy I and Ferihegy II, departure from Central Bus Station, V, Erzsébet tér every 30 minutes from 6 a.m. to 9 p.m.

There is no escaping the newspaper vendor

Streetcars run every three or four minutes during peak periods

Check before starting which airport your flight leaves from.
By municipal bus from Kőbánya-Kispest subway station: Bus 93 (black number) to Ferihegy I only, bus 93 (red number) to both airports.
Minibus to airport: bookings Tel. 157 8993.

Airline offices

Open Mon. to Sat. 8:30 a.m.–4 p.m.

Air Canada, I, Lovas út 1, Tel. 175 4618.
British Airways, VIII, Rákóczi út 1–3, Tel. 118 3299.
Delta Air, V, Apáczai Csere János utca 4, Tel. 118 7922.
Malév, V, Apáczai Csere János utca 19, Tel. 267 4333; V, Dorottya utca 2, Tel. 266 5616; airport, Tel. 157 9123.

Danube shipping

International services:
Mahart Tours, V, Belgrád rakpart, Tel. 118 1704, 118 1586.
Local riverbus: May–Sept., Boráros tér — Margit-sziget — Pünkösdfürdő and intermediate points.
BKV, XIII, Jászai Mari tér, Tel. 129 5844.

Bus

Central bus station: V, Erzsébet tér, Tel. 117 2318 (domestic routes), 117 2562 (international).

Rail

MÁV booking-office (domestic and international): VI, Andrássy út 35.
Information, 6 a.m.–8 p.m. (at night from the main stations): Tel. 122 7860 (domestic), 142 9150, 122 4052 (international times), 122 9035 (international fares).

Stations

Keleti pályaudvar (East), VIII, Baross tér, Tel. 113 6835.
Nyugati pu. (West), VI, Teréz körút 57, Tel. 149 0115.
Déli pu. (South), I, Krisztina körút 37, Tel. 175 6293.

Index